Journals in the Classroom:
Writing to Learn

D1710768

Journals in the Classroom: Writing to Learn

By
Chris Anson and Richard Beach

Christopher-Gordon Publishers, Inc.
Norwood, MA

Credits

Every effort has been made to contact copyright holders for permission to reproduce borrowed material where necessary. We apologize for any oversights and would be happy to rectify them in future printings.

Chapters 1–7

All student work included in these chapters is used with permission.

Chapter 6

Excerpt reprinted from "Journal of a Solitude" by May Sarton with the permission of W.W. Norton and Company, Inc. Copyright © 1973 by May Sarton.

Christopher-Gordon Publishers, Inc.
480 Washington Street
Norwood, MA 02062

Printed in the United States of America

10 9 8 7 6 5 4 3 2 1   99 98 97 96 95

ISBN: 0926842331

Table of Contents

Preface

Almost ten years ago, when the two of us started collaborating on various projects, we began to share some of our preliminary ideas by photocopying and swapping our personal journal entries. At first we felt almost embarrassed to show each other material that was, after all, sloppy looking and tentative, filled with questions, unexamined assumptions, bits and pieces of disconnected thoughts, and reminders to ourselves to look something up. But as we worked, we began to see the enormous benefits of this type of writing in the formulation of our thoughts and indeed in our overall scholarship. At one point, when we wrote a brief article about journal writing for a student-oriented collection of essays, we found that what had been for each of us a personal mode of writing was becoming something more like a dialogue. We swapped journal entries and then responded to each other's entries in the same loose and exploratory way, which then led to more entries and more responses. The process was so illuminating that we decided to turn the exchanges into our contribution to the collection.

For many years, we have also watched the same process seep into the learning of our students at all levels. Convinced of their education value, we began experimenting with journal writing and with dialogue journals in a range of contexts. Several years ago, we introduced dialogue journals to university lecture classes with over 200 students—with remarkable results. In some of our smaller classes, we asked students to write and respond to each other in journal-like entries on an E-mail network. Some of our courses have involved service-learning components or off-campus internships, and we have asked students to keep experiential logs to record and reflect on events in their extracurricular work. In all these cases, the journal writing convinced us that our students were delving into the material of our courses more deeply, with more sophistication, than if we had asked them to write only formal papers or essay exams. The journals also became the center of our courses, the intellectual space where the students could explore ideas without risk of being criticized for their expression, organization, grammar, or style. In some cases, we found that our students' journal writing, released from these inhibitions, demonstrated a control and expression of thought that far exceeded the quality of these students' more formal papers. Intrigued, we began exploring the nature and function of journal writing in various descriptive and experimental studies. We also wrote about these phenomena in our own journals, which, in turn, offered us new insights into journals that we have tried to express in this book.

While journal writing has come to mean specific things for us, we acknowledge that, like varieties of speech, journals can take many forms and are used for countless functions. In this book, we have tried to recognize this reality while also offering a principled and unified theory that places this unique kind of writing at the center of students' learning experiences. Throughout the book we have held to a model that privileges thought and meaning—in part because journals do not lend themselves to critique as texts. But we are also convinced that when students write a lot, even when they write the kind of associative, unstructured, and expressive material typically found in journals, they become better writers in the process. Like speech, writing cannot be learned in short, isolated experiences; it must be used continually, in functional contexts where it is important to make and convey meaning, even for oneself.

The book is designed so that a reader can jump in at any point without feeling lost. Chapter One places journals into the context of our inherited traditions, and suggests that when we think of journals in too limited a way, perhaps governed by one of these tradition, we may not see the full potential of journals in the classroom. Chapter Two describes a variety of purposes that journals can serve in secondary, and college settings. Chapter Three offers a wealth of practical advice on using journals in the classroom. Throughout this chapter, readers will find boxed examples of journal writing in action either in excerpts of students' entries or in more general descriptions of their work when it was impractical to include the original material. Chapter Four turns to methods for developing journal-writing assignments, perhaps as a supplement to more "self-sponsored" entries in which students decide their own focus. Chapter Five offers more specific advice for journal-writing in English classes, with a special focus on the use of journals in the reading, interpreting, and discussing of literary works. Chapter Six is a resource chapter of the study of professional authors' journals and on the role of journal writing in the lives of well-known people. Sections in this chapter conclude with lists of books and articles that can be of use in the study of journal writing. Chapter Seven turns to the difficult process of reading, responding to, and evaluating student journals, as well as how to coordinate student responses to each others' journal entries. The book also includes a special list of reference works on journal writing that supplements the works cited in the body of the text.

In writing this book, it has been our sincere hope that we can contribute to the widening acceptance of journal writing as an important mode of development for learners at all levels. We see this as a starting point for readers who may not have experimented much with journal writing; it may also serve as a compendium of additional strategies and ideas for journal writing for those who may have explored a few functions of the genre already. If any of the tips, examples, or convictions in this book lead to a principled, successful use of journals in an actual classroom, we have done our job. But most of all, we recognize the importance of teachers doing theirs—experimenting, assessing, and finally developing their own thoughtful ways of employing this unique form of writing.

Acknowledgments

We want to express our appreciation to the many teachers who provided us examples of their journal-writing assignments; their imaginative and principled materials and ideas inspired us to keep pushingv ahead on the book. We also acknowledge the many contributions of students in junior high, senior high, and college classes whose work we have excerpted or described; they served as models of what journal writing can do. To the publishers and editors at Christopher-Gordon we owe a hearty thanks for their many helpful contributions to this book: Hiram Howard, whose enthusiasm began over a long Italian lunch in Minneapolis and never flagged over the several years it took us to draft and revise the manuscript; to Susan Folan, for her helpful counsel as we worked on content and structure of the book; and to Beth Cronin, who saw the manuscript through to publication and worked hard to realize our vision of the final product. Toby Fulwiler, Diane Barone, Carol M. Santa and Susan Reed, gave us many insightful comments on several revisions of the manuscript. Finally, we thank our families for another test of publishing endurance—to Geanie, Ian, and Graham Anson, and to Nancy and Ben Beach.

Chapter One

The Legacy of Journals

In the following excerpts from her English class journal, Jan, a senior in high school, is writing about Nathaniel Hawthorne's short story "The Birthmark":

> May 13. After reading "The Birthmark" I sat back and thought about what I had just read. I'm still confused by a few things but not so many that I don't know what the story line is. Yet, I don't know what the story is trying to say.

> May 14. After looking over The Birthmark one more time I think I see the meaning in it. I think that, given the "age of science" had been around at this time, everyone thought that it could do everything. The fact that Georg. died is maybe saying something re. the fact that you don't fool with Mother Nature. Where do you draw the line. I think this relates to today as far as Baboon hearts, etc. The question is when do we draw the line. Is this an area for science to manipulate? I think this is one of the main issues. I'm going to re-read to see if I can find cases. And maybe more evidence.

If we reflect for a moment on these bits of prose, immersed as they are in the daily life of Jan's class, several interesting features come to light. First is the nature of the text Jan has written. She begins retrospectively, reflecting on her experiences (and confusions) reading the story. After a pause of one day, when she looks over the story again, her journal writing propels her into a moment of discovery, a kind of exploratory "present tense" in which she tentatively examines the story's theme and connects it with her own world. Toward the end of the second entry she then projects her next move, a move that will take her back into the story again to test out her assertions. Jan's entries show us the process of her explorations—her first experience reading the story; then, at an important juncture, a moment of critical reflection; and finally a plan to test out her new ideas and hypotheses—a re-reading that will doubtless lead to more revisions in Jan's interpretation. The entry shows her thinking about her thoughts, a metacritical act that drops the seeds of new ideas into the fertile soil of her consciousness.

At the same time, her entries violate many of the conventions of prose that we, as teachers, may associate with "clear thinking." It is largely an associative kind of writing. Retrospection leads to reflection, reflection to projection. Puzzle leads to hypothesis, to a new reading of the story. The entry lacks the carefully wrought structure we expect from formal writing: a clearly articulated "point" followed by a sequence of evidential statements and quotations. Instead of marching the line of logic, her thoughts wander, off balance: a musing-like question ("where do you draw the line?") followed by a contemporary example (transplanting baboon hearts into humans) followed by a repetition of the question with a new degree of rhetorical certainty ("where, indeed, do you draw the line?"). Scanning this text for its control of surface mechanics and correct grammar, we might circle half a dozen problems, such as the sentence fragment at the end of the second entry; the abbreviations "re." (for "regarding") and "Georg." (for the name of one of the characters, Georgiana); the lack of correct punctuation on questions; the redundant hyphen in "re-read"; the missing quotation marks in the second mention of the story's title; the questionable syntax in the second line of the May 14 entry; maybe even the excessive use of the personal pronoun in a text otherwise thought to analyze a piece of literature in a clinical, objective way. In other words, Jan's writing turns upside down many of our most firmly-held standards for "successful" prose. If this piece of writing pushes into the background our usual criteria for success, we have no alternative but to read Jan's work as a display of her responses as a learner. We witness her development, not its outcome. Instead of experiencing the comfortable place that her struggles for meaning might finally lead her, we're actually involved in the struggles themselves.

Jan's journal illustrates a recent development in education, especially at the secondary and college levels, from the passive accumulation of information to the active integration of new knowledge into old. Even beyond literature classes, where response journals have become quite popular, teachers are beginning to use informal, personal writing to encourage active, critical thinking about complex academic material. Proponents of the "active learning" movement have advocated the use of informal, exploratory writing, the journal being perhaps the most favored mode because of its flexibility and adaptability to most school settings. Writing-across-the-curriculum (WAC) and language-across-the-curriculum (LAC) groups encourage teachers to adopt informal journal-like writing under the assumption that such writing makes more active, critical thinkers of students. Hundreds of articles on the benefits of journal writing, most of them short and testimonial, can be found in the pages of countless educational journals in every part of the contemporary curriculum (Anson, Schwiebert, & Williamson, 1993). The zeal for journal writing is illustrated in a typical classroom-oriented article from *English Journal*. In it, Anne Sullivan describes her use of student journals and claims that, based on her experiences and students' comments, "[journal] strategies (even in their rougher forms) have helped lead many students to lifelong writing" (Sullivan, 1989, p. 55). In short, the journal has found various niches in the world of teaching and learning, a positive sign that on a national scale we see education as something more than memorizing information and taking objective tests of accumulated knowledge.

In spite of the voluminous anecdotal writings about journals, in spite of the constant discussions and sharing of journal techniques at conferences and inservice workshops, we still need to formulate a coherent approach to using journals in the classroom. This book is an attempt both to reveal the great diversity and variety of journal writing in academic settings at different levels as well as to develop a central theory to guide those many uses. What you will find in its chapters is not advocacy of a single kind of journal writing—as a tool for exploring one's own consciousness—but rather a celebration of the rich genres and functions of academic journals.

At the same time, we offer an approach to journals that places them at the very center of students' learning, a kind of hub from which the spokes of a class or a curriculum radiate. Placed at the center of classroom experience, the academic journal can develop and flourish for individual teachers, and suffer less from the abandonment or growing skepticism that comes from using them in unprincipled ways or placing them at the margins of students' learning. By placing journal writing at the center, we are advocating a powerful method for enhancing students' thinking and learning.

The Ephemeral Popularity of Journals

Journal writing like Jan's, until the late 1970's, would have been found only rarely in schools, and then almost entirely in the language arts. There is some scattered evidence of journal writing in the less recent histories of elite institutions of higher learning. Serving a tiny proportion of the population, such institutions until the end of the nineteenth century adhered to a master/apprentice model of education. In these settings, reflective writing and certainly less formal written dialogues between teachers and their pupils would not have seemed unusual. The "commonplace book" was popular in the eighteenth century as a context for "lifelong education" (Murray, 1985). But from the beginning of the twentieth century, the increasing numbers of students in public education and the growth of what Lunsford (1989) calls the "factory" model of schooling placed a much higher price on formal and assessable writing at the cost of work like Jan's.

Today, most teachers have heard about or seen student journals even if they haven't used them. Unfortunately, journal writing is often perceived as less intellectually rigorous than formal essay writing. A survey by Arthur Applebee (1993) found that only about one-third of literature teachers in 450 secondary schools place a primary emphasis on journal writing in exploring literature, compared with two-thirds who emphasize formal, critical essays. In grades 6-8, about half the teachers use at least some journal writing, but that percentage drops dramatically, to about one-fourth, by grades 11-12. "Nonacademic-track" teachers in high school tend to value journals more—about half use them in some capacity—but use of journals in the college-prep track declines to only one-fourth of teachers.

These statistics say much about common educational views of journals: teachers don't often associate journal writing with the sort of higher intellectual work demanded of high school and college students. The problem may originate in a failure to clarify how journals promote students' thinking and learning. Advocates present well-reasoned claims, usually supported by compelling anecdotal evidence, that journal writing works: that it helps students learn, invigorates classroom settings, creates a social and collaborative atmosphere, gives teachers a window into students' developing minds. But for all these promising examples, we need a better reasoned and more fully articulated set of principles underlying the use of journals. What we have at present is a hodgepodge of functions, methods and mediums—a bewildering array of success stories from every conceivable course and school. In emulating one or another approach, in borrowing this instructor's journal assignment or that instructor's grading rubric, teachers can end up importing process without principle (see Phelps, 1988). In Chapter Two, we describe some of this diversity as evidence that journal writing, unlike some canonical forms in schooling, provides a flexible genre for experimentation and manipulation. But regardless of the uses to which journals are put, we must strive for a unifying, integrated approach that guides how we assign them, what and how students write in them and how we should read and respond to them.

The Inheritance: Three Public Visions of Journals

Of the many and varied ways that journals are used in the classroom, we perceive three dominant functions from the body of literature and instructional materials on journal writing; the expressevist journal, the scientific observation log and the prewriting journal. Each of these functions carries with it an interesting history, complete with public or educational stereotypes, well-known examples and ideologies of writing.

The Expressivist Journal. Probably the most widespread public stereotype about journals emerged from what educators now generally call the "expressivist tradition," (Berlin, 1988; Fulkerson, 1979), an approach to learning that privileges the expression of "individual voice" and development of identity and self-awareness. Historical antecedents of this tradition range from the Romanticism of nineteenth-century writers to the rugged individualism of American pragmatism, beliefs that value an individualistic theory of learning—that we are all unique people. Such a theory deemphasizes the ways in which individuals are shaped by social and cultural forces that create multiply defined selves.

Metaphorically, the expressivist tradition conjures up images of famous writers exploring themselves, their lives and their thoughts in journals and diaries. It is not so much that any one of these writers consistently wrote in an expressivist mode; it is clear, that the functions of their journal writing are many and varied, even in single writing episodes. Rather, these personalities have come to represent such an expressivist tradition, and their texts are held up as models of self-exploration. A good case in point is the work of Henry David Thoreau, particularly *Walden*. Although Thoreau's voluminous journal writing gives us an excellent example of multiple functions and can serve as a model for students' work (see Pinkston, 1989), he is usually thought to be an exemplar of the expressivist tradition.

Today, expressive journal writing appears in approaches to language and English instruction that privilege the individual, the teacher's goal being to "develop the writer's autonomy, self-worth and self-ownership" (Mosenthal, 1983), or to focus on "the experiences and emotions of the students," all "aimed at fostering personal growth" (Kroll, 1980) that "satisfies a basic human need for self-expression and self-exploration" (Sullivan, 1989). Peter Elbow, perhaps best known for his extensive popularizing of "freewriting" and other forms of expressive discourse, offers the following example of his own journal writing as evidence of allowing himself a kind of discursive practice impossible in his usually controlled "public language":

> I'm being driven out of my mind by ———. What power can I gain over it by this process. Maybe the fact that it is exceedingly hard to get myself to sit down and deal with it on the typewriter is clue that it will be effective—ie, that the demons inside don't want me to do this. (Elbow, 1989, p. 44)

Typical of the expressivist tradition, this bit of Elbow's freewriting displays an engagement with his own experiences and a preoccupation (allowed by the act of writing) with his own state of mind—a process that can be intellectually meaningful and can lead to further discovery, learning and change.

As we will explain in later chapters, many express-ivist uses of journal writing can be supported in the context of students' academic learning. It is hard to claim, for example, that by exploring their own subjective relationship to course material, students are wasting their time or impeding their learning. Feminist approaches to journal writing, in particular, argue for the centrality of the "personal" connection in academic journals (see Gannett, 1992). Yet in the face of widespread (and often unfortunate) attention to education as "skill," and the cry for formal assessment that is always heard at its heels, teachers who advocate using journals solely for expressive purposes must face the challenge of accountability. Diaries, critics argue, waste valuable school time that could be devoted to more rigorous modes of learning. Board work, drill, memory, calculation, note-taking, lecture-absorption—these strike the uninformed parent or news reporter or principal as the stuff of hard thinking. From this tough-minded perspective, journal writing can be stereotyped and marginalized as "soft," "personal" and ultimately "non-academic." In a world of excessive vocationalism and a relentless educational drive for measurable skills, there is little place for the image of the lonely garreted writer pouring out his soul on the pages of a self-indulgent journal. And, as Gannett (1992) shows, the public stereotype of diaries is both highly gendered and fearful to conservatives: men "dread" the proximity of the "female diary" to their own journal-like daybooks, logs and travel accounts (p. 166), and many critics write with paranoia about the "invasion of privacy" that personal journals in the classroom are thought to promote (pp. 34–42). The rejection of the personal journal as a tool for learning and intellectual development owes as much to these stereotypes and romantic constructions as it does to the unfortunate pressures on the schools to prepare young people for the world of work—and no more.

These tensions in which academic journals are caught—tensions between "rigor" and "self-expression," between a need to teach "skills" and a desire to awaken students to themselves and open the gates to learning—have many antecedents in the history of American education. Around the turn of the century, for example, English educators had mixed reactions to progressivists such as Fred Newton Scott, who advocated a more "expressivist" curriculum in which students could explore the "interaction between the experience of the external world and what the perceiver brings to this experience" (Scott, 1926, p. 47). A critique of the expressivist movement, written in 1910, sets down many of the sentiments echoed today in arguments against journal writing:

> Since we may seldom take for granted that the immature student is in the possession of a valuable truth, and since the first inquiry of the teacher should, therefore, be concerning the truth and accuracy of the pupil's communication, it follows that the teaching of expression can never safely be made the primary aim of any course. (Cooper, 1910, p. 425)

Rejecting academic journals on the basis of their expressivist uses, however, denies them their true educational potential. Perceiving journals only as cumulative expressions of random feelings fails to recognize the academic *and* personal uses of a less formal and formulated medium than the traditional theme or the in-class essay exam. In thinking of journals as texts that encourage more than self-absorption, students and teachers may recognize that they derive from a range of other texts—formal and informal—and that what is expressed in their pages reflects students' knowledge of these genres as well as the content of their coursework. Students can freely express their feelings in the journal, but in the context of *academic* learning rather than simple self-absorption. Therefore, we advocate a reconceptualizing of the school-based journal as academic, a notion that builds on the expressivist tradition but also emphasizes a certain quality of intellectual rigor and more sharply defined outcomes for learning and growth.

The Scientific Observation Log. Another public conception of journals borrows chiefly from science, exemplars including Darwin, Thomas Edison and Margaret Mead. Many models come to mind of famous inventors, scientists, scientifically-minded explorers or anthropologists, archaeologists and others who kept copious journals. There is a strong reflective and exploratory function of such journals, perhaps best exemplified in Darwin's many field notebooks. Yet still a public stereotype has formed around the image of the clinical, usually male scientist, holding a clipboard and jotting down measurements or observations from a highly objective experiment.

Teachers involved in writing-across-the-curriculum programs creatively stretch what they perceive to be the "scientific" edges of journals-as-observation, so that students keep impression logs in art, reading logs in literature or behavior logs in social studies and psychology. But these are the exceptions. In most cases, journals as observation logs remain the province of science, especially in classes involving laboratory experiments—biology, earth science and the like. The "data" in the social sciences—for example, anthropology—not thought to be readily available in school, don't become grist for observation logs.

This social-scientific model of journal writing has unfortunately been limited to specialized uses within particular disciplines. Such disciplinary requirements can strip away the reflective potential from journal-writing. An interesting example of this tension between disciplinary requirements and the reflective potential of journals came to light not long ago in comparisons between famous anthropologists' "field notes" and their (hitherto unseen) personal diaries. The same events that had been clinically noted and dissected in the field journals were interpreted in quite different ways in these scholars' personal journals. Anthropologists were then faced with the question of which representation made a richer or more compelling case for understanding the culture being studied, and this has led to continued debate in the field about the nature of fact, knowledge and interpretation. In the same way, it might be useful to think about the relationship between journals as clinical logs in a biology class and journals as personal reflection. How do students think about the experiments they're conducting? Is there a difference between their personal interpretations of what happened in a lab experiment and their more constrained "clinical" conclusions? This suggests the need to merge the "clinical," scientific uses of journals with the more personal, subjective dimensions of writing, going beyond the simplistic dichotomy between "cognitive" and "affective" response.

In higher education, future nurses practice keeping patient logs and translate them into highly formulaic and format-driven reports to doctors and health-care officials. These "journals," with affinities to the Darwinian tradition, give no opportunities to reflect on what it means to be a nurse, what it means to deal with patients, how to resolve complex ethical issues in medicine and a thousand other topics at the heart of a burgeoning and ever more complicated profession. Such uses of journals at higher levels of learning are often mirrored in more basic activities in the primary and secondary schools, where children record details of flora and fauna but have little freedom to analyze, synthesize and evaluate those details in terms of their own prior knowledge and experience.

Within some scientific fields, the limitations of the journal as "objective" record of data have recently come to light. Segal (1990) argues that "something more is needed" in the teaching of anthropology than field exercises and unreflective participant-observation (with most of the focus on the observation side). Instead, "the participation, the interaction between the field and field-worker, is the locus for the essential work of gathering distinctively anthropological data" (p. 122). Clearly, we need to challenge the notion of journals as "pure" records of objectively observed data.

Such a challenge sometimes requires only small steps in curricular revision, not major overhauls. In consulting with a nationally known school of dentistry, one of us began looking for ways that dental students could increase their academic writing (Anson, Maylath, Loupe, & 1991). In their first year, the students were required to observe third- and fourth-year dental students as they treated patients in the affiliated dental clinic. Before using journals, students simply observed their senior peers—a useful exercise in envisioning their future careers, but one that did not encourage much reflection. When the idea of journals was broached to the dental faculty, there was little resistance: the students would *record* their observations, thus finding an immediately pragmatic use for writing. As consultants, however, we then proposed having the students keep double-entry journals, writing down their clinical observations on the left side of their notebooks and then, reflecting on their observations in right-hand entries. The strategy worked; the students came to class with much more to say about their observations, and their entries suggested that they were critically assessing what they saw and relating their lecture-and-textbook knowledge to the enacted practices they recorded. In this case, the narrowly "scientific" orientation of journals paved the way for an educationally broader use in a demanding course of study. Such experiences suggest that, as with the expressivist journal, we expand the functions of academic journals as we search for new ways to help students learn.

The Prewriting Journal. Most teachers characterize the "prewriting" journal as a sort of repository of ideas, musings, doodlings, diagrams, rushwritings, notes and attempts at drafting. Over time, and often through careful instructional sequencing and intervention, the writer begins moving toward a formal paper. Metaphorically, journals become the "blueprints" or the "leavings" of the refined, polished presentation. In some approaches, the teacher collects and variously assesses this messy trial work, perhaps on the basis of its quantity or diversity.

In contrast to the most free-flowing and uninhibited journal writing encouraged by the expressivist tradition, the prewriting journal seems immediately *useful.* Next to the traditional English class, where the activity of writing was rarely discussed, the strong process orientation of the journal has revolutionized instruction in those places where it is used. Students actively explore their knowledge, look for patterns in what they generate, freewrite their way toward useable text, write tentative drafts, critique these drafts and respond to the critiques of others, and revise and edit their early attempts as they slowly move toward an improved, final creation. Explained as "strategic" work for improved composition, prewriting journals have not undergone much scrutiny as to their wider intellectual potential. The limitations of the prewriting journal are more subtle than criticisms leveled against journals promoting "free expression" and exploration of the self. The problem is the way that this unique mode of learning can become trivialized and weakened—a mere dress rehearsal for a final, formally evaluated text.

The following excerpt from the syllabus of a high-school honors writing course reflects this bias. The excerpt clearly shows how the journal as a process-log encourages the free flow of ideas and intellectual exploration but constantly looks ahead to a finished product to be assessed.

> *Your Journal:* In addition to the major requirements of this class, you will be keeping a journal that will contain all the process-work you do that leads up to

your final papers. The journal will contain brainstorming notes on your topics, freewriting and other invention exercises, drafts and revisions, as well as comments from your group editors. All of this work is required and will be given a grade of "+," "√" or "-" on the basis of overall quality and amount of material. Keep in mind that your journal is a chance for you to produce *better final papers that will receive higher grades if you do the work thoroughly.*

The limitation here is one of vision. The journal *contains* disparate notes and false starts that look outward to a different kind of text world, the kind that measures 8 1/2 X 11 inches, with 1-inch margins, typed on high quality bond. Once such a text is produced, the journal turns into mere ephemera.

The focus on journals as "pre-writing" or preparation for more formal text production, as Gannett (1992) puts it, "not only reduces or restricts the meaning of the term [journal] to a 'strategy' or 'tool,' it also disconnects the concept of the journal from the long and rich set of traditions associated with its use . . . " (p. 34). Instructors eager to make journal-writing procedural and operational in the process class "may fail to distinguish among the complexities and subtleties of journal keeping behavior":

> The writing process researchers generally place journal-keeping within the Pre-writing stage, which then emphasizes the journal as a subservient activity for the essay and more formal writing. This view is deceptive because it discourages thinking of the journal as a separate genre. The entries in journal- keeping are apt to be seen as tentative steps toward the draft. Conceptualizing the journal as Pre-writing leads to the assumption that the main or only purpose of journal-keeping is to facilitate more formal writing. (Lowenstein, 1982, pp. 150-151, quoted in Gannett, p. 33)

Lacking from the prewriting journal is a sense of its intellectual equality with formal, archetypal texts. Placed side-by-side with such formal texts, especially in "content-rich" courses across the curriculum, prewriting journals can soon blossom into learning logs and eventually replace the formal texts altogether. Classrooms that require overly mechanized prewriting journals miss opportunities for intellectual and interpersonal growth that more principled uses of journals can inspire. Eventually unimpressed with the results of their students' labors or unconvinced that process journals really results in better formal papers, some teachers soon abandon them in favor of what they perceive to be less messy forms of instruction. The assumption that process logs simply make visible what proficient writers and thinkers do internally leads to their systematic abandonment from higher levels of the curriculum.

Each of these three public and often stereotyped conceptions of journals—as expressive diaries, as scientific observation logs, and as prewritten grist for final texts—has served to keep journal writing at the edges of the classroom, undermining its potential as a significant tool for learning. To place journals where they belong, at the very center of the classroom, we need to reshape and reconceptualize their underlying supporting theories having to do with how writing fosters learning. To do this requires us to redefine the functions of expressivism, clinical observation and invention exercises in terms of a larger, more holistic vision of writing in students' learning.

The Inadequacies of the Communication Model

The place of language in the schools, as Marland (1977), Britton, et al. (1975) and Martin (1983) have reminded us, must be at the center of learning. The gradual fragmentation of the school curriculum into discrete, discipline-specific areas pushed speaking into "speech" (and occasionally drama), writing into "composition" (or English), and reading into remediation, at least in high school and beyond. The effect of this splitting off and dividing up of language learning has gradually become apparent to educators around the country, as they notice its disappearance in the "non-language" parts of the curriculum. Even as "writing-intensive" courses are introduced to solve this problem, their designation as sites for written language can ironically justify the reduction of writing by teachers in "non-writing-intensive" classes (see White, 1992).

Yet we can't entirely blame teachers for not saturating their classes with writing, for example the isolation of writing in departments of English, composition and ESL owes to the perpetuation of a myth that one group ought to be "doing" language while others do science, math, social studies or physical education.

Teachers at all levels across the curriculum express concern about using writing in their courses because they (1) don't feel it's their job; (2) don't think it is "relevant" enough to the subject they teach; (3) think it may "get in the way" of their "coverage" of the subject they teach; (4) think it takes an inordinate amount of time to read, respond to and grade; and (5) often feel, and sometimes confess, they are insecure about their own writing abilities and can't call themselves expert enough to "teach" it to their students.

All these concerns are valid. If we assume that by "writing" we mean formal, carefully assigned papers that take students time to prepare and take teachers much time to read and grade, the issue of workload becomes crucial to writing across the curriculum. Some teachers really do have little time to "teach" writing to their students if that means lecturing on the proper form of an essay, diagramming sentences on the board or reading, analyzing and critiquing model student essays on an overhead projector. Many teachers believe that their colleagues in the English department really do know everything one could possibly know about grammar and punctuation and that such erudition is necessary to "teach" writing. And if the history of western civilization consumes most of the school week, commas, semicolons, sentence fragments, even thesis statements begin to look less and less relevant to knowing about the French Revolution, Robespierre and Bastille Day.

The problem, as anyone who has run or participated in a writing-across-the-curriculum workshop knows, originates in the way we think about *writing*. In schools we adhere to what is commonly known as a "communication" model of language, one with a powerful and lasting legacy. That legacy echoes in the language that teachers across the curriculum often use to talk about writing—language that reveals how our school culture thinks about and values writing words on paper.

The communication model has many roots. Perhaps the most important influence on language in the twentieth century is the work of structuralist linguists, who suggested that language requires "senders" and "receivers" who communicate through a kind of "speech chain." Listen, for example, to Saussure's model of communication, which profoundly influenced many theorists after him and eventually trickled down into the schools:

> In order to separate from the whole of speech the part that belongs to language, we must examine the individual act from which the speaking-circuit can be reconstructed. The act requires the presence of at least two persons; that is the minimum number necessary to complete the circuit. Suppose that two people, A and B, are conversing with each other.
>
> Suppose that the opening of the circuit is in A's brain, where mental facts (concepts) are associated with representations of the linguistic sounds (sound-images) that are used for their expression. A given

concept unlocks a corresponding sound-image in the brain; this purely *psychological* phenomenon is followed in turn by a *physiological* process . . . . (Saussure, 1959)

When we privilege this model, we have almost no alternative but to see journal writing as peripheral to our main academic interests in the classroom—a process log or a repository for general trivia. If language—formally and properly—must *communicate* between senders and receivers, and if journals display a reflexiveness characteristic of solitary musing, it is assumed that journals will not provide students with the skills required for good communication. We may lurch toward the other extreme and justify classroom journals simply because we assume that everything else is "communication." However, doing so takes us perilously close to expressivists who use journals for a while to foster students' self-expression but then abandon them because they don't seem to be effective in helping students to learn.

But let's entertain for a moment the idea of altering the communication model. Imagine that the sender—a journal-keeping student—writes and sees what she has written. She communicates with noone beyond herself initially. The journal writing is the expression of a part of herself at a moment in time. Then she rereads—or reads while she writes—and tastes the concoction of her words and is compelled to write some more. Something new arises—a fresh insight. She realizes, midsentence, that she is conflicted about an issue. What *does* she think, really? Some more words appear on the page, tentative. She reflects: she has finished a thought "automatically." No, that's not what she meant. She writes some more. A memory unfolds before her. She tries to recall her feelings. Now another. What does it add up to? More ideas. More words. More reflection. More learning.

Writing in this mode of thinking and reasoning can't possibly yield polished prose. The whole process must be associative to work. Ideas need to contradict each other, at least occasionally. There must be space to be wrong, or to recognize that one is wrong, or to criticize what one has just argued. And there must be space, at least during the act of writing, to be uninhibited by the constraints of the "receiver"— most especially if that receiver is a teacher. As Mina Shaughnessy clearly revealed in the opening of her book *Errors and Expectations* (1977), those constraints can be especially paralyzing when they turn students' vision away from their ideas and toward the correct form of their prose. Commas and apostrophes take the place of assertions and support for hypotheses. The mind spins, caught in the fearful vortex of error. And before long, incentive, exploration and growth disappear as the student spirals down to a place where what you say no longer matters.

Later in this book, we discuss the nature of audience in journal writing and the central role that teachers and other students should play in much academic journal writing. But interestingly, journal writing isn't *defined* by an audience in the way that formal writing—writing that "communicates"— is. With the exception of dialogue journals, in which a student writes directly to and with another student or a teacher, journals assume no direct outside audience. When we read solo journals, we look over the writer's rhetorical shoulder, not at her rhetorical face.

The communication model compels us to focus on the quality of the linguistic code that writers employ to send messages to receivers. Undesirable "static" in this code amounts to exactly the sorts of features we saw in Jan's journal writing at the beginning of this chapter. For decades, teachers have been systematically trying to improve the lines of communication between student writers and their audiences— almost always teachers responsible for painstakingly "decoding" the garbled messages and showing how they could have been sent more clearly to begin with. Placing so much emphasis on the quality of the code for communication strips some of the writer-centered, learning-based and exploratory potential from writing.

By denying the power of the communication model to define writing in our classes, we can take an important step toward placing journals at the center of learning. We no longer need to fear the process of evaluation—at least not as we traditionally conceive it. Evaluation shifts from commas and thesis statements to the thing we know best as teachers; learning, growth, intellectual development. We no longer need to fear that writing will "take over" our classes because it becomes an integral part of the way students learn the subject matter. We no longer need to fear that writing will butt that subject matter aside just when we fear we can't get to everything we want to cover. Instead, *writing becomes learning the subject matter.*

We have watched, for example, as a teacher of a senior high school psychology course experimented with the substitution of writing for lecturing. He typed up his lecture notes (altruism, aggression and other concepts from social psychology) into a reading and gave it to his students at the end of his Monday class. They were required to read the essay and look for cases of the concepts around them, then write the cases in a journal and reflect on them. On Tuesday, in the hour he would have spent literally reading the notes they had already read, he led a discussion by soliciting their cases and asking the class how or whether the cases illustrated the concept at hand. Measured even in simple terms, this substitution of active reading, writing, reflecting and talking yielded much more intellectual engagement than if the teacher had read notes to them as they sat passively absorbing the abstract concepts, unintegrated into their prior knowledge.

Language education, especially in speech and composition, is about formally presented communication—communication with or to "receivers" whose reactions will lead the writer or speaker to success in school and on the job. Without the concept of audience, without the pressure to make texts conform to criteria of organization, clarity, style and correctness, students may not create prose that will serve them well in the future. And all the journal writing in the world, if it ignores or turns those criteria on their head, won't show students how to control and manipulate their writing to impress audiences who will judge them.

In contexts where formal writing already plays a key role, the journal can become instrumental to learning such criteria. As the student produces a piece of formal writing, the journal takes center stage, not simply a prewriting tool for inventing ideas but the place where the very activity of writing for audiences can be understood and raised to a higher level of consciousness. The formal paper takes its place next to the lab experiment, the difficult reading, the field trip or the documentary film as the grist for the learning journal.

In contexts where there is no formal writing, and probably never would be, the journal doesn't need to "substitute" for experiences gaining control of communicative texts. Interestingly, journal writing may actually foster more formal writing in contexts where, before the journal was in place, that formal writing would not have appeared. Teachers who latch on to the idea of informal writing, writing that requires little of that "technology" of writing that they may fear or dread, often find themselves slipping in assignments whose communicative criteria can be more readily specified. This happens frequently in scenarios and case studies, which seem generally journal-like but subtly introduce the concept of audience through texts that must respond to the problems or issues described in imaginary settings.

But more important is the principle now espoused by whole language theorists that learning to write (or speak) well requires first and foremost an immersion into a community where such activities are central. Language acquisition experts show us incontrovertibly that children learn to speak the language of their parents largely because they are immersed in that language incessantly and its use is functional and highly social. Teachers who believe students must learn the proper forms for "communication" can't justify assigning ten or fifteen papers in a single course, so they assign one or two. Students' experiences with writing are then limited, not unlike a situation in which a young child is asked to prepare three or four speeches each year for her family but remains silent the rest of the time. In a setting where writing plays a more central and functional role, like speaking, we can easily picture journals of fifty or a hundred pages. Both of us routinely assign journal writing in large and small classes and expect students to write a page a day for the ten-week term, yielding at least 70 pages. Unused to journals, most students gasp in horror on the first day of class when we announce these average page lengths, but soon come to understand what we mean by journal writing and often go well beyond the suggested amounts.

Journals—At the Center

By doing away with the notion that writing must communicate in a traditional way and by reassessing what we mean by communication in the learning process, we stand a chance of enhancing the role of journals in the academic experience. To do so takes an adjustment of priorities for some, a leap of faith for others. What other principles can support such a move? Is it enough simply to reject a model of writing as communication?

Writing and the Informal. In the rest of this book, we propose a use of journal writing that places thinking and learning at the center and specific language forms around it. This model essentially reverses the priorities established by a strict adherence to a communicative view of writing. The "code" doesn't disappear, but its potential is elaborated and extended way beyond our traditional criteria to include forms, structures and even idiosyncratic quirks that can both energize and reflect learning. The interpersonal, cognitive, social and affective become our concerns, rather than about the language that enacts these.

It is useful in this context to consider Halliday's (1979) three language functions, the interpersonal, the textual and the ideational. The interpersonal function refers to the social nature of communication, while the ideational function refers to the role of language in mediating thought. The textual function is the *medium* of language—its form and expression. All of these functions gain prominence in formal writing, but it is the nature of the textual—specifically the criteria we impose on our readings of texts—that stands above and infuses the interpersonal and the ideational. We fault students' word choices, style or tone for not showing an "understanding" of their readers (interpersonal), and we critique the structure of their arguments and even the form of their sentences for not conveying their "meaning" coherently, persuasively or logically.

In informal writing all three dimensions still exist; but the distribution of our emphasis looks entirely different. The textual recedes into the shadows of the discursive frame, while the ideational is bathed in brilliant light. The interpersonal takes on a very different quality depending on the social function of the journal in the classroom. "Solo" journals may look beyond their borders and into the other activities of the class: they give life, through students' enhanced thinking, to discussions, group work, experiential learning activities and the general intellectual quality of the classroom. "Dialogue" journals or journals used in highly social ways—through sharing in groups or pairs—become the most important medium for interpersonal interacting, assuming that some of the oral work in the class involves discussing both the writing and reading of journals.

In the redistribution of emphasis along Halliday's three functions, we privilege the "informal." But the use of this term is problematic in education. "Informal" conjures up images in which learning lacks "vigor" or "rigor," in which students are "permitted" to "slack off" or in which teachers "go easy" on them. Although learning theorists have shown that the assimilation of new knowledge doesn't have to be painful or even highly effortful to be successful, we have come to value energy so much in education that casting journal writing in the language of the casual does serious harm to their further use, through the public stereotypes we've already discussed. Instead, while the language of journal writing may be thought non-traditional, the intellectual processes it encourages both require and lead to thoughtfulness of the kind we value in all educational circles. We have seen students so engaged in journal writing, and in such productive ways, that we couldn't imagine assignments, tests and other measures of accountability through which the student could have been any more connected with the material. Indeed, we might imagine a setting where such typical modes of learning and assessment could stifle creative thinking, block learning through anxiety or refocus the student's attention away from the ideational and toward the textual, denying her the opportunities to become intricately connected with her material.

The Classroom at Site for the Construction of Learning. Students may be more motivated to use their journals to learn if they assume they are constructing their own knowledge. Many writing activities in school assumes that knowledge consists of bits of information to be memorized and recalled. Such assignments may also imply that the teacher knows all and the students know little. To demonstrate that they have acquired the teacher's knowledge, students may read a story and then take a quiz in which they must recall the names of characters or something about the setting or plot. Or, in E. D. Hirsch's (1987) pedagogical program, students learn certain facts and details that are thought to be part of our "cultural literacy" and will then become more facile readers and writers because of the "efficiency" with which they recognize these culturally shared bits of information (Anson, 1988). This approach suffers from the age-old problem of accommodation and assimilation: simply knowing or being able to recall certain facts doesn't guarantee that students will understand the wider phenomena or principles that unify them. Simply memorizing names and dates may not lead students to change or modify their existing knowledge or ideas. Engaging students in what Bereiter and Scard-amalia (1987) call "knowledge-telling"—recalling or regurgitating bits of information in writing—may not lead to deeper or more intellectually sophisticated understandings of the knowledge in question.

To know something requires synthesizing and integrating it into existing knowledge, and then examining it and bringing it to a level of critical awareness. Through this process, students construct knowledge for themselves. Constructivist theories of learning posit that by building their own knowledge in classrooms as "constructivist sites," students know something in the sense that they understand it. As Eleanor Duckworth notes, "All people ever have is their own understanding: you can tell them all sorts of things, but you can't make them believe it unless they construct it for themselves" (1992, p. 4).

The traditional notion of acquiring knowledge by accumulating and regurgitating "facts" is particularly problematic for the discouraged or at-risk student who, marginalized into low ability level tracks or groups, faces instruction that emphasizes skills and knowledge of grammar, usage and mechanics. Offered skills-driven assistance for years—non-functional, non-audience based and often purposeless—these students soon learn to perceive knowledge as something "out there" to be mastered, not as something they can construct from what they already know and can assimilate. In contrast, students in high-ability classes are encouraged to express their own thoughts and ideas; their literacy becomes more highly functional and inter-personal, project-oriented and engaging. In a traditional approach, for example, students studying drama might be given a presentation or lecture about the various charac-teristics of comedy. Having read and studied these "basic" ideas, they are then tested, sometimes objectively, on their accumulation of facts. This knowledge then becomes a "base" on which more meaningful experiences can be con-structed. High-ability students are assumed to have the base, and they are placed initially into contexts where the social dynamics of education, role-play, active learning and the like can be enacted immediately. Lower-ability students again and again miss these sorts of opportunities as the "bottom-up" educational model tries to plug information into their already dulled and unmotivated consciousness. This hierarchical program can be found in most areas of study, especially in writing and the language arts, where "remediation" involves courses in the "basics" of gram-mar and mechanics—often in instruction that doesn't per-mit texts longer than single paragraphs—and where advanced work permits highly social, functional and en-joyable writing activities.

Constructivist approaches assume that all language is and should be highly social, dialogic and interactive; that texts can't be divorced from their contexts or trivialized into exer-cises without turning them into what Russell Hunt (1989; 1993) calls "textoids," disconnected and often meaningless fragments of language that serve little purpose in students' development except the learning of isolated skills stripped of their functional meanings.

Placing writing at the center of learning through the use of journals doesn't guarantee that students don't write textoids; we have seen journals turned into simple reposito-ries of quite meaningless assignments. But even the slightest attempts to systematically work with journals in the class-room makes it difficult to deny writing its social and inter-personal functions. In the next chapter, these functions are described in detail as we consider the many and varied intellec-tual, academic and social purposes possible in journal writing.

Chapter Two

Purposes for Using Journals

The other day on the bus, we noticed a student writing in her journal. She was writing quite slowly, stopping to glance out the window and ponder her thoughts. While she may have been fulfilling an assignment, it was interesting to see how actively she was constructing meaning through the journal, her long, thoughtful gazes giving way to bursts of writing, her frowns of deep thought dissolving into looks of resolution. She seemed to be enjoying her work, as if driven by a sense of meaning and purpose.

Students who keep journals learn to think of their writing as purposeful, and fulfilling their academic and personal needs. For some, journal writing gives focus to their thoughts or enables them to concentrate on a particular topic in a reading or writing assignment. For others, the journal helps record and organize their reactions to readings or generate new ideas. If students know that jotting down responses to a story helps them write a paper, they are more likely to perceive journal writing as useful, rather than as just another onerous assignment. This new conception may lead them to use the journal on their own as a valuable tool for learning.

By putting the journal at the center of classroom instruction, we help students to see the range of different purposes their journal writing can serve. Figure 2.1 depicts a number of fairly distinct purposes for journal writing related to three larger goals of schooling—especially in English and the language arts—*improving thinking, enhancing formal writing* and *enriching the social context of the classroom.* As a seventh-grader makes observations in his journal about a reading, his learning of concepts and ideas is enhanced. As a high school junior engages in planning activities for a paper, she becomes more fluent and skilled at organizing her ideas for an essay. By sharing their entries on a short story, students in a senior literature course are drawn together, collaboratively, into a lively classroom discussion, anchoring their social relationships and engaging them in the course.

In this chapter, we describe more fully the various purposes shown in Figure 2.1, illustrating them in the context of students at different stages of development. In doing so, we do not want to imply that students come to journal writing with some predetermined purposes. Rather, the exploratory nature of journal writing leads students to discover new purposes for their writing. For example, in writing out her reactions to a novel, Dana described her perceptions of the character Conrad's behavior in the novel *Ordinary People*. She then realized that her jottings related to her paper on how families in literature react to traumatic events. With that purpose in mind, she returned to her entry, reread it from a new perspective and wrote another entry. In that process, she learned to use journal writing to discover a topic, even though her journal assignment made no overt connection to her formal paper.

As we suggest in this chapter, such purposes must first be structured and modeled in the classroom, leading students to recognize how these purposes can enhance their thinking,

Figure 2-1
Purposes for Journal Writing

Enhancing formal writing
- developing material for essay writing
- generating categories for organizing drafts

Enhancing the social context of the classroom
- enhancing classroom discussion
- constructing social inden-tities and relationships

Improving Thinking
- develop fluency
- learning to concentrate
- attending to intuitions
- discovering alternative modes of learning
- expressing emotional reactions
- recording, summarizing and organizing perceptions
- exploring and extending thinking
- formulating and testing beliefs

learning, writing and interaction with peers. Then, as they grow accustomed to the journal, they begin using it to fulfill their own purposes.

Improving Thinking

As writing theorists have long argued, a powerful connection exists between thought and written text as it emerges from a writer's pen (Emig, 1977). The act of making thoughts tangible and visible engenders new thinking, which leads to new text. The writer scans and rescans a fresh assertion, testing it with a reader's scrutiny and then reformulating it with a writer's new vision. By simply expressing their thoughts in writing, students are learning to think—describing phenomena, organizing perceptions and lodging new ideas more firmly into their consciousness. Of all the many claims for journal writing, the most powerful for teaching in all contexts is the belief that it makes more skilled, astute and creative thinkers of our students. This section describes the many ways in which journal writing can help students to think—and learn.

Developing Fluency

Sam is a seventh grader. When asked to write a paragraph, he produces only a few halting sentences. He can give "correct answers" on worksheets, but he doesn't like to write, especially when he must formulate his own ideas or explore his thoughts.

One reason for Sam's lack of fluency, is that most of his writing consists of short answers on tests and worksheets; he is rarely asked to write more than a paragraph of continuous prose. This common observation is supported by several surveys of school writing (Applebee, et al., 1994; Nystrand and Gamoran, 1991). In the survey of Applebee, et al., about two-thirds of eighth- twelfth-graders reported writing papers of only one paragraph on a weekly basis. Yet as Nystrand and Gamoran (1991) show, students who engage in extended writing of more than a page are better able to interpret literature than those who do little extended writing. The raw quantity of students' writing seems strongly related to how much and how well they learn.

Accustomed to giving "correct answers," many students rarely learn to compose—to formulate their own ideas or knowledge. This lack of experience integrating new knowledge into old—feeling and exploring it, intellectually turning it over and shaping it through their own understandings—

soon leads students to a sense that they have little or nothing to say about the world. In this dualistic perspective, "experts" create knowledge, and students absorb and regurgitate it (Perry, 1970). Lacking confidence in their own ideas, they simply defer to external authorities or the teacher as the primary source of knowledge.

Many students who have done little or no extended writing in or out of school need practice expressing and exploring their thoughts in writing. In using journals to enhance fluency, students simply fill up the pages with whatever they want to write. These experiences quickly lead students to develop confidence in their ability to express their own ideas. As we suggest in Chapter Five, response to this writing by teachers and peers acknowledges the validity of the student's ideas, leading to continued growth in confidence and self-esteem, characteristics of successful writers and communicators.

Being fluent also entails feeling comfortable about writing. Students who are uncomfortable or apprehensive about writing simply avoid it. For highly apprehensive writers, journal writing can build confidence and comfort in writing. Free from the constraints of formal essay writing and the inevitable corrective comments, students can learn to express their thoughts openly. Fear of the red pen can be quickly alleviated, as we propose in Chapter Five, without entirely removing "evaluation" if students can receive readerly comments through journal exchanges. They soon begin to perceive their writing as evoking positive responses in others. While journals are not a panacea for instant relief from writing apprehension, their informal nature and spontaneity can encourage some reluctant writers to develop a sense of voice and possibility to replace some of their fears. By putting words to paper in an uninhibited, freeflowing manner, students grow less concerned about being "correct," "neat" or "relevant."

Learning to Concentrate

Enter into the mind of an eighth grader, Mark, who is reading a short story in his classroom. Like many early adolescents, Mark feels like everyone in the class is watching him. He also has a lot on his mind—a fight with his mother at breakfast, a test scheduled for next period and a game after school. Distracted and troubled, he has difficulty concentrating on his reading. The story's events and characters seem to swirl around in his mind without adding up to anything meaningful.

Journals at Work: Building Confidence

Mary Ellen is a ninth grader who, like Sam, writes very little. In asking her to talk about her previous writing experiences in school, her teacher Dawn discovered that Mary Ellen had received a lot of negative "red-pencil" comments on her writing."Whenever I got my paper back," Mary Ellen told Dawn, "it was all marked-up with red ink. I became afraid of handing in any writing. Noone ever liked my writing." Dawn also discovered that Mary Ellen is a perfectionist. She wants to do it "just right." When she wrote her papers, she was concerned with following the prescribed guidelines for the "five-paragraph theme." Mary Ellen's lack of confidence and her preoccupations with form made her a reluctant writer, unable to express or explore her ideas freely and fluently. As Dawn helped her to write freely in a journal, Mary Ellen soon lost most of these inhibitions and began exploring her thoughts without fear. Her entries grew longer and more exploratory. Even when she wrote essays, they reflected a new-found confidence in her ability to express her own ideas.

Journal writing may help students like Mark to concentrate. By jotting down his perceptions of or reactions to the characters in the story, Mark is more likely to focus on the particulars of the text. Or, by writing about a topic, idea or issue, he can sustain his thinking about a topic. For example, as part of their discussion of the novel *Catch 22*, Mark's teacher asked her students to write a journal entry on the meaning of power and share their perceptions of the concept. As a bridge to the story, the teacher then asked the students to list examples of who does and does not have power in the novel and what it means to be powerful or to be powerless. With these topics in mind, Mark learned to explore an idea in a more sustained way.

Attending to Intuitions

In spontaneously expressing their own thoughts, students learn to attend to their unarticulated intuitions, what Perl (1980) calls their "felt sense." Once raised into consciousness, these feelings and intuitions can help them to explore the nature of their relationship to academic material. As they record these momentary insights in a journal, students begin listening to their own inner speech, conducting "an intimate conversa

> ### Journals at Work: Attending to Intuitions
>
> Jane, an eleventh grader, reads an article in the school newspaper showing that students are generally having difficulty completing their homework because they lack the drive to succeed. But Jane knows that the long hours many students work in after-school jobs interfere with their homework. In her journal, she explores her dissatisfaction with the newspaper article. At the same time, she also senses a lack of validity in her generalization that long working hours interferes with doing homework. As she openly expresses her feelings about these topics, she learns to rely on her intuitions to guide her thinking.

tion" with themselves (Belanoff, 1991, p. 21), listening for "other voices" representing different perspectives or attitudes. The thinking that results, as Ann Berthoff (1981) describes it, can be "chaotic." But this chaos then yields to a sense of uncertainty, as students question the status quo because they are not satisfied with simply restating what is already known.

Discovering Alternative Modes of Learning

Much of students' learning in school is limited to logocentric modes of learning—reading and writing with an emphasis on logical/rational thinking. But as Howard Gardner (1985) has argued, students bring different forms of intelligence to school in addition to these school-based modes of thinking and reasoning. Some students have a highly developed sense of visual and spatial intelligence which is manifested in artistic expressions. The journal allows students to express themselves in ways that may be more in keeping with their thinking and learning styles.

Visual/spatial expression. From a logocentric perspective, it is assumed that language precipitates thought and writing. However, this is equally true of images and visual representations which, as writing theorist Stephen Witte (1992) has argued, may precede the verbal expression of thoughts in writing. A more visually-oriented journal invites students to express their ideas creatively both in language and in images. In some cases, writing triggers images or illustrations, while in other cases, the images or illustrations trigger writing. For those students with a strong visual/spatial orientation or learning style, incorporating visual images into their journals helps them express their thoughts and ideas.

Journals at Work: Visual Learning

One of our students, Dana, illustrated her journal using a range of different magic-marker colors and icons to highlight and emphasize concepts, clips of newspaper headlines, magazine ads and drawings. Her writing, which sometimes wound around cutouts from magazines, served several purposes: from labeling parts of a clipping, to commenting or analyzing its features, or to connecting something visual to her own experience. Often she related an advertisement newspaper cartoon to a piece of literature she was studying in a class.

Oral expression. Some students are more proficient as speakers than writers. Students with learning disabilities that hinder their capacity to write fluently are often more confident expressing their ideas orally than in writing. For such students, taping their thoughts may help to facilitate their expression of ideas (see Chapter Three for discussion of tape journals). Extended monologues build confidence in students' own "voices," which can lead to greater fluency.

Students may also use journals to tape oral anecdotes or narratives. Many students are adept at entertaining the class with accounts of the latest car accident in the parking lot or fight in the hallway. For these students, as Jerome Bruner (1986) has argued, narrative serves as a powerful way of knowing. Rather than approach learning from strictly a logical/deductive approach, these students may employ narratives to capture their understanding of a phenomenon or topic.

Expressing Emotional Reactions

Many students are reluctant to express their emotional reactions or engagement in writing. When asked to cite reasons for their emotional response to a text, only one-fourth of 13-year-olds and two fifths of 17-year-olds taking the 1980 NAEP assessment were able to do so (Education Commission of the States, 1981). The reason stems from a lack of experience exploring their responses in class discussions. Numerous studies of classrooms discussions show that only a small percentage of talk is devoted to expressing feelings. Writing, even more distanced and formal, is often associated with an "analytic" mode of thinking that devalues the emotional. Males, in particular, find it difficult to express their feelings in written journals, possibly because they associate journal writing

---

Journals at Work: From Oral to Written Fluency

Chuck, an eighth grader, generally said little or nothing in class discussions. As he began to use a tape journal, he started to "hear" himself express his thoughts in an extended form. He told stories into the microphone about his hiking trips and how satisfying it was to reach the top of a mountain after a long climb. Once he became comfortable with the tape journal, he began to talk more in class. Similarly, Joseph, an African-American student, told a series of stories on a tape journal about being harassed by police officers and security guards at a local shopping mall. In reflecting on these stories, he began to think about why he was perceived as a threat. He recalled his descriptions of the police officers and guards, then considered the possibility that they are insecure and need to harass others in order to maintain a sense of power and control. He also reflected on his role as a black teenager in a white-dominated culture. Instead of beginning with exposition about his experiences, his story-telling led him to new and interesting insights.

---

with "being feminine" (Gannett, 1992). In adopting a detached stance, males avoid expressing their feelings.

The tendency for writing to be used only for objective analysis is unfortunate not only in its reinforcement of genre stereotypes but, also because emotional reactions can often precipitate analysis. Expressing one's doubt about an idea may lead to a more intelligent critique. For example, given the spontaneous nature of journal writing, students may begin an entry by stating an emotional reaction to a text, presentation or event: "I really liked that story;" "that was a really dumb film;" "I was bored by the end;" "I can't believe something like that would ever happen." Describing their identification or empathy with a character or person may lead them to consider possible reasons for these feelings. Emotional reactions may also trigger autobiographical connections. Emotions of anger, envy or love may evoke recollection of experiencing that emotion in the past.

Many adolescents have difficulty reflecting on their response experience. In his research with adolescents, John Thompson (1987) proposes a hierarchy of responses related to the levels of students' reflection: "unreflective interest in action," "empathizing," "analogizing," "reflecting on the significance of events and behavior," "reviewing the work as the

Journals at Work: Exploring Emotional Responses

William Steig (1989) cites the example of a college student, Marian, who wrote about her first reading *Wuthering Heights* at age seventeen. She experienced "the intensity of the emotion between Catherine and Heathcliff, recalling it as a love quite apart from physical, sexual or natural love" (54). She also recalled a similar intimacy with her boyfriend Ted in the eighth grade. Her intimacy then deteriorated as she rejected Ted and Ted changed as a person. In reading her past journal entries about her relationship with Ted, she associated her hurt feelings with her feelings about Heathcliff's relationship with Catherine. This association didn't give her a complete answer; instead, she used her writing to ask deeper questions: "If Ted does play a Heathcliff role and I, a Cathy role, why is it that I sympathize with Heathcliff? Perhaps our tales are closer than, even now, I care to admit" (57). Steig notes that this kind of writing helped Marian "understand [their relationship] as it seemed to be reflected in *Wuthering Heights*, first to an adolescent girl and then, in a quite different way, to the same person as a young woman" (61).

author's creation," and "defining one's own and the author's ideology." Most of the adolescents in his studies responded on the first three levels; unless prompted, few went beyond those levels to reflect more fully on their responses.

The sort of metacognitive awareness proposed in Thompson's higher levels encourages students to explore their own attitudes, beliefs and values. For example, having described the fact that she was angry about a guest speaker's presentation on government and taxes, a student then considers possible reasons for her anger, reasons having to do with her beliefs about government. Her emotional reactions trigger deeper thinking—and fuller learning.

Recording, Summarizing and Organizing Perceptions

Students often use their journals as a study aid to record and summarize their responses to a reading, a story, a film or a lecture. Such writing involves more than copying the information presented in the text. Recasting information in their own words allows students to incorporate it into their existing knowledge. During lectures students usually copy down the teacher's words verbatim, assuming that they will review these later—most often to cram before a test. By rendering a teacher's points in their own words, students must understand and reflect on the material, reformulating the teacher's ideas to match their own knowledge.

The influence of purpose on note-taking is evident in several research studies. Durst (1989) examined the processes of 11th graders as they wrote summaries from notes. The more successful summary writers were more aware of task goals, the relationship between new information and what they already knew about a topic and the significance of information relative to the topic. In another study of college freshmen writing from sources (Kennedy, 1985), better readers were more likely to manipulate and revise their notes prior to writing their drafts. In contrast, the less able readers often simply recopied their notes without relating them to the purposes of their draft. The two groups differed primarily in the degree to which they were willing to transform their reading notes into their own ideas and agendas. As Kennedy notes:

> The truly fluent group read the text with pencil-in-hand, overtly employing many spontaneous learning activities like underlining and providing comments that revealed they were interacting with the authors in a deliberate way. Conversely, the not-so-fluent group were passive processors who read the texts with hands tied behind their backs, rarely using study-type strategies or acting upon the texts in an assertive way (p. 451).

Observing phenomena. The dominant educational view of knowledge assumes that students learn facts and information that exist independently of them, in a prepackaged form. Even in recording perceptions students are engaged in constructing their own knowledge. The active role of meaning-making is especially evident when students use their journals in ethnographic investigations of some context or phenomenon. In these projects, students observe and record observations of behaviors at sports events, in classrooms, the lunchroom, shopping malls, meetings of clubs or religious organizations or television dramas.

Organizing Perceptions. Recording perceptions is just the beginning of a process that involves later arrangement, comparison and analysis. Informal, spontaneous journal writing is, unfortunately, often thought too messy and associative to foster the "hard thought" that leads to the logical arrangement of ideas. In freewriting, students are assumed to use a

Journals at Work: Recording Perceptions

Kennedy cites the examples of a less-fluent reader, Dave, and a fluent reader, Tracy. Both of these students read from sources and wrote a rough draft. Dave's plan was simply to include information from the articles he read. He mechanically inserted author's ideas into the draft, "stringing them together in a piece-meal fashion" (452). In contrast, Tracy went beyond Dave's plan to take notes on the articles, defining connections between the articles, creating a contextual framework and outline for organizing her perceptions and then using her notes to guide her drafting.

Tracy was able to rework and organize her notes to construct her own knowledge because she had a defined plan or strategy for doing so. This suggests the need for instruction on how to go beyond Dave's regurgitating of notes to reworking and constructing a framework for organizing notes. A key step in this process is the ability to extract a set of categories for organizing the notes.

Students may also define their purpose or plan for note-taking *socially*—to impress a peer or teacher, convince a friend to do something or to lead a group discussion. An eleventh grade teacher asked certain students to be discussion leaders for Eudora Welty's short story, "Why I Live at the P.O." One student, Jill, jotted down her thoughts about what she planned to do in her discussion with four of her close peers. On one side of the journal, she jotted down her responses to the story. On the other side, based on her responses, she wrote about what she hoped to accomplish in the discussion—to get her peers to express their reactions to the story, to explain the characters' behaviors, to compare their own family to the family in the story and to explore the credibility of the narrator. On the same side, she also jotted down some things her peers might find interesting in their own lives—"ways into" the story. She then returned to the other side and, with her objectives and student interests in mind, described some possible questions or activities related to her responses. She used her perceptions of her social role as discussion leader to organize her thoughts.

> ## Journals at Work: Observing Phenomena
>
> In *Living Between the Lines*, Lucy Calkins (1991) describes how a group of fifth grade students investigated the plight of the homeless in New York City. The students talked with homeless people, public officials and social workers. Throughout their project they recorded their observations in notebooks, which served as the basis for their work. They wrote reports and letters to authorities that drew on these observations. Rather than simply reading or listening to presentations, they were able to develop their own understandings of the homeless.

"what-next" strategy (Hillocks, 1986), writing down whatever pops into the heads in a linear, pell-mell manner. For more careful, logical thinking, formal essay writing is the preferred genre. However, as Richard Haswell (1991) has argued, this view equates "organization" with a formalist, text-governed notion of structure (the five-paragraph theme being one well-known model). Haswell proposes a more "reader-based" definition of organization that draws on Kenneth Burke's (1969) notion of a subjective sense of arousal and fulfillment. In responding to a story of a quest, a reader's experience may be organized through empathy with the hero's journey. That journey, with its culmination at the end of the quest, transcends the traditional models of text structure to which much of our instruction is tied—models that include such well-known forms and patterns as "problem/solution," "cause/effect," or "comparison/contrast." In his research, Haswell (1991) found that when students engaged in freewriting, they organized their perceptions according to this "reader-based" sense of arousal and fulfillment. In his analysis of hundreds of freewriting entries from freshmen composition classes, Haswell noted that more than half of the freewrites were "point-driven" (Vipond & Hunt, 1984); two thirds of the entries were written with a definite purpose. He also found that most of the freewrites exhibited a "claim-driven," logical organization in which students stated and defended certain ideas or positions. His analysis seriously questions the common assumption that journal writing is "disorganized" and "non-logical."

Using visual display to organize entries. In writing an entry, students may simply put down whatever words or phrases come to mind. This "visual display" invites them to adopt a reader-based perspective (Emig, 1977), from which they can

---

Journals at Work: Organizing Perceptions

Donna, a ninth grader, was writing about her experience organizing a debate on gun control in her English class. She developed an extensive body of information on the topic and was prepared to argue her case for the need for gun control based on an extensive set of facts. But during the debate, her opponent used emotional arguments for individuals' rights to own their own guns for self-defense. These claims appealed to the other students in the class. Donna was upset that these emotional arguments carried more weight with her classmates that her factual evidence.

In describing her experience in an entry, she organized her recollections around her growing frustrations with the direction of the debate. While she never explicitly stated an underlying point or thesis, her perceptions revolved around the idea that the emotional pleas were carrying the day. As she wrote, she intuitively began to develop an underlying point—that factual arguments may not always be effective. Rather than writing a series of disconnected perceptions, from her own reader-based, "point-driven" stance (Vipond & Hunt, 1984), she experienced a kind of internal logic concerning her expectations about the most effective forms of argument.

---

infer various relationships and interconnections. By putting a word or phrase next to another word or phrase, a student may literally "see" them as related—a phenomenon noted in a great deal of work on invention and pre-writing.

Exploring and Extending Thinking

In addition to describing perceptions, students may also use the journal to explore and extend their thinking about a particular topic, idea or issue. While students may have difficulty extending their thinking in an entry, in every day social conversation, other students provide the prompts that encourage them to keep thinking about that topic. When one student falters, another jumps in. The force of this social interaction does not always transfer to the students' writing, in part because they see writing as monologic—as involving only their singular definitive voice or personae. They have had little experience taking a more dialogical, dialectical approach to extending their thinking.

Journals at Work: Visual Displays of Perceptions

As part of an observational study of cliques, a student described her perceptions of the different groups in her school:

Different groups in the school. Jocks, nerds, geeks, burnouts, brains, politicians, drop-outs cheerleaders, druggies. Some of these overlap.

jocks	politicians	cheerleaders
nerds	geeks	brains
burnouts	drop-outs	druggies

By reflecting on her chart, she posed a number of questions that led her to devise a plan for further work:

What makes these groups different? How do students see these groups as differing from each other. Some of them have more power than others. Some of them like being in school more than others. Maybe I could chart the relationships between these groups.

She then took her entry and rearranged the items as if on a graph, with power and liking school as two axes:

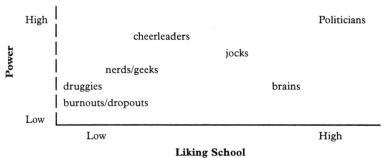

Based on her chart, she could then write about how these different groups are perceived according to the criteria of "power" and "liking school."

The journal as inner dialogue. Understanding this dialogic perspective requires a model that differs from the traditional textbook models of the "well-organized, coherent" formal essay. We propose an alternative way to explain the thinking process in journal writing: the journal as inner dialogue. To extend and explore their thinking, students learn to engage in a dialogue with themselves.

For the theorist Mikhail Bakhtin (1981), dialogue is central to existence. When people make an utterance or respond to a text, they are "answerable" for what they are saying in terms of the social effects on and responses of others. At an *internal* level, a person constructs an intrapersonal dialogue that takes into account the potential *external* dialogue. The meaning of this internal dialogue is intimately related to the social meanings of the external social context. As Gregory Clark (1990) notes," understanding is constructed in a second internal, intrapersonal dialogue, this one within the person to whom an utterance is addressed, a dialogue conducted in response to the utterance of another" (12). Similarly, in writing in the journal, students are engaged in an inner dialogue of acts and reactions. As writers, the students state a thought, an action. As readers, they may then react to their own statement in terms of how others may have reacted to their statement.

Journals at Work: Inner Dialogues

In responding to John Updike's story, "A&P," Roberta, a twelfth grader, writes, "I'm really upset that Sammy quit his job without really thinking about what he was doing. He made a really dumb mistake." In an act of self-interrogation, she reflects on her own previous assertion. She senses that characterizing Sammy's action as "dumb" may be a little too harsh. She wonders about whether or not he was simply being dumb or stupid, or whether or not there may be something else going on, speculating that, "maybe he's not so stupid after all." By sensing the limitation of her thinking, she adopts an alternative stance, exploring the possibility that his action was motivated by some thoughtful, deliberate plan. She then writes, "Or, maybe he really wanted to quit because he was so bored working in his mindless job at the grocery store." Through this inner dialogue, she is extending her thinking by reflecting on her own ideas through a series of acts and reactions.

In conceiving of journal writing as an inner dialogue, we are implying something more sophisticated than simply dialogue as aimless chit-chat that often serves to simply maintain friendly social relationships. Rather, we want to portray the inner dialogue as a dialectical exchange which has some underlying purpose associated with carrying on an argument or debate. Dialectical thinking is open to exploring alternative perspectives for the sake of continuing the discussion it-self. It avoids a premature closure inherent in a competitive concern, found in debates, for "scoring points." As George Dillon (1991) describes dialectical thinking, it is:

> concerned with the procedures of argumentation, espe-cially with argumentation pro and contra as a means of submitting claims to critical scrutiny. As such, it values explicitness and candor in the articulation of positions, the bracketing of other, potentially persuasive consider-ations, the freedom of participants to express their views fully "without fear or favor," and the agree to accede to the position supported by the best reasons (p. 145).

The ability to carry on a conversation with oneself in writing requires the ability to reflect on one's own thinking, something that many students may have difficulty doing. Given the spontaneous nature of their journal writing, students may make their own process explicit of self-interrogation as "in-ner speech." For example, having raised doubts about his own ideas, a student may state that "this just doesn't make sense. I need to go back and think about this some more," making explicit his own way of reacting and a plan for furthering his thinking.

Some students may have difficulty assessing the suffi-ciency of or doubting their own opinions, perhaps because they are not accustomed to reacting critically to texts. In his book, *Reading as Rhetorical Invention*, Doug Brent (1992) ar-gues that students need to learn "how to be persuaded by texts" when they read (105). In thinking about the persua-siveness of their own positions, students need to adopt the stance of the skeptical, doubting audience. In some cases, being the doubting audience means entertaining opposing beliefs.

Learning to reflect on a writer's believability may also help students reflect on their own believability. Having asked the question, "Do I really believe this writer," students may ask the same question of themselves—reflecting on and chal-lenging their own positions.

Students are more likely to doubt their own assertions if they are aware of alternative perspectives on a topic or issue. For example, in reading a number of articles on the topic of national health care insurance, a student quickly discovers that advocates of different health care plans hold quite differ-ent beliefs, often due to the constituency they represent—the insurance industry, private citizens, the government. To make sense of these differences, students need to do more than define each of these participants' positions. They also need to

---

Journals at Work: Doubting as Inner Dialogue

A student writes that "most people are basically out for themselves—they are driven by their own self-interest." In reflecting on this statement, he senses the limitation of the word "most." He then entertains the opposite perspective, writing in his entry that "on the other hand, some people do act out of a sense of 'doing good for others.'" By raising an alternative belief, he must then reconcile the competing statements, which he does by noting that "people may vary in their motives for acting. In some cases, they act out of self-interest, while in other cases, they act on the basis of doing good for others."

Based on a discussion of the criminal justice system, Alyn, another student, writes that "People who commit crimes need to be locked up in prisons; that's the only way that you can prevent them from conducting more crime." But after reflecting on her statement, she begins to have some second thoughts. Recalling the discussion in class, she then writes in her entry, "On the other hand, people often learn about crime in prisons, so that when they get out, they simply do more crime." This leads her to further reflection: "Maybe the key is what happens in jail: whether people get any rehabilitation in jail, or whether they just learn to become criminals." Doubting her initial thesis that time in jail prevents crime leads her to consider some counter evidence, which then suggests an alternative thesis regarding the nature of the experience in jail.

---

be able to define their own beliefs relative to the different positions being espoused. In doing so, they are defining their own beliefs towards, for example, national health care. They also need to ferret out the reasons for a writer's beliefs; why writers may adopt different positions on the same topic. Knowing that a writer who defends the current health care system is a lobbyist for insurance industry increases their self-doubt.

Students may also doubt assertions for which they have little or no evidence. Having made the claim that "nobody in this high school would want to go into the military," a student may begin to wonder if she has sufficient evidence for this claim. Adopting the stance of the sceptic, she makes explicit her own reactions: "I wonder if this is really true. Maybe I should ask around and see if there is anybody who is planning to go into the military. You never know, there just may be somebody out there who is." In this case, questioning the validity of her own claims in the journal gives way to a test of those claims, and a richer analysis of the issue.

Moving from inner to outer dialogue. In addition to learning to reflect on their own assertions, students may also explore and extend their thinking by entertaining multiple voices. In some cases, these are the voices of actual people—a friend, teacher, parent or favorite writers. In other cases, they simply represent certain positions, ideas or institutions.

These inner dialogues between voices do not take place in a vacuum. They occur within the larger context of what we will call the outer dialogue, the actual or hypothetical social drama surrounding the inner dialogue. Many students, particularly extroverts, rely on this outer dialogue to help them engage in various forms of self-interrogation.

When students exchange entries with each other they write for a real audience, anticipating possible responses. While they may not accept their partner's perspective, they are still entertaining an alternative point of view. This lifts them out of their adolescent egocentricity, encouraging them to recognize the need to consider multiple perspectives.

Students' inner dialogues also reflect the larger outer dialogue—conversations, debates and deliberations occurring in the community, society or media. Participating in the ongoing discussions about certain contentious topics or issues—abortion, equity, the environment and women's rights—they become immersed in the complex, intertextual network of different, often conflicting beliefs.

Formulating and Testing Beliefs

Much of the writing students do in schools consists of what Bereiter and Scardamelia (1987) describe as "knowledge telling": recounting or describing perceptions of texts, with some occasional interpretation. Students read a story and are then given a quiz on the names of characters or details about the setting, sometimes in order to develop their "cultural literacy" (Hirsch, 1987). However, simply knowing, memorizing or being able to recall certain facts does not necessarily mean that students will actually understand these facts or use them to modify their own ideas. To know something deeply—to "understand" it in the fullest sense of the word—students need to construct their own knowledge and formulate their own beliefs and ideas. Constructivist theories of learning suggest that by creating their own knowledge and understanding,

> ## Journals at Work: Inner to Outer Dialogue
>
> Marsha is exchanging her entries with Jill. In responding to the novel, *The Color Purple,* she writes in her journal, "I just wish that Celie had been more assertive in her marriage. Why does she put up with that man?" She then thinks about how Jill may react to her statement. Based on Jill's previous comments that Celie is a victim of a system which she is powerless to change, she predicts that Jill will answer her question, "Why does she put up with that man?" by saying that she has no choice. With Jill's hypothetical reaction in mind, Marsha then has some second thoughts. She writes, "Just as you have argued Jill, maybe she doesn't really have much choice in the matter. She can't just walk out on him—where would she go and how would she live?"
>
> Mike, an eleventh grader, is using his journal to plan a presentation to some seventh graders about conflict resolution. In an entry, he describes some possible ideas on the value of conflict resolution: "Conflict resolution helps them think about other person's point of view." He then envisions how a hypothetical seventh grader would react to that idea. In his journal, he begins to wonder "whether they are even able to grasp the idea of thinking about another's point of view. If they can't even do that, how are they going to understand the idea? I've probably got to help them understand what I mean by 'point of view.' Maybe I'll do an activity. Maybe I can stage a fight over stealing a hat and have them talk about what it feels like when someone steals your hat."

students know something in the sense that they understand it and believe it to be true. As Eleanor Duckworth (1992) notes, "All people ever have is their own understanding: you can tell them all sorts of things, but you can't make them believe it unless they construct it for themselves" (4).

Traditional "essentialist" approaches to learning may be especially inadequate for the discouraged or "at-risk" student who, marginalized into remedial curriculums, is often taught in ways that emphasize skills, the accumulation of discrete facts or the memorization of rules. Knowledge to such students becomes something "out there" to be mastered, not something constructed through their own resources and integrated into what they know. Such a view often adds to their feelings of inadequacy or powerlessness in the classroom. They learn to assume that their own beliefs, concerns or what is really on their minds are irrelevant—a process that can lead to serious disengagement and dropping out of school (Fine).

In order to truly understand a phenomenon, students need to do more than simply acquire knowledge about it. They may know enough about the idea of "free will" to be able to state the meaning of the concept. But by defining their beliefs and ideas about free will in a journal, a student achieves a deeper understanding of that concept.

Students are more likely to express their own beliefs and ideas if they feel strongly about or are bothered by a particular topic or issue. For example, asked to write a description of their school, it is unlikely that they will talk about their beliefs and attitudes. However, if asked to write about how they *feel* about their school, they are invited to express their *own* beliefs and ideas. The fact that a student is bothered by a school rule that any student who is late to class must report to detention leads her to consider reasons why she is bothered—the fact that the rule is based on a punitive attitude towards students, something she opposes.

As we have argued, formulating beliefs and ideas is not a solitary event, but rather occurs in an ongoing conversation with the beliefs and ideas of peers or the beliefs and ideas expressed in texts. In reacting to the beliefs and ideas of others in their journals, students begin to perceive the journal not simply as a private expression of feelings and thoughts. They may also begin to recognize that their journal serves as a forum for grappling with a host of voices representing a host of others' beliefs and attitudes. They learn to connect the inner dialogue with the outer dialogue. For example, in writing about the issue of pressure to succeed in their lives, students may incorporate a number of different voices—parents, teachers or friends who may have a range of different points of view about positive and negative aspects of pressure, some believing that pressure is a necessary force while others believing that it is debilitating. As students formulate these different perspectives, they may then stand back from their own entry to perceive it as a text consisting of different perspectives, as a conversation or public forum of which they are a member/participant. They may then agree with or disagree with others, a process that encourages them to extend their thinking about an issue or topic.

It is again important to recognize the strong relationship between purpose for writing in the journal and what is happening in the classroom. Students are more likely to express their beliefs and ideas if they feel strongly about a provocative topic or issue or if they are engaged in classroom activities that involve them socially in expressing their beliefs and ideas: open-ended discussions, forums and debates. They are particularly more likely to disuss their own beliefs and attitudes when they have been challenged. For example, if Bill has made an outrageously sexist remark that offends Susan, she may want to write in her journal about what offends her. Or a retort by Susan to Bill may prompt Bill to explore his attitudes in his own journal.

Some students may be reluctant to express beliefs and ideas because they feel tentative to them. Some of this stems from instruction in writing formal essays that emphasizes the need to be definitive—to "prove your point in order to win over your audience." Because they are records of ongoing thoughts, journals encourage students to entertain what are called "passing theories" (Davidson, 1984)—tentative hypotheses or hunches that students entertain on a trial basis, "trying them on for size."

Journals at Work:
Formulating and Testing Beliefs

Gail is writing about the topic of censorship. While she strongly believes that magazines such as *Playboy* present women as sex objects, she is also uneasy about suggesting that they be censored, knowing that this is an issue of free speech. In her vacillation, Gail begins to consider the notion that it is the readers themselves who need to learn to be critical of sexist, stereotyped portrayals of women. By treating this idea as a "passing theory" in her journal, she can test it out to determine if it would work. Her passing theory prompts some further reflection about whether readers could become critical of stereotyped portrayals or whether being critical would actually changes basic attitudes towards women.

Students may also use their journals to explore the problematic, ambiguous and multifaceted aspects of experience. Many secondary students adopt a dualist stance, thinking in absolutist terms, asserting simplistic opinions or ideas: "all seventh graders are nerds," "most adults don't care about kids," "girls are no good at math," "boys who play football are dumb." To move beyond dualist thinking, students need to entertain opposing opinions or ideas and to test these out against evidence.

What leads students to explore complexities in their writing? In a study of tenth graders' exploration of complexities inherent in their journal writing about beliefs and in their freewriting responses to literature, one of the authors (Beach, 1991) found that students who were willing to critically examine their own lives were more likely to explore complexities in their writing. These students frequently challenged institutional norms, entertaining other explanations or interpretations. In contrast, students who defined their social identities by conforming to institutionally defined roles of being the "good student" or "good athlete" were less open to weighing different versions of reality. In responding to literature or writing narratives, these more "reality-bound" students may have more difficulty entering into or adopting the multiple perspectives invited by the transaction with the text.

To help students explore opposing perspectives, Barry Kroll (1990) designed a course on the Vietnam War. To encourage the acceptance of complexity, Kroll asked his students to write in their journals about contradictory accounts of the same battles. Kroll found that the students began to move away from a dualistic, absolutist way of thinking and became more open to entertaining and testing out competing perspectives.

Part of formulating new beliefs and ideas involves entertaining different disciplinary perspectives, a process strongly encouraged by the writing-across-the-curriculum movement. In the typical school day, secondary students move quickly from one subject matter to another in 45 or 50 minutes periods. This structure often fragments their learning into quite different disciplinary experiences as they enter into different ways of learning and knowing. They move from a history class, where they have just considered cause/effect relationships, to a chemistry class, where they hypothesize about and observe different chemical reactions. From math, where they engage in symbol manipulation, they move to a foreign-language class where they learn to think about cultural differences in language use. In some cases they find it hard to switch from one kind of thinking to another—or they aren't able to use a thinking strategy in one class (cause/effect in history, for example) when they move to another (chemistry, where the same process is at work with different "material"). They have not yet acquired the specific thought processes associated with what it means to be a historian, scientist, mathematician or translator. By using journals in different subject areas, students gain practice in thinking like historians, scientists, mathematicians or translators.

In journal writing, students can also apply different perspectives to the same text. In a course on using film and television in the classroom, one of us asked our students to respond to the same film or television program from a range

---

Journals at Work:
Entertaining Disciplinary Perspectives

In a composition course at Central State University in Ohio, instructors had their students respond to examples of African-American art (Scott, Davis, and Walker, 1989). In their initial entries, students responded without any prompting. Reacting to a portrait painting "Ode for Two Black Dsyton Poets," a student wrote: "The portrait of the man and woman was very unclear. It looked like a plain picture of a man and a woman" (21). The students then heard a presentation by an anthropologist/art critic who discussed the work. The student returned to the painting, and wrote:

> I went back to get a better look. I realized that the man's face was painted like that of a warrior. The woman's face was painted also . . . she looked like an African woman in (tribal) dress and make-up. They seem to represent the past and present in all of us (21).

Once the students in the course acquired the anthropological perspective, they responded more to the larger cultural meaning of the images. The students then participated in a workshop with the artist, who shared his motivation and techniques and led the students in creating their own art. After this experience, the student returned again to his journal:

> The present was represented by the hairstyle and the past was represented by the paint on the faces and body . . . . When looking at old pictures of family members, the pictures are usually black and white. The style of dress and the painted faces are of the past, but in color . . . there seemed to be an inverted relationship between the two . . . ." (21).

As the student was exposed to new and different ways of thinking about art, he revised his perception of the art work and learned to construct his own evolving meanings.

---

of different perspectives: technical/aesthetic, semiotic, generic, cultural/anthropological, archetypal/mythic, feminist and economic/Marxist. At the end of the course, students noted that by applying each of these perspectives, they responded to new and different aspects of the same film or program.

Enhancing Formal Writing

To this point, we have been illustrating the many purposes of journal writing in the enhancement of students' learning, thinking and intellectual development. In many cases the writing is informal and exploratory, designed not for finished, articulate communication with an audience but for a reflexive connection with the self as it constructs new meaning. In some theories of writing development, less structured, expressive writing of the kind we have described is said to *improve writing ability,* albeit indirectly, as a kind of by-product of engaging the mind, eye and hand (Emig, 1977).

Yet as we pointed out in Chapter One, journal writing can also serve as a more direct route to improved writing ability by becoming part of the processes in which students engage on the way from an initial thought or assignment to a finished text. In this section, we briefly explore some uses of journal writing in the process of creating formal papers.

Developing Material for Essay Writing

Given the recursive nature of the writing process, in which students continually cycle between generating and organizing ideas in drafts, the journal can provide an excellent place for them to work out their thinking informally, during and even after their drafting. As with freewriting, students should not be concerned about aspects of organization associated with drafting. As Lucy Calkins notes, "They [notebooks] have served as a concrete, physical invitation to write without requiring me to view my scrawlings as rough drafts" (Calkins, 1991, p. 38). Nor should students be concerned, at this stage, with readability or clarity, which are usually best practiced later on during the revising and editing processes. Although nothing about writing can ever be entirely linear, young students often face cognitive overload if they are expected to work with too many different aspects of writing at the same time. Such overload can lead—as it often does in test-essay situations—to a high degree of apprehension.

In using the journal as prewriting, students need to learn to maintain a sense of tentativeness in exploring their ideas. Often out of concern for completing a draft to meet a deadline, they may prematurely close off their exploration of ideas simply to move to a draft and "get it in on time." As a result, they may simply rely on external sources or authorities without much reflection of their own. For these students, copying some "key quotes" expedites the whole process, which circumvents two important educational purposes of writing—to think and to learn, not simply to communicate.

Generating topics and questions for essays. Students who have difficulty selecting a topic for their essays can list a series of things they have done in their life, topics they are interested in or ideas or texts that intrigue them. After reviewing their lists, they can select one experience, topic, idea or text. They can then list as many questions as they can think of about their choice. Then, in reviewing their questions, they can combine, eliminate or collapse certain questions, generating a short list of questions. These questions then provide the grist for further developing information through observing, listing, freewriting or mapping.

Generating categories for organizing drafts. Students often have difficulty devising and organizing raw material into a coherent paper. Formulaic structures such as the five-paragraph theme may provide them with a simplistic template for arranging material, but this doesn't teach them alternative structures based on the topic or content of their writing. Journal writing offers them a place in which to try out different organizing schemes for their ideas.

Journals at Work: Generating Material

As he writes about his various friendships, Fred realizes that he needs to define what he means by "friendship." He then goes back to his journal and reflects on the meaning of friendship. First he lists six characteristics of friendship, using the names of his friends to illustrate the concept to himself: "Jodi: I go to her when I feel really down about something. Bryan: The friendship of sports and action. Eric: Best friend, can tell him anything and everything." This material, initially close to the self, then helps him to pull out higher-level abstractions, which he does in a series of short freewriting episodes. His paragraph about Jodi focuses on certain kinds of friends who are natural commiserators, and how these kind are probably friends for life because they share your down moments and lift your spirits, something Fred labels "a gift forever." After writing his six paragraphs, Fred has a good deal of material for his paper, material that now needs to be arranged in an interesting and logical way.

Journals at Work:
Generating Organizational Categories

Sharon is writing an analysis of her high school's athletic program, comparing the degree of support for male versus female teams. She has conducted extensive interviews with players, coaches and school administrators, resulting in pages of comments. She has also been jotting down her thoughts based on her reflections about the interviews. For each entry page, she then entitles that page as to its basic overall focus: "discussions with male coaches," "discussions with female coaches," "limitations of the female basketball team," and so on. These titles become the central organizing terms for her essay: "problems with the current program," "reasons for problems," "solutions," and "reasons solutions will work."

Searching journals. In keeping a journal for an entire semester or course, students can't always remember what they wrote weeks before. Once students have developed their categories, they can use those categories to search back through their journal entries to resurrect material for their draft. To readily identify material in these categories, they can also create their own visual icons or symbols that represent the different categories and write these icons or symbols next to relevant material in the entries. Alternatively, they can apply icons or symbols to identify material they believe is particularly significant or important. After reviewing their entries, they then return to those items that have been starred or circled and rewrite or revise these early entries for their papers.

Enriching the Social
Context of the Classroom

While journals have long conjured up images of personal, therapeutic and self-expressive modes of writing, it should be evident that their appropriate use in the classroom is nothing less than socially dynamic. As students write and share their thoughts, they are anchoring relationships with their peers, witnessing different learning styles, hearing different perspectives on issues and seeing first-hand that the interpretation of knowledge and texts varies from person to person. But because journals begin in the personal realm of writers exploring their thoughts, their classroom use may be more accurately characterized as a rhythm of public and private, a kind of oscillation between the self as learner and the community of selves that make up the learning in school.

This section explores some of the social functions of journal writing in the classroom, including the enhancement of discussions and other uses of oral language and the construction of productive social relationships that can lead to deeper learning among peers.

Enhancing Classroom Discussions

It's a familiar pattern. You begin a discussion by asking the students to give their responses to a poem. The same few students eagerly contribute, while the rest of the class sits in silence. How do you encourage those other students to contribute and share their responses? The eager contributors do so because they have confidence in their ability to express themselves. They can "think on their feet," formulating their ideas as they speak. The silent students, apprehensive about their ideas or speaking abilities, become further and further silenced as the glib students dominate the discussion.

Just as journal writing can serve as "prewriting," to prepare students for writing, it can also be used to enhance classroom discussions, particularly for students who lack confidence in openly and spontaneously expressing their thoughts. By writing in their journals before or during discussions, students can formulate their thoughts so that they can share them in small and large group discussions. Once the discussion begins, if they have difficulty formulating ideas as they speak, they can simply refer to what they wrote in their journal or even read it aloud if that helps. Students can also write as the discussion proceeds, reflecting on what is being said in preparation for voicing their own thoughts.

Writing prior to discussion may also result in more substantive talk. In one study of discussions about short stories *without* any prior writing (White, 1990), about half the students' responses consisted of surface descriptions of the stories. In discussions *with* prior writing, only 28% of the discussion consisted of descriptions, while 72% of the discussion consisted of abstractions about the stories. Having worked through some initial reactions or perceptions of texts in their journals, students may be better prepared to reach abstractions in discussions about the texts they read.

All of this presupposes that students can readily and easily shape the direction of discussions according to their own previously formulated written responses and ideas. But this is not always the case. Based on their observational studies, several theorists (Goodlad, 1984; Sizer, 1984; Powell, Farrar, & Cohen,

1986) charge that many classrooms are "overly-structured," providing students with little freedom to decide the direction of activities or talk. For example, an analysis of discussions in 58 eighth grade classrooms (Nystrand & Gamoran, 1991) showed that, on average, less than a minute of class time was devoted to class discussion. Only 12% of the teachers' questions were "authentic"—they were genuinely seeking answers—and only 11% of the questions were follow-up probes to students' answers.

Similarly, in his analysis of discussion among high-ability high school students, James Marshall (1990) found that teachers generally dominated the discussions. After a teacher's question was answered, the focus or floor returned to the teacher. The teacher's turns, which were two to five times longer than the students' turns, were used to inform, question and respond to students, while the students used their turns primarily to inform. The teachers also asked questions in a way that established their own framework for keeping the students "on track." For example, 73 percent of the teachers' questions focused on the text. The teachers typically described the text, applying their own background knowledge, followed by an interpretive question. The students then responded with the appropriate interpretive answer. Marshall cites the example of the following sequence about:

The Grapes of Wrath:

Teacher: "Who's the first one who sees (Casey)? Through whose eyes do we meet him?"

Student: (inaudible) "Tom Joad."

Teacher: "Through Tom Joad, the main character. So through Tom we meet the preacher. And they talk. What do you know about the preacher? Maybe I shouldn't call him that. Why not? What shouldn't I call him the preacher?"

Student: "He has strange ideas."

Teacher: "He has strange ideas, a little strange."

By framing responses according to their own interpretive agenda, the teacher forecloses the possibility that the students will explore their own opinions or ideas. In the process, students are learning what Bloome, Puro and Theadoreu (1989) define as "procedural display," responding according to the expected script or scenario or trying to find "correct answers." As a result, they are less likely to explore differences of opinions or ideas.

The openness of classroom discussions may retroactively influence the quality of students pre-discussion journal writing. If students anticipate discussions in which they have little opportunity to voice their own beliefs and ideas, they will have little reason to write in their journal. In authoritarian schools or classrooms, some students, particularly students of color in "lower track" classrooms, have been silenced for voicing opinions and ideas that challenge prevailing beliefs and attitudes. As Michelle Fine (1990) discovered in her analysis of drop-outs in an urban high school, there are various forms of silencing. Students may be ignored, may not be given an opportunity to express their ideas, or may simply be told to be quiet.

If students anticipate actively expressing their beliefs and ideas, they may value their journal writing as a covert rehearsal for expressing their ideas in their small or large group discussions.

Constructing Social Identities and Relationships

In a traditional model of education, the teacher's goal is to impart certain knowledge or skills to students. Classroom instruction revolves around "learning the material." In this context, students' writing usually serves the purpose of assessment—to gauge whether the students have accumulated the required information or to sort them on the same basis into those who may move on and those who need remediation.

However, more recent social models of writing suggest that students use writing to construct and establish social identities and relationships. Students define, establish and convey their "selves," roles or persona through their writing. As Lucy Calkins (1991) puts it, writing serves to "validate a child's existence" (36) as a knowledgeable, contributing member of the classroom community. In reading to the class a description of a vicious, hair-pulling fight in the lunchroom, a student reveals her own moral outrage to her peers. In sharing a recollection of his deceased grandmother, a student conveys her capacity for love of others.

Through their oral and written discourse in the social context of the classroom, students communicate their roles ("class clown," "teacher-pleaser," "burn-out," "school politician") or their knowledge or expertise in certain areas ("animal lover," "hockey fan," "mystery buff"). Given a basic need to be known and respected by others in the classroom community, students are continually using their behavior, talk and writing to establish these role identities in the classroom. By participating in athletics and extra-curricular activities or wearing certain clothes, students align themselves to a pro-school "jock" group. By resisting academic norms and expectations and by behaving or dressing in "deviant" ways, students align themselves to "burn-out" groups (Ekert, 1989).

Journals at Work:
Establishing Social Identities

A group of students in an eleventh grade class are writing articles for different "special interest" magazines to be published for the class (sports, movies, music or ecology). Through their early journal writing on their chosen topics, they maintain and construct social relationships with their peers. By sharing notes for an article on a current rock star, Kim defines her own status in the eyes of her peers as an authority on that topic. Given their immersion in multiple social contexts—both in and out of the classroom—these students also use their journals to reflect on their roles, purposes and audiences. Entries focus on what others thought of their work or how impressed they were with one student's research on the decline of streetcars in America.

Adolescents are continually experimenting with alternative social identities and voices. Rather than express a singular "authentic voice," they use their writing to adopt multiple voices. By writing down her strong negative reaction in a dialogue journal to another student's sexist remarks, Susan is defining her own identity through her writing—an identity associated with her more "feminist" beliefs. Given its informality, the journal can become a place for students to readily experiment with alternative voices associated with a range of different identities.

Students are very much aware of what they perceive to be the role of the "good student." Being a "good student" and responding the "right way" means that one performs according to the teacher's dictates and criteria. Students also resist this "good student" role in various ways. By not responding to a teacher's questions, a student publicly conveys to her peers that she doesn't care about being the "good student." In passing notes to each other that mimic or parody a teacher's behaviors or those of studious class members, students are displaying what Robert Brooke describes as "underlife" behaviors. In doing so, they are expressing the fact that they are more complex and unique than the roles given to and assumed of them in the classroom.

In addition to classroom roles, students may also use their writing to construct roles in terms of gender, class and race. For example, male students may be less likely to express themselves or their feelings in journals, which they associate with "being female" (Gannett, 1992). In responding to texts, they may adopt a more detached, objective stance than females (Bleich, 1988; Flynn, 1983; Fox, 1990). In contrast, females have more positive attitudes towards in journal writing, particularly dialogue journal writing, because it provides them with a way to use language to construct personal relationships, a use of conversation preferred by women (Tannen, 1990).

Similarly, males and females may use their journal writing to respond in quite different ways to literature, adopting the gender stance invited by the particular text. After reading John Updike's story "A&P," a male student may respond positively to the grocery boy Sammy's sexist remarks and "male gaze" stance, while a female may resist or be offended by them. In recounting narrative events, males may emphasize physical actions, while females may emphasize interpersonal perceptions. When British adolescents were asked to write narratives, males typically wrote action-adventure stories in which they dramatically defeated their opponents in feats of physical prowess (Moss, 1989). In contrast, the females wrote stories focusing on the development of interpersonal relationships. Moss argues that these stories are not simply playing out traditional sex-role stereotypes; rather, they represent adolescents' need to define and explore the complications of gender roles. She found that many of the stories contained some of the underlying tensions and ambiguities associated with defining these roles. For example, the female students' romance stories frequently grappled with the issue of male power. As Moss notes:

> The male view of women, the female view of men, are seen as being in conflict. The women's view of the man includes the knowledge that the man's view of her is wrong, and that if she succumbs without a struggle to his initial view of her, fails powerfully to contest it, she will be the loser. [They are] depicting the tensions between alternative ways of reading masculinity (the thriller) or masculinity and femininity (the romance) (114-115).

Through their journal writing, students engage in acts of "doing gender," of defining their gender roles. Students may also construct selves in terms of class and race, employing those discourse practices associated with certain social roles. Students who perceive themselves as "burn-outs" often resist what they believe to be the middle-class norms of the school, norms inconsistent with what are often working-class attitudes (Eckert, 1989). Because much of large secondary schools' bureaucratic management style serves to marginalize these students, the "burn-out" does not feel part of the school culture. To express their resistance, these students may write very little or they may express themselves through relatively unconventional forms: rap lyrics, profanity, doodles or drawings—forms they associate as "anti-school." Like students' expression of "underlife," it is important for us to understand this writing as a way to construct class identity, even though it is often difficult to condone anti-school behaviors.

Differences in students' racial background may also influence their journal writing. In their study of African-American and white adolescents' journal responses to visual art images, Scott, Davis, and Walker (1989) found that the African-American students were more likely to draw on oral narrative traditions, particularly a "preaching style," in responding to the images. In contrast, the white students were more likely to respond in an abstract, analytical manner. Given certain attitudes towards an appropriate "school discourse," Scott argues that teachers need to recognize the value of African American students' rhetorical style and register, particularly in journal writing. As Anne Dyson (1989) has found with younger students, learners with different racial backgrounds bring different experiences and attitudes towards language use that are manifested in journal writing. Scott's work suggests the value of having students respond to visual images, responses that serve to reify their own attitudes and beliefs.

As we have suggested, journal writing encourages students to experiment with different voices and roles, experiments that help them to define their social identities within the classroom context.

In this chapter, we have suggested a range of purposes for journal writing which improve students' thinking, learning and writing, and which can turn classrooms from places where students are relatively passive receivers of knowledge into socially dynamic, learning-rich settings. As the next two chapters show, these many and varied purposes can become a guide for designing specific journal activities and using them in the classroom. By defining their own purposes for journal writing, students can also begin to understand how journal writing serves their needs. As they begin to perceive journal writing as purposeful, they will be more likely to treat their journals as central to their classroom experience, rather than as an added frill.

Chapter Three

Using Journals
in the Classroom

Many teachers who are convinced of the educational value of journals nevertheless worry about a reaction they often hear from students: that journals are a waste of time, a lot of busy work piled on to the more important activities of reading, writing formal papers and studying for tests. Faced with this pressure for justification, some teachers simply stop assigning journals. The reason for these negative perceptions of journals often stems from how the journal is being used. All but the most self-determined students, when simply assigned a journal and then left to their own devices, are bound to resist what they perceive as useless busy work. Classrooms where journals are successful are almost always those in which teachers carefully assign, discuss, coordinate and oversee the daily use of journal entries. Integrating journal writing into a class or curriculum involves many important instructional decisions and a willingness to monitor and be thoughtful about how the journal is affecting students' learning.

In this chapter, we turn to some strategies for assigning and incorporating journals in your classroom. Because every classroom community reflects unique curriculums and educational objectives, you will need to adapt and particularize many of the suggestions we offer.

Before They Begin: Introducing Students to Journals

In teaching a course or unit, you have decided to build your activities around journal writing, making it a central part of your teaching. Because your students have not had much experience with journals, you may need to spend some time introducing them to what may be a new and different way of writing.

To introduce students to journal writing in our own classrooms, we ask students to talk about their experiences with journals in previous classes. Many students tell us that their teachers offered little direction for writing journals, used them solely as a reading check to see if they had done their homework, or graded the journals based on errors in spelling or punctuation.

Given these and similar experiences, students often come into our classes with negative attitudes towards journal writing, even to the point of groaning when journals are first brought up and assigned. One of your first goals may be to bolster your students' attitudes toward journal writing, either the collective attitudes of the entire class or those of individual students who are especially apprehensive or resistant. The following issues are among those most often in need of attention in the early stages of assigning journals.

Conceptions of journal writing. Students may bring certain conceptions of journal writing that can limit their use of the journal. They may think of journal writing as a series of formal "mini essays." This suggests that they are not familiar with the difference between formal versus informal writing. If this is the case, try comparing formal essay writing with examples of more spontaneous, open-ended, exploratory and subjective informal writing. Avoid simply talking about these differences; instead, first show students actual samples of previous students' entries and then engage students in a short activity in which they write for a few minutes on an interesting topic.

The following excerpts from the journal of Lisa Treichel, a senior in high school, demonstrate the stylistic and intellectual differences between "formal" writing and "journal" writing on the same topic: Hemingway's short story "Hills Like White Elephants."

> Excerpt from Lisa's Early Journal Entry on "Hills Like White Elephants"
>
> "Hills". After reading this story I was confused. They (the man and woman) are sitting around drinking and talking, but their conversation doesn't seem to mean anything. Or maybe it's that what it means is a kind of private thing between them, but then we're like eavesdroppers just kind of hanging around near them, so we don't really know what they are talking about, just piecing it together. Then there are all these physical descriptions of the dry hills, and I can't figure out who is going

where and why they seem sad. It's a WEIRD story! It
seems so simple but it makes no sense.

Excerpt from Lisa's Paper, "Avoiding Subjects:
Conversation in Hemingway's 'Hills Like White Elephants'"

```
. . . . Another device that Hemingway uses to
have his characters avoid dealing with sub-
jects directly is to have their statements
"trail off." This gives the impression that
either the subject is too difficult for them
to talk about or that they begin statements
knowing that the other character can complete
it in their mind. The trailing off strategy
is cleverly used to hide important details
from the reader, giving the story a sense of
mystery. ....
```

Using such a pair of samples, you might lead a discussion contrasting their features. The formal excerpt seems, in
some ways, less freely exploratory and more preoccupied with
form than ideas. The journal entry includes errors—an issue
that many students will be interested in discussing—but seems
less constrained and stylistically more appealing.

Familiarity with journal writing. When assigned to keep a journal, many students will feel uncomfortable writing in a less
formal mode. They may be unfamiliar with journal writing or
may not understand your particular approach. Once they
begin, however, they may develop a more positive attitude
towards keeping a journal. Keeping students motivated will
be one of your early goals. Consider assigning some fairly
structured, specific entries at first and collecting them or using them in class on a daily basis. As students become accustomed to the kind of writing you are asking them to do, they
may redefine some of their attitudes.

Purposeful uses of the journals. Students may also perceive little
purpose in journal writing related to helping them in your
course. By providing them with activities associated with the
purposes described in Chapter Two, you can help them understand that journal writing involves more than simply fill-
ing up pages. For example, if students recognize that taking
notes about their reading helps them remember details from
their texts, they may begin to appreciate the value of journal
writing. If rewards for journal writing aren't at first obvious
and "automatic," think of some ways to demonstrate their
usefulness. We sometimes ask students to reflect on a specific
topic or question in an early journal entry. That topic or ques-

tion then appears on the first quiz in the course. If the students have responded to the early prompt, they usually feel more confident writing a short answer to the question and begin to look on their journal as purposeful.

Associations with the term "journal." The word "journal" itself may conjure up negative stereotypes among some students, especially those who think it means a diary. In introducing the journal, you may want to use an alternative name, such as "log," "scrapbook," "writing book," "daybook" or "reflection pad." Each of these names, in turn, may begin to define the journal in ways you want to avoid. In our own introductions to the journal, we usually list several names and use them to talk about how we want students to define the journal. In courses focusing on specific content, one of us stresses the term "academic" when we describe the journal, disallowing entries not focused on the course material or clearly related subjects. In writing courses we loosen this restriction in the service of helping students to explore their thoughts and find topics to write about. In your own classes, finding appropriate terminology and labels can help reflect your focus and goals in using the journal.

Writing apprehension. Some students who had negative experiences with writing or are poor readers may be apprehensive about writing (for more on writing anxiety, see Rose, 1985). Such students are often concerned about writing the "correct way," and fear negative comments from their teachers. Such students may not have experienced the kind of uninhibited freewriting typical in most journals. Your positive reactions to their thoughts may also lessen their anxiety about writing and help them to become more fluent. As they begin expressing themselves without fear of formal conventions or negative comments, they may develop a more positive attitude towards journal writing. This may take some patience as you allow students to lessen their apprehension through their writing experiences.

Issues of Gender. As we previously noted, males often perceive journal writing as a "female" activity (Gannett, 1992) and may be reluctant to use journals. Some females, tapping into generally negative stereotypes of diary writing, may likewise resist keeping a journal. If you sense such resistance you may need to discuss the issue of gender overtly with your class. To counter the stereotypes, you may also want to share and analyze examples of men such as Thoreau who kept diary-like journals and women such as Margaret Mead who used journals for professional and scientific reasons (see Chapter Five).

You may also have students share reasons for their attitudes toward journals. Males may begin to hear reasons that challenge their stereotypical notions of journal writing.

Starting Out: Fostering Fluency

As we noted in Chapter Two one purpose for journal writing is to help students develop fluency in their writing. As your students begin journal writing, emphasize the idea of fluency—of expressing thoughts in an open, spontaneous manner. As in freewriting, students write to fill up the page without concern for editing for syntax, mechanics or spelling—or even whether their writing is "important." As Brenda Ueland (1987) notes, by writing quickly and "recklessly," students avoid the self-consciousness that often hinders expression: "If you write fast, as though you vomited your thoughts on paper, you will touch only those things that interest you. You will skip from peak to peak. You will sail over the quagmire of wordy explanations and timidly qualifying phrases" (139).

If students have difficulty writing something, a list such as the following relatively generic topics or promts can help:

- my biggest gripe
- what makes me happy
- a fond memory
- my favorite pastime
- things I'm good at
- things I'm no good at
- "If I were President, I'd . . ."
- what bugs me most about school
- things I admire

Students can also write everything they know about a certain topic, idea or issue they happen to be studying, a process similar to what Peter Elbow (1981) describes as "focused freewriting." For example, if your class is studying the topic of "the family" as portrayed in literature and on television, you might ask your students to write whatever thoughts and feelings they associate with the prompt, "my family." Then, when reading their journals, you can become more knowledgeable of the students' experiences, attitudes and beliefs related to their own families—information that can help to plan further classroom activities and discussions.

The more students write in their journals, the more confident they may be about expressing their own ideas. Some students, particularly those with little previous journal writing, may need to more time to develop this self-confidence. This is particularly the case for:

- Middle school/junior high students who have done little or no writing in elementary school or whose instruction there focused primarily on surface mechanics. These students usually need practice in writing so they gain confidence in their ability to express their thoughts.

- Students whose handwriting is too slow to keep pace with their thoughts. Quick-paced journal writing may show students shortcuts so that their pens can keep up with the quick progress of their ideas.

- Students who lack confidence in the validity of their own ideas or who are apprehensive about writing. With their history of being ignored, shunned, silenced, or shamed by peers and adults, these students often assume that no one cares about what they have to say. As Ueland (1987) notes: "everybody in the world has the same conviction of inner importance, fire, of the god within. The tragedy is that . . . they stifle the fire by not believing in it and using it." (158)

To encourage fluency, especially early on in a course, you need to avoid forms of evaluation that might inhibit students' expression. As you read their journals, find some specific things to praise or engage in their ideas in a kind of dialogue. Hearing this praise, students begin to perceive their writing as having some effect on a reader, perceptions that bolster their self-esteem and identity as writers. If you need to evaluate your students, do it on the basis of quantity. This can also help you to keep track of whether your students are increasing their fluency as writers.

Choosing a Format for Classroom Journals

Most teachers assume that a journal must take the form of a lined, spiral-bound notebook light enough to be carried around. As we suggested in Chapter Two, journals come in many forms depending on the uses to which they are put. The following are some suggestions from veteran users of journals. You might experiment with those that seem appealing until you find the right form for your own purposes as a teacher.

Taped Oral Journals

Some students, particularly those with learning disabilities, have difficulty with the act of writing. Taped journals help them learn to orally articulate and extend their thoughts. As they gain confidence in their ability to express themselves aloud, these students may eventually translate that confidence to their writing.

In creating a tape journal, students purchase a cassette on which they record their reactions to readings or classroom discussions, interpreting and responding to texts orally, or "prewriting" thoughts for a paper.

In asking students to talk on tape, you may want to start them out with an oral "think-aloud" response to a text. In "think-alouds," students can respond to an entire text after reading it, or they can react line-by-line, making explicit their free-associations. Think-alouds tend to work best with shorter texts such as poems or sections of longer texts.

Initially, you may want to model how to do a think-aloud for students, stressing the idea of making explicit one's thinking without editing one's thoughts. In describing think-alouds, consider making analogies to processes with which your students are familiar: the student can imagine him- or herself as a sports commentator, creating a play-by-play of their own mind. As they become more adept with the method, your students will develop confidence in their ability to extend their thinking (Lytle, 1982).

Students may have difficulty sustaining a monologue without an audience providing them with immediate feedback, especially because they may not be accustomed to the internally dialogic nature of journal writing or oral free-association. To help them sustain their monologue, you might suggest that they imagine an audience such as a peer or teacher reacting to their own talk. Or, as they are talking, they could refer to cues or prompts such as the following that may help sustain their thinking:

> "for example..."
> "and the next thing thing that happened..."
> "in contrast..."
> "because..."
> "furthermore..."
> "on the other hand..."

A wealth of material is available for taped journals. Some more common activities include the following.

*   *Interview comments.* As part of their monologue, students interview peers and adults about their experiences and ideas. For example, in his tape journal Mark talks about various reasons students don't attend the school-sponsored dance—the music, the decor, the intrusive chaperons. To document his contention, he records comments by a number of his friends who voice their own reasons for not attending the dance.

•   *Multiple voices.* Students can create a dialogue containing a range of different fictional "voices" or roles who each comment about a particular event, topic or issue. In lieu of including interview material, students create their own cast of peers, parents, teachers, fictional characters, celebrities or historical persons, who represent a range of different perspectives. Students could read brief biographies of famous people or authors and then create a conversation with these different voices about an event, topic or issue (see Ann Bourman's *Meeting of Minds* [1990] for further activities.)

Students could imagine a host of different voices reacting to their own statements, carrying on an inner dialogue between a "you" and a "me" (Baldwin, 1991). Or, they may entertain the voice of an alter-ego "you" who raises devil's advocate questions of the "me:" For example, in responding Maya Angelou's book *I Know Why the Caged Bird Sings*, a student carries on the following inner-dialogue between the "you" and the "me:"

You: "So, what's bothering you about this book."
Me: "I'm really bothered by the way the dentist treats Maya's grandmother, telling her that he wouldn't treat her toothache because he'd rather put his hand in a dog's mouth."
You: "I wondered why she just didn't strike out against those people when the 'poor-white-trash' girls teased her grandmother and she just ignored them."
Me: "Yeah, but if you strike out against them, you're getting down in the gutter with them, the violence just create more violence."
You: "Well I know that I would have a hard time just sitting back and taking it."

Students can also respond to their assertions in terms of "other" current selves that represent different sides of their own personality. A student may perceive herself as a "sports hero," anticipating that she will be successful in a sporting event. Another student may perceive himself as a "loner" who has difficulty making friends. After describing this "other" self, they can then address it directly, adopting a different or even opposite perspective. In creating a dialogue with the "sports hero," a student may recall instances in which she was not a hero but still enjoyed playing the game.

This sort of internal dialogue works especially well when students grapple with complex issues. Colin is writing a paper on the issue of ecology versus economic development in the timber industry:

Colin: "If people in this town lose their jobs in the lumber mill, then this town faces some hard times ahead."

Other side: "You have to look at the bigger picture. If we don't protect the forests, then there won't be any woods left to cut, so there won't be any jobs anyway."

Colin: "But the lumber industry is very careful about not cutting down too many trees and about replanting new trees. You environmentalists are more interested in simply preserving a bunch of owls. Why should owls be more important than people?"

Other side: "It's not a simple either/or issue. The industry is just using the spotted owl regulations to try to get rid of all environmental controls. And when that happens, then they'll just cut down all of the trees."

By adopting others' perspectives, students may ultimately gain some understanding of their own perspective. In asking them to use their journal to reflect on their own attitudes and beliefs, try having them address the following questions:

Who is speaking and in what voices?
What attitudes and beliefs are being espoused?
What are the motives for assuming a certain voice?
How do these voices reflect my gender, class or race?
How do these voices serve to define relationships with others?

• *Oral performance of a text.* One way to display an interpretation of a text is to "perform it" through dramatic readings or other staged methods. To prepare for their oral interpretation, students initially think about the meaning they want to convey through their performance. They then perform the text using a number of different techniques. For example, they may read a Langston Hughes or Gwendolyn Brooks poem "straight" and then read it again with a syncopated beat. Working with other students, they may create a "stereophonic" production in which different voices are juxtaposed against each other. Students may also add background music that reflects the mood or attitude they want to convey with their language—romantic music for a love poem, the sound of machine-gun fire for a poem about violence or war.

- *Group tapes produced collaboratively by a pair or group of students.* In a group tape, students record their discussions of a topic or experience and their follow-up comments about that discussion. Alternatively, they can produce a group oral interpretation or dialogue in which different members of the group adopt different roles. Groups of students record a role-play of the characters in a short story and then discuss their feelings about assuming the different roles. They can also construct "video journals" in which they investigate a problem, demonstrate a particular technique or examine the workings of an institution in the form of a mini-documentary. A group of junior high students created a video showing different aspects of their school for viewing by prospective students.

Loose-Leaf Notebooks

The journal may also take the form of a loose-leaf notebook. Unlike a spiral notebook, a loose-leaf notebook allows students to insert and remove materials. Students can include previous writings, handouts from other courses, clippings of newspaperor magazine articles or other students' entries, and their own responses to material. They may write their reactions to this material or explain why they included it in their journal. For example, JoAnne, an eleventh grader, collected some of her writings from her elementary and middle-school years. In a subsequent entry, she wrote about changes in her writing and about why she wrote little in elementary school but then, in sixth grade, began writing pages of reactions to her earlier schooling.

Students also find that the loose-leaf notebook is handy for sharing writing with peers or the teacher. Students can insert and comment on entries they receive from peers or teachers. They can also remove certain items from their journal as they develop a "showcase portfolio" (see Chapter Seven).

Dual-Entry Journals

Dual-entry journals make use of a format designed to encourage students to go beyond simple reactions and into more sophisticated reflection. In a dual-entry journal, students record reactions or perceptions on the left side of the journal. Then later, they can reflect on and analyze their reactions on the right side of the journal (Lindberg, 1987). On word-processing programs, students can also use the two-column feature to juxtapose perceptions and reflections on the same page.

The physical separation of the two entries encourages students to analyze their perceptions, a recursive process in which the perceptions on one side of the page trigger reflections on the other side, which, trigger further perceptions. Ideally, in moving back and forth between the two sides of the page, students enter into an inner dialogue.

In responding to the PBS American Short Story series film, "Bernice Bobs Her Hair," by F. Scott Fitzgerald, Ben listed his reactions to and perceptions of the images, events and persons in the film on the left side. Later, he reflected on his responses on the right side. The film, based on F. Scott Fitzgerald's story, shows the attempt of Marjorie, a popular socialite, to help her reserved cousin Bernice to become more popular with males.

Marjorie is so conceited that she's blind	Marjorie thinks that she's the center to her own limitations of the universe
Bernice is more honest and self-reflective than Marjorie	Bernice is quite shy and reserved, but seems to be aware of her limitations
Marjorie is really quite sexist	Marjorie assumes that being popular with males is the most important goal in life
Bernice's appeal comes from her honesty	Bernice becomes more popular with the males
I'm on Bernice's side: she sees through the fact that this is all a big game	Bernice begins to see the limitations of Marjorie's flirting games
All of this says a lot about how females are forced to learn to be popular	Bernice realizes that Marjorie set her up to bob her hair so that she would no longer be popular with males

The dual-entry format can also encourage students to reflect on events in their own lives. On the left side, they might recount an important experience in their lives. On the right side, depending on your instructional goals at the time, they might embellish specific vague memories with lists of descriptive details or they might reflect on what they learned from the event, what they would be like if the event had never happened or what the event reveals about their own attitudes or identity.

Some students may be able to record but not reflect on their perceptions. In responding to *Julius Caesar*, they may understand what the characters are doing or saying to each other, but may be incapable of inferring larger meanings or significance of the characters' actions. They may see that characters in the play are continually suspecting each other and testing each other's loyalty, but they may not be able to place these details in the larger interpretive context of the play.

Students may be more likely to reflect on their perceptions by working together in small groups. As facilitator, you might ask a student in each group to describe his or her perceptions to the other members, who then reflect and comment on those perceptions. Modeling the process first in the large group may help the students to begin their group work. As they work in small groups, they will demonstrate various styles of responding to each other's perceptions.

In reflecting on each other's perceptions, students may also ask questions about the meaning of their own terms or concepts. Responding to *Julius Caesar* in his perceptions column, Judd wrote that "many of the characters were primarily interested in achieving power." In his reflection column, he posed the question, "what do I mean by power?" and then explored his own conceptions of the term.

Other ways in which students can reflect on their perceptions include the following:

- *Reasons*. Students may formulate reasons for their statements. If a student states that "In the beginning of the story, Bernice agrees to let Marjorie help her learn to flirt with males," the simple question "why" may lead to further explanation and reflection: "She wanted to be popular."

- *Assumptions implied by their statements and reasons*. As students reflect on the reasons for assertions, they can continue to probe the assumptions underlying their reasoning. Asking "why?" again for "She wanted to be popular" yields, "She's assuming that being popular is the ultimate goal in life."

- *Beliefs/attitudes implied or represented by their perceptions*. As they continue to explore their reasoning, students eventually discover that certain ideas they think are universal truths are in fact personal or socially determined attitudes and beliefs. After writing "Bernice realizes that being popular isn't what she expected," Jill shifts into her own opinions, testing them in writing: "I believe that girls need to recognize that there are other things more important than being popular."

- *Oppositions/tensions/ambiguities inherent in their perceptions.* Students may also reflect on dissonance in their own perceptions. In thinking about Bernice's behavior, a student notes, "I wonder why Bernice, after she had her hair bobbed, was both angry that she'd been set up by Marjorie and also happy that she was no longer Marjorie's star pupil."

Peer Dialogue Journals

Most people think of journal writing like diaries, as a solitary and very private activity. Without an immediate audience some students may find "solo" journal writing difficult or purposeless. Exchanging entries with a teacher and/or peer in a dialogue journal provides them with the social interaction and motivation to extend their writing.

As illustrated below, peer-dialogue journals represent a hybrid form that combines the characteristics of formal written essays, oral conversation, solo journals and teacher-student dialogue journals.

By sharing their entries with others, students enjoy participating in the social exchange associated with oral conversation—a reciprocity "closer to talk written down than any other school writing" (Shuy, 1988, p. 81). This conversational exchange, according to Michael Halliday (1979), tends to focus on unfolding processes, while written language tends to focus on products. As Halliday notes, "writing creates a world of things; talking creates a world of happening" (p. 93).

Figure 3-1
The Peer-dialogue Journal as a "Hybrid Genre"

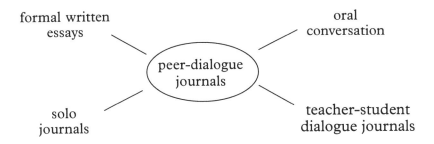

Participants in oral or written conversation also anticipate their audience's reactions by posing questions to be answered by their audience. Their social transactions create an on-going support system for exploring responses. As research on teacher/student dialogue journals indicates (Peyton & Seyoum, 1989; Schatzberg-Smith, 1988; Staton, Shuy, Peyton, & Reed, 1988; de la Luz Reyes, 1991), by providing ongoing feedback, teachers model strategies for extending their thinking. De la Luz Reyes compared ten Hispanic middle school students' "literature logs" and similar reaction logs they exchanged with their teacher. In the solo literature logs, students were asked to respond to specific questions summarizing perceptions of the text. She found that the students wrote longer entries in the dialogue journals than in the literature logs, particularly when they were writing about their own families or culturally relevant matters instead of school-related topics. They also reported that they enjoyed the dialogue journals more than the solo logs. Additional research also shows that dialogue journals can develop self-confidence among learning-disabled or highly anxious students (Johnson & Hoover, 1989).

Most of the literature on dialogue journals describes them as interactions between a teacher and his or her students. Many teachers find it impractical or impossible to keep a dialogue journal with all their students. In our own work, we have experimented extensively with "peer" dialogue journals, in which pairs of students exchange regular journal entries and begin carrying on a conversation in writing, typically focusing on the subject matter of a class. Peer dialogue journals provide an immediate, often trusted audience (another student) without burdening you with dozens or even hundreds of daily or weekly entries to which you must respond.

In addition to removing the burden of extensive teacher response, peer dialogue journals have other advantages over teacher/student exchanges. While they lack the immediacy of oral conversation, peer-dialogue journals remove some of the intimidation of face-to-face contact, even among trusted peers. Furthermore, if students perceive teachers as superiors, they may less likely to share feelings, doubts and concerns than with peers. In one study of 38 college students engaged with dialogue journals with their teachers, only twelve students posed questions, and they only posed eighteen questions (Schatzberg-Smith, 1988). In contrast to the teacher-student dialogue journal, students engaged in peer-dialogues create their own social support network.

Criticism of informal, "note-like" exchanges as being less intellectually rigorous than formal papers may be unfounded.

Even such disparaged practices as note-passing in class result in substantive levels of thinking. In a study of notes written by eighth graders, Roberta Jackson found that most of them, particularly those written by high achievers, included information reflecting a high level of cognition. The notes also served to define social roles and relationships. As one student said: "It's like it is with friendships. Your best friends are jealous if you write to one more than you write to the others" (Jackson, 1992, p. 56). Another student assumed the role of a central switchboard operator:

> People from all groups write to me and I pass on the information. Say that there's a fight brewing, one kid would write to me, and I would write to the person he is mad at and get his side. Then I sometimes try to patch things up. But this can be risky. Say like my group doesn't like me passing notes to the cheerleader types. They might think I'm stuck-up or something. Then I would have no one to write to!
>
> (Jackson, p. 56).

As this comment suggests, students are reluctant to share their responses without a positive social relationship. Because they often do not know each other personally, students need to use their entries to build their relationship by disclosing personal experiences or sharing their own opinions. In our own research with peer-dialogue journals (Anson & Beach, 1989; Beach & Anson, 1993), we found that by initially revealing their own personal interests or concerns—disclosing themselves and addressing each other by name—the partners set the stage for a collaborative relationship. They also established a bond with each other by sharing difficulties with the course assignments or texts. When one partner admitted confusion over a text or concept, their partner often shared similar difficulties, or offered advice or consolation.

At the same time, there were certain barriers to building social bonds. In some cases, students addressed the instructor as their primary audience, describing their partner in the third person: "Like myself, Melanie was also perplexed by the assignment." Other students had difficulty accepting their partner's attitudes and learning styles. While one student might use her entries to carefully and "logically" summarize the class discussions or text, the other student would use the entry to explore, in a more subjective or emotional way, some of the same ideas. Or one partner in a pair would assume a dominant stance, creating an unproductive competitive relationship or silencing the other partner—a tendency found in a study of peer-conference dialogues on a computer network (Selfe & Meyer, 1991). In that study, males, particularly those with "high-profiles," sent more messages, raised more new topics and expressed more disagreements than females. Because the males dominated, the females were more reluctant to participate. This suggests that partners need to treat each other as collaborators rather than competitors.

Setting up peer dialogue journals. In setting up dialogue-journal writing exchanges, you will either ask students to pair up with partners at their discretion, or assign the pairs yourself. (Threesomes can also work, but be aware that the regular exchanges can become complicated, especially with student absences.) You may want to consider the social dynamics of your classroom in making decision about partners. Will some less popular students be left unpaired if the students choose their partners? Are there issues of gender, culture, personality or disposition that might play a role in your setting up of the pairs?

We have found that even in college classes, among very bright students, the sharing of journals takes effort to coordinate. Most students are unfamiliar with dialogue journal writing in the classroom, though creative analogies will help them understand their form and purpose—many students will be familiar with "chat lines" and electronic mail bulletin boards and will soon understand dialogue journals when they are explained in these terms. A handout describing the procedures may be useful, and it is important that you spend time showing typical dialogue entries from previous classes or even your own dialogue journals with friends and colleagues. You can then point out effective characteristics of dialogue journals.

You may want to allow students to choose their own partners for the exchange of entries, or you may want to establish the pairs yourself. The former method has the advantage of allowing some freedom of choice to the students; however, they may choose friends who think very much like they do, and shy students or "outsiders" may feel ostracized if they are not immediately chosen by a partner. You will also find that in most cases female students will pair off with females and males with males, or there will be pairings based on ethnic or racial similarities. A productive use of dialogue journals is to help students of different genders, backgrounds and intellectual dispositions to write to each other from their various perspectives. For this reason, you may wish to pair students yourself, thinking carefully about these issues.

Once the pairs are established, the partners should establish a positive social relationship. In their initial entries, as in building a friendship, students can share their previous experiences, likes or dislikes, leisure-time activities or career plans. As a possible warm-up activity, try asking the partners to pass notes about some immediate concerns or interests (Jackson, 1992).

You will also want to establish specific guidelines for how and when students should exchange entries. Students can simply swap entries or copies of entries, at least once a week if not more frequently. As we noted in Chapter Two, if students are keeping their journals on a word processor, they can exchange discs and respond to each other at a particular place on the file. Each student uses a different font, to keep track of who is writing what.

Reacting to peer entries. When students begin exchanging entries with each other, you need to model ways of reacting to their partner's entries. Students may react by noting that, as readers, they were engaged, intrigued, confused, puzzled or overwhelmed by their partner's entry. Or they may respond to their partner's entries by describing similar texts or experiences. To demonstrate these responses, try showing students one or two entries and model your own reactions to them. Then hand out some additional sample entries and ask the class to share different ways of reacting to them. Typical kinds of reactions include the following:

- Positive reactions expressing liking, enjoying, empathizing with an entry.
- Questions or reactions expressing need for more information, clarification, doubts.
- Related experiences or texts.
- Intellectual engagement in a topic: taking issue, disagreeing, providing counter-examples (see Anson & Beach, in press).

A sample exchange. The following excerpts from an exchange between three ninth graders, Rachelle, Lynette and Adam, illustrate some of the positive features of dialogue journals. Adam is a student who did little or no writing in response to regular classroom writing assignments. In contrast, he readily and enthusiastically participated in an exchange with Rachelle and Lynette.

In this exchange about a number of different topics—the novel *Watership Down*, playing softball, a law on high school employment, and an episode involving punishment for missing a team practice—the students were highly respectful of each other. They also actively sought out each other's thoughts and advice.

Rachelle: Do you guys like this Rabbit book [Watership Down]? I admit, I wasn't that excited about it at first. I mean, 475 pages about rabbits? Rabbits!! But I guess it's OK now. I finished the book yesterday. I guess I'm a pretty fast reader, but I read all the way to my cousin's wedding Saturday, 2 hours, so I was almost done and then I just finished it off. Some of the things in the book stick with you. Yesterday, I was playing tennis and I missed a super easy shot. I said, "Oh, frithrah!" I have no idea why, it just came into my head. I was playing with Danelle Jutz, who is also reading this book, so she didn't give me too strange of a look. We were just being silly anyway. Some of the things in the book are hard to understand though. Like when the train came, I could not figure out what it was! I though it was a bomb or something maybe, like if the humans were building something. Sometimes I'd be reading along and think, "What just happened?" so then I have to read it over. My favorite character is Pipkin, because he's the nicest one. And I like the El-Ahrairah stories. I hate the Efrafan rabbits, though, the ones at Cowlip's warren. The thing that bothers me is that rabbits just aren't that smart. I'm sure they would know how to dig and stuff, but I can't really buy a rabbit having ESP. Or talking. Or having a town like Efrafa. But I guess if it's just a story, the author can do whatever he wants. I like how he takes things from the rabbits' perspectives, like the white stick instead of a cigarette. I also like how they give the rabbits personality. At the end, you can tell which is which, finally, like Blackberry is the smart one.

Lynette: I felt the same way about the book. Oh great, a stupid book that is going to take me forever to read it. I've been able to keep on pace and it's not as bad as I thought. I'm not as far as you Rachelle. I'm only on 294. I wasn't able to really read this weekend. Friday night I went out with my boyfriend, Shane. Saturday I was shopping. Sunday I went to the cabin. I guess I have to admit that it is an okay book. Some of the El-Ahrairah stories are good, but I had trouble understanding the one about the Black rabbit.

I like Pipkin too. That's probably because I always like the smallest of the bunch. This stuff does grow on you. Just this morning I was thinking how I wanted a hurdudu.

Not to change the subject, but I don't really feel like talking about the book anymore. Do you guys have your permit? I don't yet because I just turned 15 on May 1st. I get to take classes when this summer starts. My dad already lets me drive though. Some days he'll take me to empty parking lots. Lately he's been teaching me how to drive a stick shift. Once you get the hang of it, it's alot of fun. I always feel more under control. Up at the cabin yesterday my dad let me drive our mini van.

Adam: I thought that the rabbit book, *Watership Down*, by Richard Adams (cool name!) was stupid at first. I hardly read it. Then the day before the test last Thursday I thought I should just read as much as possible so I could pass the test and I kind of got into it. I thought that it was kind of interesting. I don't really like Pipkin. He is a wimp. He is scared of everything.

[Rachelle's marginal comment: Hey Pipkin's isn't such a wimp! He's just tiny and afraid of everything. Okay, so he's kind of a wimp. I guess I just feel sorry for him.]

[Lynette's marginal comment: He's little! I bet you were a big stud as a 5-year-old, huh Adam?]

[Adam, continued]: I like El-ahrairah and the Black Rabbit of Inle the most. He is cool because he brings mystery into the story. He is evil and sly. However, I don't know why he wanted El-ahrairah's tail, whiskers and wars. I guess that he's just a nut!

So far I think that you two are nuts too because you use their strange language. It hasn't really grown on me that much, you couple of narm marli's. Ooppssss! Just kidding! Do either of you know what that thing was that saved Holly and his little band of outlaws. That said that Frith had sent it to save them and it was loud too. At first I thought that it was a helicopter but now I think that maybe it was a train. I don't know. Do you?

[Rachelle's marginal comment: You know what I thought it was a meteor. (I don't know if I spelled that right. Then I realized it was a train later.)]

[Lynette's marginal comment: Yeah, it's a train, but I thought it was a bomb!]

[Adam, continued]: Tonight our softball team (Red Sox) is playing Excel Engineering for the first game and Tolleffson Construction. Our current record is 1-1. I think that TC is 0-2 but I'm not sure so don't quote me on it. Excel Engineering is 2-0. Chris Fandall is on that team. [Rachelle's marginal comment: Are you sure? I haven't head him talk about it at all.]

[Adam, continued]: He thinks that he is so cool now because they beat some so called tuff teams. He keeps bragging about it to me had bad they are going to whop us.

[Rachelle's marginal comment: Don't listen to him. He like's to get on your nerves.]

[Adam, continued]: I hope we kick their tails. You probably will want us to knock them down a peg tonight so that school can be spared from his big bragging mouth too.

Rachelle: I think that a law forbidding high-school student from holding jobs is about the stupidest thing I've ever heard. I don't understand the reasoning at all. Why would they do this? To give kids more time to study? Like they would use their free time studying! They'd probably just goof off after school, watching "Duck Tales"! No, I'm sorry, but that is just stupid. A lot of kinds need those jobs to help each money for their families. They might be the biggest source of income. Besides, even if it wasn't crucial to your family for you to get a job, how could you do anything without money? How could you buy a car? Go to college? For most kids, these are reasons they get jobs, and they couldn't have these things without it. Besides, whatever happened to a job teaching you responsibility? This idea is so ridiculous, it would never go through. Wait, I just thought of another reason. Kids that really need the money would drop out of high school to get a job and support their families . . . .

Here it is, my final writer's notebook entry for the year! It's about time. I wonder if we'll have to do this again next year. Probably, huh? I like this partner writing stuff better than alone. It's more interesting . . .

Lynette: Great entries guys! This notebook idea is great. I really look forward to reading it and then responding back! I actually like this better because I always have something to respond. Usually I spend all my time trying to think about something to write about. Ms.____ was right, I got to know you two better.

Rachelle, I'm not sure I agree with you on the law forbidding high-school students from having jobs. I should say I agree and disagree. I know some kids get a job to help support the family. I think that is great. I also think it's okay to want extra money to save up for a car and college.

I don't think having a job is okay when it starts to interfere with your studies. I think it is so important to get good grades, and I won't let anything get in the way of letting that happen.

I don't know if you guys are going to write anymore, but if you do I want you to respond to this. On Monday, Anne C & I were walking to swimming. I looked up & 2 guys turned around. It was my boyfriend Shane & Anne's boyfriend Pat. They had come to watch our swim practice. As we walked in our coach Nicole had a cow because they were there. We didn't know that they were coming. They had come from Anoka. What were we supposed to do. Tell them they were supposed to leave when they would have done no harm? If anything Anne and I would have worked harder to try and impress them.

We turned around and walked out. Nicole said we had to be back in 3 minutes. We didn't come back. Anne decided not to go, and then I kind of followed her decision.

That night I told my parent what I had done. I asked my mom if she would write me a note to excuse me so I could swim in the meet. Nicole had told the team that she might not let us swim in the meet.

When we got to swim practice on Tuesday the coaches had a long talk with us. The reason why we left was because they didn't give us a chance to prove that we could perform well with them there. They had decided not to let us swim in the meet. I understand why they didn't let us swim, but they are punishing the team more than they are punishing us. Anne & I get first, seconds, & thirds. We have beaten Coon Rapids before 89 to 82. We ended up losing the meet 69 to 102.

Rachelle: I know what you mean and I have a perfect example. On Wednesday the A team had a game (for softball), so we had practice. Some people didn't show up for the practice, so they didn't get to play in Thursday's game. We only had 8 players then, so we used two outfielders and lost 21-4. (Don't laugh, they were really good.) Maybe not being able to start or something would have been a better punishment, instead of punishing the whole team.

On the surface, these exchanges seem highly informal and social—much like the kind of interaction one would expect the students to have during a lunch break. Yet beneath the social nature of the exchanges lies educationally purposeful material. In responding to *Watership Down*, the students shared their experience reading the novel, especially the way their initial impressions (that it was "stupid") gave way to greater engagement and interest. They also talked about their reactions to specific characters, disagreeing as to whether or not Pipkin was a wimp. By posing questions and making assertions, they invited each other to respond.

In sharing their opinions about the law, forbidding high schools to work, Rachelle and Lynette argue their positions by citing evidence and consequences—a reflection of relatively mature persuasive writing for ninth graders. They also seem to be formulating their arguments with their partner's position in mind, which gives them a sense of purpose for their writing. Similarly, in describing her punishment for not returning to practice, Rachelle frames and organizes her narrative around her purpose—to convey her sense of injustice. As often happens in peer dialogue journal with partners of equal status, Lynette then mimics Rachelle's narrative, citing her own example of unfair punishment. The social relationships created through the written dialogue encouraged purposeful, extended writing in a range of different modes.

In sharing their thoughts, the students are also engaged in what Nel Noddings (1991) calls "interpersonal reasoning." In contrast to the competitive, aggressive, argumentative stance characteristic of debates, they demonstrate care for their partners' ideas, a flexibility in defining the goals or purpose of the exchange, an effort at maintaining and cultivating the relationship, and a search for an appropriate response. The potential of socially supportive writing to encourage the same kind of cognitive complexities as traditional oppositional forms such as argumentation has been receiving increasing support among theorists of discourse (see Anson & Beach, in press).

When asked what they liked about writing dialogue journals, the ninth grade students in Rachelle, Lynette and Adam's class pointed to their enjoyment receiving responses from each other: "It was fun to hear what others thought about things I wrote. The teacher can't take the time to comment on everything so it was great feedback." Another student noted, "It seemed as though I was really communicating with someone and they cared about my thoughts. Receiving responses was like waiting for a letter in the mail. I was always very curious to find out what the other person thought."

Because their partners were reading their entries, students noted that they were particularly concerned about the quality of their writing: "What I was writing, I 'talked' to my partner and wrote better because I knew someone else was going to read it. I seemed more careful about how I wrote as well as what I wrote."

This sense of audience led to consideration of their partner's needs as readers: "Since you're writing to someone, you must really explain your ideas and thoughts. They don't know what you're thinking, so you must use as many examples and details as possible." Another student remarked, "I felt more like I had to give much more detail because your partner had to understand you so they could respond. When you're talking to someone, there's more feeling, you stress certain things, it's not like some old boring thing you have to do."

The students disagreed whether partners should be assigned or self-selected. Some argued that by assigning partners, teachers could insure that students worked with persons of dissimilar backgrounds. In writing to less well known partners, some students noted that they were more likely to honestly express their opinions to "someone who did not know us so well that they weren't just telling us what we wanted to hear. We could say so many things that would sometimes be hard to say to even a friend." Others preferred selecting their own partners because "we know what their interests are and know what they would like to read." Others suggested beginning with a self-selected partner "until they get the idea of what they have to do," and then switching to a randomly selected partner. Still other students recommended that the teacher select partners based on students' nominations and/ or previous analysis of the students' journals. Because there are good arguments for assigning partners and for having students select their own partners, you may need to make this decision by accommodating to your students' particular abilities and preferences.

The Class "Walking Journal"

Another dialogue-based journal is the class "walking journal" or "dialogue bulletin board." In this method, students contribute to journals that are passed around among students. They can also write their entries on three-by-five cards and put them on a bulletin board. Other students read these responses and react by adding other three-by-five cards or "Post-it-Notes" adjacent to the original cards.

E-Mail Peer-Dialogue Journals

Electronic mail has become a popular form of written communication and could serve as another form for the peer-dialogue journal. In some cases, students participate in an on-line exchange within the same networked computer lab, with students responding and reacting to each others' messages as entries (see Handa, 1993, for techniques for setting up computer network exchanges in the classroom). If students have access to modems, they can send e-mail messages to each other. By sharing their e-mail addresses, students can send messages to particular peers or to the entire class. In some settings, it may also be possible to set up a class listserve, which allows students to write to an entire class by sending their messages to a single address. Based on their interest in a particular topic, students can join discussion groups or newsgroups located on the internet system.

There are a number of advantages to using e-mail for writing. Students can readily and immediately communicate with a wide range of different audiences. In a networked classroom, they can send messages to whoever they wish and receive immediate reactions. They can also incorporate downloaded files from previous writings into their messages or scan images from newspapers, magazines or books into their messages. This interactive environment creates a strong sense of community in which students can assume an active role as a participant.

Another advantage of e-mail exchanges in a networked classroom is that it serves to de-center authority. In many classrooms, the teacher dictates the nature and focus of topics in a discussion. When a student contributes to a discussion, a teacher typically guides the direction of a discussion by accepting or rejecting that student's contribution. When a student makes a comment deemed to be irrelevant according to the teacher's agenda, that teacher can simply discourage the student from making such comments.

In contrast to this teacher-directed discussion, in a networked classroom students create their own exchanges, often free of any teacher direction. As Lester Faigley (1992) argues, this shifts the focus of authority from the teacher to the students. While the teacher often sets the agenda in teacher-led classroom discussion, in e-mail exchanges, the students set the agenda according to their own interests and voices. In analyzing the exchanges between students in his own class, Faigley (1992) characterizes their discussion, now freed of his own authority, as composed of mutiple, equal, competing voices that is:

> more wavelike, with topics ebbing and flowing intermingled with many cross currents. Not only do the many voices act out Bakhtin's principle of the multiaccentual nature of the sign, but the movement recalls the opposition he described between the monologic centripetal forces of unity, authority, and truth and the dialogue and the dialogic centrifugal forces of multiplicity, equality, and uncertainty (p. 183).

In participating in these on-line exchanges, students share their concerns, ideas, reactions and frustrations knowing that they will receive some supportive reactions.

Another advantage of e-mail exhanges is that students can communicate with audiences in different schools, communities, regions or cultures. In a study of students' participation in the QUILL program, Bruce and Rubin (1993) found that students are often highly motivated to write to audiences whom they are not familiar with but whom, given the fact that they live elsewhere, hold a certain fascination for the students. In writing to these unfamiliar audiences, students are then challenged to create social relationships with students who espouse different cultural perspectives.

Electronic-Mail Messages: Lonely Alaska Females

As part of the QUILL program, students in Alaska could send messages to other students all over the world. Two eighth grade students in McGrath, Alaska wrote the following message, including some deliberately misspelled keywords which readers use to call up messages (Bruce & Rubin, 1993, p. 90)

```
                    Calling All Men
Sheila Forsythe              Althea Jones

Hi,
    This note is to all you good looking guys
our there in the worl. There are two of us
writing so we'll tell you a little bit about
ourselves. Our names are Sheila Forsythe and
Althea Jones. We're both 14 and stuck in a
small town in Alaska called McGrath. We have a
pretty big problem and we hope that you guys
will help us out. We have a very short supply
of foxy dudes here. So if you are a total fine
babe PLEASE I repeat PLEASE write us!!!

    Keywords: /McGrath/Male Order Men/
```

Two other eighth grade girls in Holy Cross, Alaska developed a "personal ad" specifically for boys in Juneau (Bruce & Rubin, p. 91):

```
                Good Looking Juneau Boys
Two Holy Cross Girls          Josie and Evelyn

    Our names are Josie Adams and Evelyn Fields.
We like skiing, basketball, hockey, writing
letters to cute boys, and we could be more than
pleased if any of you cute boys would write to
us. We don't have any boyfriends. So you don't
have to worry about that! We also would like
you to send a picture when you write. (You are
going to write aren't you?) We will send you a
picture too. Josie if 14, and Evelyan is 13.
Well, please write soon! We are waiting for
your letters!!!
                    xxx xxx
                   xxxx xxxx
                xxxxxxxxxxxxxxxx
                 xxxxxxxxxxxxx
                  xxxxxxxxxx
                   xxxxxxx
                     xxx
                      x
            WE SEND YOU OUR HEARTS!
          SINCERELY, JOSIE AND EVELYN
    Keywords: /Juneau Boys/H.c.r Girls/
```

Another advantage of e-mail is that it can minimize differences in students' sense of status or power. Differences in status or power related to gender, class or race influence students' participation in everyday conversation. Students with status or power often dominate the conversation. As a result, women are often more likely to be interrupted, to speak less, to ask more questions and make more apologies and to defer to a focus on male-initiated topics than do men (Fishman, 1983). However, when participating in e-mail exhanges, particularly when adopting pseudonyms, these gender differences are minimized (Selfe, 1992; Selfe & Meyers, 1991). If students are less intimidated by these perceived social markers that operate in everyday social conversations, they may be more willing to express their ideas and opinions without fear of ridicule or shame.

At the same time, there are a number of disadvantages to e-mail exhanges. The very immediacy of participating in on-line written exchanges may detract from a student adopting a reflective, contemplative stance about their writing. Students may be so concerned about promptly responding to a peer's messaage, that, as in oral conversation, they do not stop and reflect on their own writing. Moreover, students may be reluctant to challenge their peers given the social pressure to achieve group consensus. Greg Myers (1986) argues for the need to encourage students to challenge the emerging group consensus, something that may require more reflective effort by students than is the case with immediate, on-line responses.

Furthermore, the very anonymity that eliminates status markers can lead to a lack of concern for or accountability to others. As Faigley (1992) found, college students who were using pseudonyms in an on-line computer exchange often included sexist or racist comments designed to deliberately provoke or offend other students in the class, the practice of "flaming." Because the students were anonymous, they assumed they did not need to be concerned about the consequences of their statements. This suggests the need for some clear statement of rules of etiquette regarding participating in an e-mail exchange.

There are also some logistical problems with using e-mail. Students may not have easy access to computers and/or modems. This raises serious questions regarding the equity of a communication system that allows some to participate but not others. Students also may not know if their audiences actually received or read their messages. Or, having sent out a lot of messages, students may be disappointed to find that they are not receiving any themselves.

On balance, the advantages of e-mail outweigh the disadvantages. For many students who write very little, e-mail has enhanced their interest in writing because it serves to connect them to a network of social relationships.

The Planning Journal

Samone is thinking about what looks like a hectic two weeks: soccer practice every day after school, a biology lab report due, a social studies test and a paper on *Summer of My German Soldier*. She uses her planning journal to develop a "to do" schedule with deadlines. She also uses the planning journal to specify the strategies or techniques, the "how to do it" processes, that she needs to accomplish her various tasks. For example, in order to write her paper on *Summer of My German Soldier*, she lists the following:

- review my notes on Patty's actions
- compare her relationships with her father, her mother, Ruth, Anton and Charlene
- talk about how these different relationships affected her

Linda is holding a conference with Margaret about her draft paper on her summer job at a camp for disabled children. Margaret gave her a lot a helpful "reader based" comments that suggested to Linda a number of specific revisions. To remember what revisions to make, she gets out her planning journal and jots down a list of needed revisions: "add more descriptions of the setting," "describe the camp's philosophy in more detail," "talk about my own reactions to the one boy with crutches," and "show how some of the children had difficulty participating."

These two students have learned to use their journals to plan how to organize their work for writing these papers. Many students have difficulty knowing how to organize their time, often leaving assignment to do at the last minute. They lack what Deborah Brandt (1990) describes as the "to do" strategies—knowing what specific strategies or processes to employ next. As a result, they may experience a loss of control and self-esteem. By using their journals to formulate plans, students may then further appreciate the use of writing to not only organize, but also to define goals and specify tasks that meet those goals.

Scheduling and Organizing Activities. Using a journal to schedule activities involves more than simply recording due dates and appointments. It also involves learning to organize activities to insure that activities can be completed in ample time. To organize their activities, students copy a calendar and staple it into their journal, noting due dates and appointments. For specific days they list activities they want to accomplish for that day and, to indicate their priorities, they put an "A," "B," or "C" next to each activity.

Must be completed "★"	Priority for completing "A," "B," "C"	Activity

For example, George and his team are planning a video production on shopping for bargains in local area stores. Given the options of "selecting camera equipment," "working on the script," "requesting permissions of store owners" and "studying ads for potential bargains," George decides that "working on the script" and "requesting permissions of store owners" are the most important. In his planning journal, he ranks these items with an "A." He also considers which activities involve short-term versus long-term commitment, noting that requesting the permissions can be completed soon, while working on the script will take a longer period of time.

Students may also use their planning journal to define and assess their goals. In the beginning of the year, Beverly is meeting with her teacher Mark, to define a set of goals that she wants to accomplish for the second trimester. Based on a portfolio assessment of the first ten weeks, Mark also has some expectations for Beverly's growth. Beverly has noted in her planning journal that she places a high value on learning to express herself more openly in classroom discussions. As she reviews these notes with Mark, they discuss activities that would best fulfill Beverly's goals, when she records in her journal. Mark also keeps a record of her plan to assess the degree to which she fulfills her goals. Rather than using a unified set of criteria, Mark evaluates his students according to their ability to fulfill their own negotiated goals.

For specific tasks, students may create "to do" lists, which have the effect of shifting their focus from topics ("what to say") to actions ("what to find out, what to do next, etc."). To help students distinguish between these two kinds of focus, you can ask them to list topics on one side of the page and related strategies on the other side. For example, Derek is planning to write a paper on the characteristics of mystery, citing examples from mystery stories and films. In a planning entry, he lists the possible topics on the left side and the strategies related to developing those topics on the right side:

topics:	strategies:
the detective character type	review different detective characters to list common traits
the sidekick character	same as above
the criminal types	same as above
the plot	compare stories/films to determine similarities
red herrings	compare how the red herrings are used
solving the crime	compare techniques used by detectives
my involvement/engagements	write out responses and think about ways I'm engaged

Students may also plan strategies from a set of questions about a certain topic or issue. For example, Rosie heard from her friends that they get little or no useful advice about colleges or college applications from their guidance counselors. She decides to write a paper on the issue of college counseling in her high school, a paper she can then circulate to the principal and the head of the counseling unit. She begins by listing some questions to which she wants answers (see question-listing):

- What information do students believe to be the most important for selecting schools and applying to college?
- How much do the advisors know about different colleges?
- How much time do they do they spend with students talking about colleges?
- What advice to they give to students who may not be planning to go to college?

Once she has developed a list of questions, she can then determine how she will obtain the necessary information. For each questions, she specifies the strategies she will use to answer it. To determine how much advisors know about different colleges, she plans develop a list of highly-familiar and less-familiar colleges as a basis for gauging their knowledge.

**Creating a Classroom Community
Through Journal Writing**

Journal writing can be an excellent medium for creating a sense of community in the classroom. Just as journal writing can build positive social relationships in the classroom, so the quality of the social community in the classroom can influence students' willingness to share their writing. In a classroom community built on trust, mutual respect and accountability to others, students are more apt to express honest, unconventional ideas.

Creating a Classroom Community

In creating a classroom community, you inevitably need to consider the students' attitudes toward the culture of the classroom. Consider two ninth grade classes taught by the same teacher, Joyce. The students in Joyce's third period class described their class as a "family." In the culture of that class, students supported each other as members of a community. When a student left the class to go to another school, the class experienced a sense of loss, which led them to write letters to their former classmate. In this class, a group of female students continually assumed the roles of social organizers/facilitators, setting the tone for the class and offsetting the males' attempts to dominate.

In contrast to the third period class, fourth period was, "the class from hell." In this class, the students, particularly males, expressed their resistance by slouching at their desks, congregating around the door or in the back of the class, shouting taunts across the room and openly bragging about not doing the work. Unlike the first class, the males had the upper hand and there was a general lack of community and trust.

While the students in these two classes were very similar, the classroom cultures led to quite different behaviors. Joyce often felt intimidated and even threatened by the students' behavior in the fourth-period class, and was often tempted to rely on her authority to bring order to the students' experience. She resisted using punishment, assuming that such measures would be counterproductive and only mask the root causes of the problem. She attempted to build relationships with individual students, particular the ringleaders in the class. In one-on-one conferences, she helped students define a specific set of goals and plans relating to their behavior. Removed from the public limelight of the classroom, the students no longer felt the need to display their macho behavior. In negotiating these goals, Joyce was holding the students' accountable for their own emerging sense of integrity. As she noted, she was resisting their stereotyped self-image of "bad students" who would prefer punishment or detention to owning up to their own integrity. At the same time, through her willingness to negotiate, she was suspending her own role as authority, conveying a trusting relationship with her students.

Creating a positive culture enhances the quality of journal writing and journal writing contributes to building this culture. In order to reflect on her own concerns, Joyce kept a journal. She was able to record instances of differences in students' behavior, body language and talk between the third and fourth hours that reflected differences in the cultures. She was able to devise some possible strategies for coping with her concerns.

She also turned to the journal to improve the quality of classroom discussions. Before discussing a short story, the students listed questions that related to their own interpretations. During the discussions, she would stop students and have them write their thoughts about the topic(s), which had the effect of recharging the students' thinking so they could interject some new ideas or push the discussion in new directions. In a large group the students had been discussing the issue of the inherent self-interestedness of human nature. Some students argued that humans are by nature "out for themselves," while others argued that humans, given their need for others, do care about others. During a "writing time-out," Joyce asked the students to cite some examples of people acting purely out of self-interest versus out of concern for others. The students then shared these examples, discussing the extent to which they serve to affirm or refute their positions.

At the end of the discussion, her students wrote about what they learned from the discussion, reviewing to synthesize their perceptions. Because the students wrote something about the discussion, they could connect it later on to subsequent tasks—drafting a paper, completing a new reading assignment, participating in another discussion or writing an article for the school newspaper. By studying these reflective "learning entries," Joyce could determine differences in her students' perception of their classroom experience.

From these journal writing experiences, the quality of discussions improved over time in both of Joyce's classes, particularly the "macho" class. As the sense of group cohesion improved, so did students' willingness to express themselves openly and honestly. Thus, the journal writing and the sense of classroom community each served to bolster the other.

Creating a Social Context Through Role Play

Journals can also create an enhanced social milieu in the classroom through a large-group writing role-play in which students exchange written messages in lieu of verbal exchanges (Beach & Anson, 1988). By being assigned different roles, students must break out of their usual classroom persona to experiment with alternative ways of behaving and speaking. Quiet student who venture little in class may suddenly come alive now that it is safe to deviate from their usual roles.

In preparing for the the role play, students select an issue of concern to them, discuss the different positions regarding with that issue and construct a number of roles associated with a hearing or trial about that issue. Students then exchange memos and try to influence each others' beliefs about the issue. At various points in the role play, students stop and read their memos aloud. At the end of the role play, students then reflect on the social strategies employed in their memos. They may note that some memos began with descriptions of the writer's relationship with his or her audience: "As a voter in your district . . . ," "As someone who has always supported your policies . . . ," or "As someone who is concerned with your future . . . ."

In Mary Beth's tenth-grade class, the students were exploring the issue of censorship using role play. This role play was set in a small rural community in which a parent complained about a book her son was assigned to read in school. The school board was meeting to address the parent's complaint. In preparation for the role play, students assumed a role—parent, school board member, principle, teacher, student, town major, newspaper editor. In their journals, they wrote their responses to the novel and explored their positions (through the lens of their imagined persona) on censoring the novel. During the role play, they exchanged written messages in which they tried to influence the school board to vote for or against censoring the book. Through the message exchange, they built a power base by seeking others' identification and political allegiances. At the end of the role play, the school board members voted.

Students then used their journals to reflect on how they felt in their particular role. A student who assumed the role of the mother wrote about her awkwardness in having to defend the need for censorship. By writing about their feelings, students grappled with differences between their own attitudes and those associated with their role.

Negotiating Learning

A more social community can also be created in the classroom by giving responsibility to students for designing their own learning. This does not necessarily entail a completely "student-centered" as opposed to a "teacher-centered" classroom. A happy median between the two is something the

British describe as "negotiated learning." By negotiating with students you are allowing students to define their own goals and plans according to their needs and interests. In negotiating learning, students can use their journal as a "planning journal" to define specific goals and plans for completing a task. At the same time, you are maintaining your responsibility for providing students with some possible direction and assistance in achieving their goals.

Yunhee, a twelfth-grade student, has developed a strong interest in justice and students' rights within the school setting. In negotiating a plan with her teacher for an independent study project, she lists in her journal some specific questions she wants to explore:

- Do students have legal rights or due process when disciplinary decisions are made?
- How are school rules defined and for whose purposes?
- What are the reasons students are punished?
- Does punishment serve to deter misbehavior?
- Are some groups in the school (males versus females, low-ability versus high ability, "jocks" versus "burnouts") treated more fairly than others?

Based on these questions, she then lists some techniques for exploring answers to these questions in her journal:

- talk to students and administrators
- observe teachers or administrators dealing with discipline problems
- read the school rules
- interview students, teachers and administrators about their perceptions of specific cases

Once her teacher approved Yunhee's plan, they discussed ways of using the journal to keep field notes, including strategies for making generalizations based on those notes.

Another example of using a journal for developing learning plans comes from an eleventh-grade English class. The teacher asked the students to select a novel they read during the year and to analyze its portrayal of gender roles. Sharon chose John Steinbeck's *Of Mice and Men*, a novel she characterized as "real sexist." The teachers asked the students to use their journal to define the purposes and strategies for their analysis, a process she modeled for the students. Sharon listed her purposes in her journal:

- To determine the differences in the portrayals of the male characters—George, Lenny, Curley—versus female character—Curley's wife.
- To compare behaviors associated with being male versus female in the novel.
- To discuss my own reactions to these differences.
- To explore possible reasons for these differences.

She then listed some techniques for analyzing gender portrayals in the novel:

- For each character, list some specific behaviors.
- List other characters' reactions to those behaviors.
- Divide those behaviors for male versus female.
- Look at how the behaviors are valued—positively versus negatively.
- List my own reactions to the behaviors.
- Consider the ways that readers in the 40's and 50's might have reacted.

She then reviewed her plan with her teacher, who suggests some ways of associating character behaviors with the cultural categories of "male" versus "female."

Both of these are examples of negotiating learning. Because the students are formulating the assignments, they have more investment in completing the assignment. Rather than dictating tasks to the students, the teacher negotiates with them on how to completing their projects.

Teacher Reflection

In addition to having students use journals, you may also want to consider keeping your own journal to reflect on your teaching. You might begin with a narrative recollection of what happened in a particular classroom, and this may serve as a springboard to subsequent reflections. As one student-teacher noted about her journal writing, "A lot of times I would start writing while something would happen, a specific incident or something, and I'd start writing like a story format. I'd just keep going." (Mass, 1991, p. 218). In her narrative, a teacher, Marjorie, writes about a role-play activity. She sets the scene—a classroom in which the students rarely expressed their emotions or experimented with optional roles. She then describes the students as enjoying the role play, particularly those students who adopted roles quite different from their usual classroom roles. In reflecting on her narrative, and now consciously noting her highlighting of the classroom context, she recognizes that the role play represented a welcome deviation from established classroom norms, something she was not aware of during the event or even while composing the narrative. She then discusses possible explanations for why the role play served to break the classroom norms and expectations.

You might also use classroom narratives to reflect on social roles. In reflecting on her student teaching, Majorie noted that she was often caught in the role-ambiguity of being the "teacher" but not being the "real teacher." She also perceived new attitudes toward her role as she became less teacher-centered and more facilitative. Journal writing helped her to reflect on her own beliefs and strategies, reflection that was essential to her improvement as a teacher.

You can also reflect on some of the tensions or conflicts that are an inevitable part of teaching. Student-teachers are continually grappling with the role ambiguity of assuming the role of "teacher," but still being a "student teacher." In his journal, Arnie, a student in our University program, noted: "I think going into the school as a student teacher is like driving down the road with a big 'student driver' sign on you car. People look at you as if you are in between worlds—not really a teacher but yet not a student."

You can also reflect on tensions between different opposing teaching strategies. In a reflection on a literature assignment, Rachel defends the value of a close reading of the story against a "response-centered" approach:

> I am having some resistance to focusing on the personalizing of the text. My guided assignment is very text-centered. I am assuming that the students can become involved with the text without immediately connecting it to their lives. Relevance. So Suzy, what did you do in school today? Talked about swamps. Is that relevant? Maybe not in terms of short term goals, but in the larger context of the class it could be. I don't think I can force myself to avoid issues that I feel strongly (at least not for long). After honing some of these close reading skills, it would be great to turn them onto some of the more charged and controversial ideas within the text (i.e. the ethnic and gender politics, etc.).

In this reflection, she adopts multiple voices representing competing perspectives, whose meaning is constituted by her social relationship with the methods instructor. She adopts the voice of the parent who may represent a practical perspective representing a concern with acquiring relevant knowledge in the classroom. She also adopts the perspective of her literature professors who have taught "the power and joy one can have in reading through a text, weaving through the interconnected meanings and images within it." And she adopts another voice of a teacher who wants to grapple with political issues and ideas in the classroom. These different voices represent a an underlying tension between different theories of teaching literature. What's important is that she is aware of these tensions, an awareness that leads her to begin to grapple with assumptions underlying literature instruction.

You may also experience conflicts between your need for security, control, approval, maintaining the system, integrity, success, etc. and actual classroom experiences. One of our student teachers, Donna, has a strong need for affiliation with others, particularly her students. In a narrative account of her first day at an urban junior high school, she describes a meeting of an interdisciplinary team, with expectations that they would "share concerns as well as ideas and provide for each other needed peer support." However, she finds that "the players were tired, frustrated and ready to move to another league":

> Sitting in a circle, the six adult members squashed themselves uncomfortably into the junior high-sized desks and eventually came to stare at me. Mr. F. was busy cutting out a new seating chart for his first hour class and made no effort to introduce me to the gang. Therefore, I took the initiative to introduce myself, including some background information about my program. Without my prompting, the Geography teacher, Mrs. P, and Mr. F., who was apparently listening after all, began to tell me how they couldn't wait to get out of teaching junior high and instead move on to high school instruction. Biting my lip until I tasted blood, I finally let out the assertion that I indeed had chosen this setting and this age group because, for some inexplicable reason, I really liked junior high students. The "team" just smiled at me knowingly and said, in confidence-shattering unison, "You'll learn, honey. You'll learn . . . ."

In reflecting on the conflict between expectation—as driven by her need for affiliation with students and the reality of her colleagues' attitudes, Donna perceives the school as constituted by a culture whose attitudes she rejects. As she notes, "The students at this school and other schools like it deserve more than tired teachers with tired ideas."

Another student teacher, Sue, perceived a conflict between her own high expectations for accommodating to all of her students and the reality of having too many students:

> Sharon [her cooperating teacher] laughs at me because she say I want to care about them all, but it's impossible, and after a while you just get the pink slips about suspension or hospitals or babies and think, "oh well" and throw it in your pile and that's it. This tends to conflict with our lofty goals of student-centered teaching and reaching each one and making a difference.

She also perceives a conflict between her standards and unmotivated students. She has "plenty of patience with students who are trying to learn but little patience with students who are unmotivated or disruptive. I am not patient with myself, which can lead me to become frustrated quickly."

You may also reflect on the instances in which your strategies lead to success. Rachel describes a conference with one student, Corey, who is writing a sketch on Nat Turner for a school event in which student assume the roles of notable, historical people. She finds that Corey is overwhelmed with a lot of notes he has taken about Nat Turner and doesn't know how to begin his paper. So she asks him to reflect on "what do you know about this guy? What is he famous for?"

> Boom. All he needed was a chance to speak. His lack of writing was not an act of rebellion; his slump against the wall was not directed at the assignment itself or at me, I self-consciously worried. He was stumped. He had all this information—he was bursting with it—and simply didn't know how to place it, didn't have a clue as to when to begin, how to share it with someone else through his writing. He talked and I listened, asking questions to fill in the gaps of the story he told. I took brief notes as he spoke, noting the highlights of his telling, what he was focusing on. By the end I was able to help create a frame, a loose outline, in which he could then fill his wealth of details. When I left the class that day he had a screen full of writing.

Rachel recognizes that her strategy to help Corey to "create a frame, a loose outline" for his writing was successful. And you can reflect on instances in which plans and expectations are not fulfilled, leading to a sense of frustration. Rachel describes a discussion in which one of her three students made a lot of sarcastic remarks:

> Sarcasm. Witty comments. What do you do with them? When do you acknowledge them? What if they are demeaning towards you or one of the other students? I am fairly sarcastic myself and know I am going to have to use caution. Throughout the role play it was Gordon who threw out (but not up) the challenging comments. I either ignored his comments completely and moved

on with the group or a few times worked to involve him in a more constructive way (i.e. asked him to read, to offer a suggestion for our list). What if you have ten demanding such attention? Would establishing ground rules for discussion help?

In reflecting on this discussion, she uses her journal to define the tension between her discussion scripts and challenges to those scripts, reflection that leads to an awareness of the need to change her strategies.

Many of these teachers built their reflections around narratives. Writing about your recollections of a specific classroom incident can provoke further reflection. You could even use a dual-entry format in which you put the narrative recollection on one side of the page, and your reflection on the other side.

You may be more likely to reflect on your teaching in collaboration with colleagues. By sharing or exchanging your reflections with a trusted colleague as part of a peer-dialogue journal, you can then provide each other with some supportive comments and reactions that leads to further reflection. In her study of six teachers with whom she wrote dialogue journals, Miller (1990) found that teachers frequently described their own constraints, tensions, ambivalences and uncertainties associated with teaching. One teacher, Beth, a mathematics department chair, wrote about her difficulties of being an administrator who missed teaching her classes. She is reflecting on the tensions between dependency versus autonomy within institutional constraints.

> I don't think it is the need to go back and be a teacher again but to find a space that allows me to be me, to feel that what I have to say is important. The only place there is for me where I can be me to the greatest degree is our teacher-researcher group. I wonder if in administration that environment is dropped because of self-interests talking a priority, because of the fear of being shown as incompetent, because of a false self built upon successfully landing a job? I do not own this job yet and cannot "see" what that could mean. The struggle is either with me always having to ask, or with the subtle controls emanating from those who are my superiors (p. 125).

In her response to Beth, Miller (1990) responded in an entry that acknowledged Beth's need to examine her own ambivalences:

> I can see how you are struggling with all aspects of this job right now. The job itself seems to bring a lot of issues to the surface for you. And I know that you fight

that shutting down and shutting out that the pressures sometimes force you to do. You talk about trying to resist the compartmentalized, sequential, logical aspects of your job as the only ways to do it, and yet sometimes, maybe your shutting down is an intuitive way of protecting your sanity, of knowing where you have to stop pushing, for the moment, anyway!

Rather than denying or imposing her own advice, Miller attempts to describe or explain Beth's ambivalence, a reaction that provides Beth with some perspective for coping with her ambivalence.

In another exchange, two high school English teachers, Randy and Mitch are discussing their students' perceptions of their roles as teachers in the classroom. Randy begins by quoting from an article he has read.

Randy: From Zemelman and Daniels: "Students are always uncomfortable when their expectations are not met, and they will try to redirect the class experience back into familiar channels and patterns." I get this a lot in my classroom. I do things differently than many English teachers. My students sometimes resist this because they are familiar with what they think an English teacher should be, and I come in and shatter that conception for some. Often what happens is that students get a new impression, equally distorted, the you're "one of those different teachers." They have a schema for that. Unfortunately my experience has told me that because of this, the students don't always think they have to work for me,"after all, he's such a different teacher."

Mitch: Yep. But you can be a different teacher who requires work. That's a different-different teacher.

Randy: This takes the form of a student coming into my classroom and expecting me to bend my rules on something, "because you're not strict, right?"

Mitch: Yeah, they want you to be what they want you to be.

Randy: Actually, I don't consider myself strict, but I am consistent. If I tell students the rules, I expect they'll follow them. Why don't they get that? Is this making any sense to you Michael?

Mitch: Of course it does.

Randy: Do kids come to you and expect greater latitude with rules on the assumption that since you're innovative and are excited about teaching you'll cower to any student need?

Mitch: See, and one of the things that I do is I tell my students that there are some rules that I won't bend. Some of them are not mine to decide. The nice thing about having high school students is that I can ask them if they've ever had a job where they had to do something that they didn't want to do. Most of them can relate to that.

Randy: I don't know if that pertains to the quote as I think it would, but the bottom line is this: Kids have trouble with things that don't match their school schemas. I, as a teacher with a sense of humor, should not have rules...or something like that.

Mitch: Yep. That's what they want—funny and no rules. But when you think of it, humor probably has as many rules as anything.

Randy: Related Babble: The kids generally complain about the music I play between classes, but let me forget to turn it on one day and all I here is, "What happened to the music?" "I thought you hated the music." "We do hate the music, but that doesn't mean we don't want you to play it! We like the music; just not the music you play!" Go figure.

Mitch: Maintain the status quo no matter how much I don't like it. What I have that I know is better than having something I don't know. It's the dysfunctional family axiom.

Through their exchange, Randy and Mitch are reflecting on the tension between being innovative and maintaining rules. Randy is also perplexed about his students' attitudes towards his own attempts to enforce rules in his classroom: "why don't they get that?" In posing his question, "Is this making any sense to you, M.?", Randy is seeking Mitch's own reflection on their dilemma. Mitch shares his own sense of ambivalence as to whose rules to follow—the school's or his own, noting notes that he has no choice but to enforce the school rules. At the same time, he verifies Randy's perception that "kids have trouble with things that don't fit their school schemas," noting, "that's what they want—funny and no rules."

Randy then explores another perplexing matter: his concern about awarding passing grades to mainstreamed students:

Randy: I have an ongoing disagreement with our director of special ed. in our building over the "mainstream model" of dealing with special ed. students. I'm for mainstreaming special ed. kids. I love having G., a special ed. teacher in my classroom. I think these students deserve special attention and should be given special help. Where do we disagree? The director thinks that any student who tries should pass. I disagree. It isn't really all that hard to pass my class for an "average" student who puts in a minimum of effort. But one has to "play the game" to a certain extent. A student who receives a failing grade in my class has one or two problems, a lack of effort or a lack of ability. I don't want to damage youngsters, but pretending they have abilities they don't have is lying. Are these students better served, emotionally or otherwise, by getting a high school diploma which is meaningless? How long will it take for an employer to discover that student A has no skills? At what risk to a student's confidence do I lie about a student's ability. I think we owe it to special ed students (and all students) to move them along in their academic abilities. To find ways/strategies so that they CAN learn to read and write and think. This may or may not work in my classroom and if it doesn't something else needs to be tried. Except that I'm pressured to move these kids along through the system, because THEY TRIED.

Mitch: It's one of those battlefields they talked about in one of the readings. But the thing that I'm getting in touch with is that a high school diploma doesn't mean that much. I think more and more we are warehousing lots of kids. I don't want to lose sight of the kids who are good and working hard, but there are some kids who don't belong in high school, but to do that would mean we'd need your paradigm shift. No small thing that!

Randy: By ignoring their needs, I don't think that *we've* tried enough for them.

Mitch: Perhaps, and maybe this is my cynicism—maybe it just doesn't matter that much!

Again, Randy is grappling with his ambivalence towards mainstreamed students whom he is "pressured to move along through the system, because THEY TRIED." Mitch then raises the question as to the value of a high school diploma, in noting that ". . . there are some kids who don't belong in high school, but to do that would mean we'd need your paradigm shift." By receiving that perspective from Mitch, Randy can then reflect on his own attitudes towards mainstreaming.

In their reflection, Randy and Mitch are focusing not only on their teaching, but also the ways in which larger institutional forces constrain their teaching. One of the major criticisms of the teacher reflection movement has been that it assumes that teachers focus on their own behaviors rather than the ways in which the perspectives or ideological orientations constituting teaching and learning. When student teachers experience difficulty in adjusting to a school or classroom culture, they often blame themselves for their difficulties rather than the institutional forces that shape their attitudes and behaviors. As Deborah Britzman (1991) documents, during their student teaching, preservice teachers are often socialized to adopt an individualistic, "sink-or-swim" model of teaching that assumes that teachers must make it on their own. In reflecting on her experience, a student teacher may then blame herself rather than turn her critical attention to the larger institutional constraints limiting her experience. It is therefore important that you also focus on institutional forces shaping and constraining your teaching.

(For further reading on journals and teacher reflection, see Bolin, 1988; Slift, Houston, & Pugach, 1990; Holly, 1984; Mass, 1991; Miller, 1990; Newman, 1988; Smith, 1991; and Yinger & Clark, 1981).

Chapter Four

Developing Specific Assignments for Journal Writing

In addition to the general uses for journal writing which have already been described, there will be many instances in which you will give assignments for journal writing in order to accomplish specific teaching objectives. Without specific assignments, some less experienced students may lack the motivation or the knowledge to write in a self-sponsored way. At the same time, to preserve the spirit of journal writing, these assignments need to be purposeful, open-ended and inviting.

Instilling a Sense of Purpose and Audience

In formulating assignments, it is important to provide students with a sense of purpose and audience connected, if possible, with a meaningful context. Students may be more motivated to write if they know why and for whom they are writing something. If you ask students to write about an issue in the school—a simple "topic" without an overt rhetorical purpose or an imagined reader—you might ask them to assume they will submit their paper to the school principal, who has pledged to listen to students' concerns. Providing students with an audience other than yourself means that you can then assume the role of coach rather than judge, since the student's rhetorical purpose will not be to write a text for evaluation, and since the primary audience will not be a teacher in the role of an evaluator (Britton, et al., 1975).

By creating real or imagined rhetorical contexts, you can provide students with a sense of purpose. Imagine that you have assigned a short story portraying a conflict over power.

Before they read the story, you want the students to write about power differences in their own relationships. To give them a sense of purpose, you might develop a prompt that creates a context within which students write about power in social relationships:

> In our relationships with other people, we often find that some people have more power over us than others. You may think that teachers, the principal, parents, coaches, or police officers have more power over you, while you have more power over younger students, brothers or sisters.

> Write about some specific experiences with people who have more power than you, and have less power than you. Then describe your feelings about these different people. Why do you think these other people have more or less power than you? Now imagine that you are the main character in [X]. Adopting that character's voice, describe how s/he perceives other characters with more and with less power. Then reflect on reasons for the character's perceptions of power.

Case-Based Prompts

Cases and scenarios provide excellent rhetorical contexts and audiences when "real" ones are not practical or available. Cases describe concrete hypothetical situations that present a problem or dilemma to solve. This gives students a sense of context to write about what they would do if they were confronted with that situation.

We used the following case concerning language policy in a course that makes heavy use of journals.

> A sportswriter of a local city newspaper reports on the attempt of a major football team to acquire a "star" black football player in a #1 draft pick. The player is optimistic about joining the team but has expressed concerns, through his attorney, about the possible size of his salary. The negotiations have been difficult and tense. In his story, the sportswriter includes the following lines:

> We all know how great it would be to acquire such a superstar as Jones [the ball player]. But why on earth is Smith [the team's owner] being so niggardly? Come on, Smith! Ante up! So what if Jones comes with a price? You just can't find a better wide receiver, period.

> A week after the column appears in the paper, the editor publishes a letter. He says he received several com-

plaints about the racist connotations in the paper's use of the word "niggardly."

The editor-in-chief reports that he did a computer search of the paper's files over the past decade, and found that the word "niggardly" has been used fourteen times since then, in various stories. The complaint-letter file indicates that once or twice before, readers wrote to express their concern about the use of the word.

He goes on to remind readers that the word "niggardly" has no *linguistic* connection to anything racial (or racist); the word means "reluctant to give or spend; miserly," and comes from Middle English "nyggard," through a Scandinavian word with connections to Old English *hneaw* (stingy). Related words include "niggle" and "niggling." Because of its closeness (in spelling and in sound) to the word "nigger," the word has the potential to create negative *connotations*, if only by association.

The editor points out that technically "niggardly" is a perfectly good English word, and defends the various journalists who used it. But he goes on to say that because his newspaper serves its readers, if anyone routinely takes offense at the use of a certain word, it should probably be avoided. The language is rich enough to allow journalists to choose a suitable synonym. He decides to advise all his reporters to avoid using the word.

Your Task: Write a letter to the editor-in-chief expressing your views on this issue. You might consider the following questions as you frame your response: Was the editor's choice wise? To what extent should we monitor the language and change our use of it to avoid any negative *connotations*, even if these are not linguistically justifiable? Where would you draw the line on such an endeavor? Do you feel the same way about the trade name "Whopper," if it offends Italian Americans who see "wop" in it, or the word "nipper," if it offends Japanese Americans who see "nip" in it? If some group is offended by a word, should the rest of the culture avoid using it? Why or why not? Would you feel comfortable using the word "queer" (meaning "odd" or "strange") today? Why or why not? Is the shift in usage of "queer" and gay"—and "fag," meaning cigarette, in England—the same as the avoidance of "niggardly"?

Cases come in a wide variety of styles, length and formats. Some are extremely complex, with several "stages"—students might respond to the first part of the case, "turn in" their writing, and then read on to discover new twists and turns as new events unfold—(see Anson & Wilcox, 1988), others may be just vignettes of a few lines or a paragraph.

Even the simplest and most straightforward writing assignments can, turn into more interesting and motivating cases for students. Consider an eleventh-grade teacher's revision of a rather dull assignment he had given to students for almost seventeen years in his honors English course:

> **Assignment:** Now that you have read the first act of *King Lear*, write a one-two page analysis of the character of Cordelia. You might consider some of the aspects of *characterization* we have been discussing, such as round vs. flat characters.

As part of an inservice workshop focusing on assignment design, Ben decided to revisit this assignment. He was unhappy with the papers students wrote to his prompt, finding them dull or simply uninformed by the play, as if the students weren't reading very carefully. During the workshop, Ben decided to "give up" on the more academic purpose of testing out features of characterization, and instead create a rhetorical context that would ensure students were actually reading the play. Matters of characterization, he thought, could then be discussed in class, using the students' papers as a starting point.

Here is Ben's revised assignment:

> **Assignment:** Now that you've read Act I of *King Lear*, you should have a sense of how Cordelia feels, based on what she says and how she behaves in the play. Imagine that you are Cordelia. You've decided that it might be better to express your thoughts to your father in writing, and that perhaps he will listen to you more thoughtfully in this form. Write a letter to Lear expressing your thoughts now that he has disowned you. Shakespearean language is optional but encouraged!

After trying this out in his class, Ben reported that the students seemed infinitely more engaged and interested in the play, and his classroom discussions were extremely lively after the students wrote their responses. One reason for this liveliness, he reasoned, was that in order to complete the assignments, the students needed to read the play carefully, preparation that enhanced Ben's class discussions. As a result, Ben began creating cases and scenarios out of almost all his writing assignments.

Students can also produce their own cases in small groups or teams, perhaps embellishing them with pictures, "mocked-up" documents, and other props. They can circulate and respond to each other's cases. In one example from a twelfth-grade class, the teacher asked the students to create cases that involved ethical dilemmas. Of the six cases the class produced, one focused on the ethics of sterilizing seriously retarded girls who would pass on their genetic aberrations to their offspring. The case focused on one girl whose parents were split about the decision to sterilize her. Another case placed the reader/responder in the role of a judge deciding whether to revoke the driving license of an elderly man who had had several minor accidents only marginally attributable to his age and ability to drive. The case provided descriptions of the accidents, testimonies from witnesses and friends, statements from the man, and even a document the students had obtained from the state of Virginia about the revocation of driving privileges on the basis of ability. In these and other cases, the students were engaged in real-world writing and reading activities—since their case itself had to be well-informed on the issue at hand. In turn, their fictionalized worlds provided their peers with more opportunities to respond to non-academic audiences, purposes, contexts and rhetorical forms than if there were doing traditional essay writing.

Formulating Open-Ended Prompts

Students are more likely to be engaged by open-ended prompts that invite them to express their own ideas. In asking students to respond to a short story, you may give them the prompt: "define the theme of the story." In responding to that prompt, students may assume that they need to infer what you believed to be "the theme" as opposed to formulating their own interpretation. An alternative, more open-ended prompt might be: "Based on a list of your thoughts and feelings about the story, what is your interpretation of the story?" Simply by changing the wording from "the theme" to "your thoughts and feelings" and "your interpretation," you invite students to express their own responses without concern for responding according to what you may deem to be an acceptable or "correct" interpretation. The more personal prompt may also generate more substantive responses. In a study comparing students' writing in response to an impersonal versus personal prompts, Newell, Suszynski and Weingart (1989) found that the more personal prompt generated higher levels of interpretation of a story than the impersonal prompt. The more personal prompt invited students to describe their own attitudes and beliefs, which then led them to generate their own interpretation.

If students perceive your assignment as just one more routine demand on their time, they may be less motivated to write than if they see it as an invitation to write. By creating inviting and imaginative assignments, you are telling students that you want to read what they write—that their writing holds some significance for you.

A Minnesota high school teacher, Memry Roessler, developed the following assignment for use with a series of texts focusing on character roles, including Paul Dunbar's poem, "We Wear the Mask." In her prompt, she relates masks to differences between private and public selves:

Let's Face It!

We are obsessed with faces—how they reveal even as they conceal. We can lose face, save face, face the music or face-off. We can be sweet-faced, straight-faced, or two-faced. We can come face to face with someone or something or take things as face value. Because the face is so public, most of us construct masks to help us cope with an indifferent and often hostile environment. Masks help us adopt to new situations as well as prevent others from seeing our private self. Masks can defy, mislead, distort, intimidate. Masks can empower, mystify and affirm. The masks we wear are always subject to change, depending on who we're with, what we're doing, how we're feeling or where we find ourselves. Most of us have masks to cover every occasion.

Write about a mask your wear and when and why you wear it. Design a mask that captures some hidden aspect of your multiple self. Be creative and honest with your construction.

The language of this prompt conveys a sense of the teacher's own strong interest in the topic, interest that may provide a sense of purpose. In some cases, the students even experimented with their own journal writing, creating "rhetorical masks" in keeping with the assignment and thus giving additional purpose to their writing.

Achieving Specific Intellectual Goals

In formulating assignments, you may choose from a range of different journal writing activities—such as note-taking, listing, drawing/diagraming, mapping—in order to encourage certain kinds of intellectual skills, to connect one set of skills with another or to move the students forward by increments toward a larger product.

Note-taking. Central to effective note-taking is the ability to summarize one's perceptions of a text or lecture in one's own words. Instead of quoting a text or speaker verbatim, students need to learn to restate or reformulate their language in their own words, assimilating the ideas presented into their own schema or perspective.

To reflect on the content of their courses, students can pose questions about what they want to learn from the material (Spires & Stone, 1989). Before watching a video tape of Joseph Campbell discussing mythology, students in a tenth grade class listed some questions about mythology, such as "What is mythology?" "What is its purpose?" "How is it passed on from generation to generation?" "How does it differ across different cultures?" In recording their questions during the video, the students were able to focus on certain key points they might have otherwise missed.

In addition to summarizing their perceptions of material, students also need to organize their perceptions logically. You can model this process by showing students how you use visual layout and icons to organize your own notes. As the Joseph Campbell tape is running, keep notes on an overhead, making explicit as to how you visually organize your perceptions of his various points on mythology.

Students may also use their note-taking journals to *extend* the material to something in which they are particularly interested. Hilary is writing a paper on the topic of women in politics. Along the way, she reads a story about a husband threatened by his suddenly assertive wife. Even though the story is not directly related to her paper topic, she sees its relevance in her journal, noting that women entering politics may also be perceived as a threat by some men.

Within the classroom, students can rotate the job of keeping notes, with certain designated students serving as "class scribes" (Edwards, H., 1992). These "scribes" read aloud their notes to the class as well as posting them for absentees to use. In assuming the role of scribe, students gain a sense of responsibility within the classroom.

Rather than lecture to students, you can write up your lecture in the form of notes, have the students read and generate questions about your notes, and then use those questions as the basis of the classroom discussion. By relying on discussions of written lecture notes, students may be more actively engaged in constructing the meaning of your lecture than if they were simply listening to your lecture.

Listing. Listing encourages students to extend their thinking by creating new categories of information or new extensions of an existing concept. You might ask students to list a character's attributes, questions about a topic, problems they wish to investigate or people they can contact to discuss an issue or get information. In some cases, different categories generate sublists or even links between ideas. In listing a character's attributes, students may draw on the categories of traits, beliefs, knowledge and attitudes. When they create a second list for another character, new categories may emerge or they may see connections between the characters along the dimension of a specific category.

Drawing/diagraming. As shown in Chapter Two, students may include drawings or diagram in their journals. In some cases, you may ask students to draw a map of the setting for a novel, like the illustration below for a map of *The Great Gatsby.* To help them generate a topic, you might ask students to draw a diagram illustrating the different aspects of an issue. These drawings or diagrams help students perceive their thoughts in visual form, something particularly appealing for those with high "visual/spatial" intelligence (Gardner, 1985).

Mapping. Another form of visual display is mapping. Students can use maps to chart out and define the relationships between the different aspects of a phenomenon. Circle or spider maps generate a range of different attributes or characteristics associated with specific concepts. In responding to Eudora Welty's short story "Why I Live at the P.O.," students can place the different characters in circles and then, with spokes emanating from each circle, describe traits, beliefs and goals associated with these characters.

Students can also devise tree maps that begin with certain "high level" concepts. Under each of these concepts, they develop "roots" or "branches" to explore more specific concepts. In the following tree map, a student explores different aspects of writing about her neighborhood, moving from general to more specific.

Extending Thinking

In formulating assignments, you are also concerned with teaching students how to extend their thinking. As we noted in Chapter Two, students often lack the heuristics or "intellectual scaffolding" (Langer & Applebee, 1987) that allows them to extend their thinking—to know what to do next (Brandt, 1990). Furthermore, students are often reluctant to extend their thinking given a "failure to be tentative" (McCormick, 1990, p. 203). They impose a premature closure, assuming that once they have said what they wanted to say, they are done. Teachers sometimes encourage this premature closure by valuing regurgitation of information through "list and gist" summary writing (McCormick, 1990). In the need to obtain closure and "get it right," students are reluctant to explore their own doubts, concerns or contradictions inherent in their texts or the course. Students are more likely to be tentative about a topic if they are willing to explore a range of different perspectives.

Figure 4-1
A Map of *The Great Gatsby*

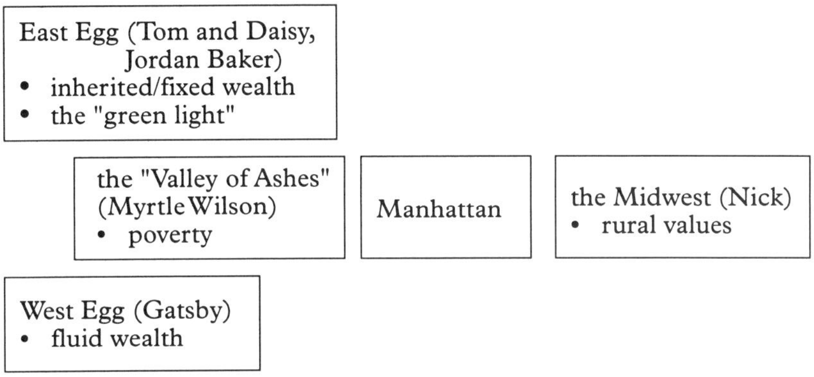

```
┌─────────────────────────┐
│ East Egg (Tom and Daisy, │
│       Jordan Baker)      │
│ • inherited/fixed wealth │
│ • the "green light"      │
└─────────────────────────┘
      ┌──────────────────────┐  ┌───────────┐  ┌──────────────────────┐
      │ the "Valley of Ashes"│  │           │  │ the Midwest (Nick)   │
      │ (Myrtle Wilson)      │  │ Manhattan │  │ • rural values       │
      │ • poverty            │  │           │  │                      │
      └──────────────────────┘  └───────────┘  └──────────────────────┘
┌─────────────────────────┐
│ West Egg (Gatsby)       │
│ • fluid wealth          │
└─────────────────────────┘
```

Exploring multiple perspectives. The likelihood that students' prior schooling has shut down their exploration of ideas suggests a strong need to encourage students to go beyond summary writing. To do so you may need to include assignments that push students to explore multiple perspectives. Some useful strategies include the following heuristics.

Five w's. The journalist's "five w's"—"who, what, where, when and why"—are a heuristic for exploring the different aspects of an event. By applying these categories in a journal, students may expand on and elaborate their descriptions of that event. If they only dealt with the "who" and the "what," they may also then describe the "where," "when" and "why."

"Describe, recall, reflect, interpret." In responding to texts, students can apply the "describe, recall, reflect, interpret" heuristic (Bleich, 1988; Beach, 1990). In this heuristic, students describe their perceptions of what happens in a story, novel, movie, essay or article. They then recall related experiences evoked by the text. In reading a story about losing a championship game, Jamie recalled her own experience in losing a girl's soccer match. She then reflected on the meaning of her own experience—what she learned from the loss. Her recollections and reflections then led to a deeper interpretation of

Figure 4-2
A Circle Map of "Why I Live at the P.O."

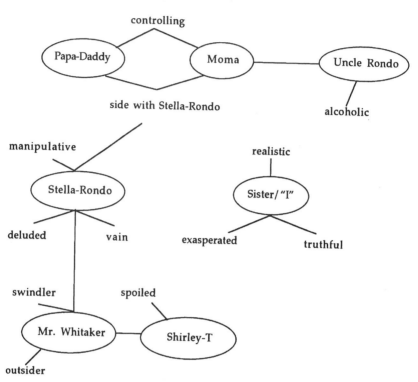

the story. In reflecting on her experience, she recognized that to take winning or losing too seriously undermines the fact that sports is primarily for fun.

Meanings to self and world. Students may also write about what a text means to them—their own personal meaning—and what it means to the world—larger implications for others. Phyllis Edwards (1992) of the Santa Cruz school district gives students categories for writing in their journals such as:

> what it says
> what it means
> what it means to me
> what it means to the world

Particle, Wave, Field. Another set of heuristic categories is based on the tagmemic system of Young, Becker and Pike (1970). They proposed the categories of "particle" (describing a phenomenon or thing itself), "wave," (describing the phenomenon or thing over time), and "field" (describing the phenomenon or thing in relationship to others of the same type). This system encourages students to explore different perspectives on the same phenomenon. A group of ninth-graders were writing about a popular main street area in their town. They first described the street itself in terms of its unique features—it has several outdoor shops and restaurants which are a popular hangout for young people. Then they described the street as it had evolved over timewhat it was like ten years ago as well as projections for what it may become. Finally they wrote about the relationships between these different aspects of time—how features of the street's past, such as the old movie theater and a nearby warehouse, were related to the street in the present (the theater was undergoing restoration while there was a major struggle over the warehouse between preservationists and those who wanted it torn down for a new parking lot).

They then wrote about the street in terms of the larger concept, "main streets," reflecting on the relationship of their particular main street to other kinds of main streets (urbanized and rural, safe and dangerous, populated and decaying, and lined with retail stores vs. manufacturing centers or office buildings). Each of these three different perspectives gave the students a different lens for examining the idea of a main street.

Similarities/differences. Students can compare or contrast phenomena in terms of similarities and differences, using Venn diagrams to determine areas in which phenomena overlap

Figure 4-3
Tree Map used in Writing About a Neighborhood

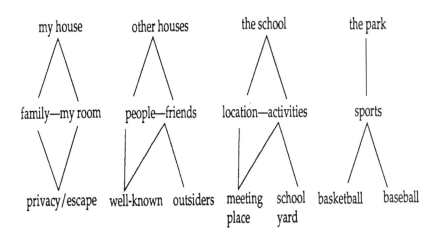

Figure 4.4
Venn Diagram for Defining
Similarities and Differences

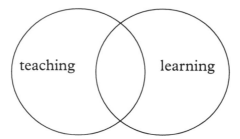

and areas in which they contrast. In writing about the relationship between teaching and learning, a student used Venn diagrams to note instances of teaching without learning, teaching with learning, and learning without teaching.

Hierarchies and Hyponymous Relations. In jotting down or mapping out relationships between concepts, students need to consider how certain concepts are subsumed under other concepts. In the field of linguistic semantics, such hierarchies are known as "hyponymous relations," which help people to organize words into categories of meaning. The word "dog" subsumes many more specific terms such as "wolfhound," "collie," and "dachshund." "Dog" is itself subsumed by higher-level words such as "mammals" or "animals." Hierarchical categories can also be developed for such concepts as parks, swimming pools and golf courses, all of which are subsumed under the larger concept of recreational services. Often a tree diagram with the higher level concepts at the top and the lower level concepts on the bottom helps students define hierarchical relationships.

Modeling Thinking Strategies

Guided journal assignments involve a range of thinking strategies, some of which may be unfamiliar or especially challenging to students. It may be unwise, therefore, to design a journal assignment and then set the students free with the assumption that they will complete the task and learn from it. For more complex assignments or ones that you know will be new to students, it's important to model the strategies you are asking them to use without making your own examples so facile and sophisticated that they lead to intimidation.

Figure 4.5
Hierarchical Tree Map for Foods

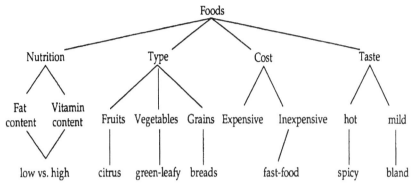

If you choose to demonstrate your own writing processes, it may help to do so "live," rather than retrospectively, since your own free associations and tentative thoughts will show students that writers are not always certain about what they think and what they want to say. As you write out your thoughts on the overhead, chalkboard or computer, provide a think-aloud commentary that makes public what Peter Elbow (1973) describes as "movies of your mind." You may want to focus on those thought processes related to your assignment. If you have asked students to keep descriptive field notes, you may want to emphasize the idea of describing specific, concrete images and behaviors. Kelly, a tenth-grade teacher, noted to her class that her description of one of her other classes ("the group was noisy today") was too vague. She then cited some examples of concrete behaviors that particularized this general statement: "Kevin was in the back of the room yelling at his friend across the room; two girls on the right side were talking about their after school job; Sam was next to the door was talking with someone who was out in the hallway."

Sequencing activities: "First things first." Some of your journal assignments will be self-contained, linked only in the most general ways to the progress of your course. Much of the time, however, it will help to sequence your assignments so that they are logically and intellectually connected, each one preparing the students for some more sophisticated activities (Beach & Marshall, 1991). A listing activity prepares students for a mapping activity. A freewriting activities prepares students for a role play activity. Attending to such sequences will help your students to acquire the "intellectual scaffolding" essential for extending their thinking.

In sequencing activities within assignments, think about

whether students are able to complete an activity in the allotted time and with existing resources. For example, Peg Finders, a high school English teacher, was helping her class respond to the short story "The Use of Force." She first asked her students to visually "map" the relationships between the story's characters. She found that they were having difficulty knowing how to draw their maps without some preliminary written responses to the story. After thinking what might logically precede the activity of mapping, she decided to have the class make a list of descriptive terms for each character. Some students wrote terms like "patient," "gentle" and "good" for the doctor, while others wrote "frustrated," "angry" and "vengeful." The class then discussed these terms and the reasons for any disagreements among them (the doctor *begins* patiently but *ends up* frustrated and finally triumphant through the use of force—details that showed the students not just static qualities about the characters but how their personalities seemed to change over time). Finders' quick thinking led to a sequence of activities that helped the students to move from one intellectual operation to the next. Completing the freewriting and listing activities prepared the students for the somewhat more complex mapping activity.

Reviewing and Extracting Ideas from Journal Entries

Journal writing is often perceived to be a process of spontaneously expressing thoughts in writing. However, equally important to generating text is learning to review entries to extract ideas for use in subsequent entries, discussions or papers. Once students have expressed themselves, they need to be able to review their thoughts with an eye to inferring what Elbow (1981) describes as the "center of gravity." In response to the question, "what I am trying to say in this entry," students define a point, position or idea they extract from their thoughts. Sarah, a twelfth grader, is writing a paper for her college admissions application on the topic of a major challenge facing the world. She chooses the topic "overpopulation," and uses her journal to brainstorm problems created by overpopulation. She re-reads her entries and, in another entry, states what she infers to be a central problem: a reduction in the quality of life due to lack of resources to feed people. She is extracting a key idea to be used for writing further entries about the relationship between quality of life and lack of resources.

Unlike Sarah, many students may not review their writing. In formulating guided assignments, you may therefore want to provide directions for reviewing entries. You may ask students to "read back over your entry and think about what you are trying to say. Then begin another entry with a statement of one or more ideas and write some more about that point or idea." You may also want to model this review process by putting an entry on the overhead, and then, as you read it aloud, conduct a think-aloud review, talking about how you are inferring your ideas.

Students also use their ideas to assess the sufficiency and relevancy of their thinking in their entries. In reviewing her entries with her hypothesis in mind, Sarah senses that she doesn't have enough information to establish a relationship between quality of life and lack of resources. That felt-sense need for more information drives her to develop some more material. Or, in writing further entries, she may discover that her idea statement needs further revision. She is therefore moving back and forth between different levels of abstraction, using her thoughts to generate ideas and using ideas to reflect on and assess her thoughts.

As part of your assignment you may include some directions for having students assess the sufficiency or relevancy of their entries relative to their ideas. You may ask them; "with your idea in mind, read over your entry or entries and determine whether or not you need to develop more information or whether your information is relevant to your point." Again, you may want to model this process of using your idea to assess your own entry or entries.

Students may facilitate their reviewing by categorizing sections of entries in the margins or at the top of the page. These categories serve as subheads for the topic or idea in an entry. Fred, a ninth grader, was writing a paper on the difficulties of peer relationships. He did not start with a preset "outline," which presupposed that he already knew what he was going to say before he had developed his material. Rather, he used his journal to brainstorm his own thoughts and feelings about his relationships with peers. He described his experience of "peer shock" precipitated by the betrayal of a friend. He listed the names of his different friends, noting those characteristics of others that led to successful relationships. He recalled and noted the reasons for conflicts and breakdowns in relationships. And he reflected on the benefits of peer relationships.

Fred then read over his entries with a eye to generating some categories. Based on summary "titles" at the top of each entry page, he arranged his entries into piles. He then wrote a new entry describing his categories, visually organizing them according to the logical relationships between three different chronological phases: "developing,""maintaining," and "ending" friendships. For each phase, he wrote the heading "difficult-" versus "less-difficult," referring to what is hard or easy about developing, maintaining and ending friendships. Beneath each heading, he then inserted illustrative examples of specific friendships. His arranging and grouping led him to produce new material useful for his paper on friendship.

Varying Assignments According to Individual Differences

Students typically differ in a number of characteristics related to their work in your class. They bring in different learning styles, strengths and weaknesses with certain cognitive tasks, experiences as writers (especially using journals) and attitudes toward schooling. In light of these many differences, you may want to adapt your assignments to suit individual students' styles, abilities and attitudes. Of course, with class loads of 120 to 160 students, it is often difficult to know much about students' individual differences. Consistent with the notion of giving students responsibility for their own learning, you might want to provide them with optional versions of assignments and let them select (with your assistance) those versions they prefer.

Creating different versions of assignments. By using a word processor you can fairly easily adapt a generic assignment to to individual differences in students' needs. High school teacher Tony Peroda revised his assignment on the short story "The Stone Boy," by Gina Berriault (contained in *Points of View*, ed. James Moffett and Kenneth McElheny). In that story, a boy accidently shoots his brother and then is ostracized by his family and has no one to talk to about his feelings. Tony's generic prompt was "respond in your journal to 'The Stone Boy,'" which he then revised on his computer to accommodate his students' individual needs. He saved his revised prompts by file names associated with individual differences for use with future assignments.

First Tony considered differences in his students' *learning styles*. Some students, he noted, prefer more structured tasks while others want more freedom. For the former group, Tony adapted his assignment on "The Stone Boy" to include specific steps that began with listing the boy's behaviors after the accident, his family members' reactions to those behaviors, and the effects of those reactions on the boy according. Tony gave these students the following chart:

The boy's behaviors	Family members' reactions	Effects on the boy

In contrast, for students who needed less structure, he asked them to simply describe the effects of the other family members reactions on the boy.

Tony also felt that some of his students worked at more "abstract" or "intuitive" levels, preferring to generate larger models or theories, to see "the big picture." In responding to stories they tried to define the overall theme instead of getting caught up in particulars. At times, these students were also prone to overgeneralizations without careful consideration of factual evidence. In formulating assignments for this group, Tony encouraged them to construct models and generalizations (which matched their cognitive styles), but also challenged them to gather information or make observations that could support their assertions.

Another group of students in Tony's class preferred to focus on specific information or facts but had trouble abstracting or reflecting on larger themes from these details. In responding to stories, they focused on matters of plot ("what happened") or characterization ("what X is like"). Consistent with these students' learning preferences, Tony provided them with activities that initially focused on collecting information about plot, setting and character. He then challenged them with structured activities that involved categorizing and making inferences about that information.

Tony also adapted his assignment on "The Stone Boy" to the *multicultural* nature of his class, recognizing that some of his minority students seemed to have been silenced in their school experiences for trying to express their own unique cultural perspectives (see Delpit, 1988). Research on use of the dialogue journals in multicultural classrooms has found that exchanges between teachers and students encouraged minority students to express non-mainstream perspectives that otherwise might be silenced (Peyton & Staton, 1993; Cooper, 1992). Tony created a safe environment by adapting his assignment to encourage personal responses that included differences in the ways that the events in the story would play out in different homes with different cultural backgrounds. He also explicitly discouraged racial prejudices and encouraged the open expression of divergent points of view.

Assigning Journals for Long-Term Use

Journals are excellent placeholders for specific, guided assignments with particular teaching goals. Ultimately you want students to use journals on a continuous, on-going basis, with as much self-sponsored writing as possible. Once students learn to use the journal writing as a habit for formulating their thoughts about readings or experiences, they don't need to be given assignments for each reading or activity. In Sharon Pilosky's senior English class her students were writing a paper on *To Kill a Mockingbird*. As they read the novel, they automatically recorded their reactions and perceptions of key events or shifts in characters' feelings and attitudes. Then, when they began to write their paper, they had an extensive collection of notes to draw on for formulating ideas. Sharon observed that once they perceived the value of keeping notes to assist them in paper writing, they were more likely to use the journal to prepare for future papers. As they jotted down thoughts before a class discussion, they also realized that they relied on their notes for sharing thoughts with others.

Weaning students from specific assignments also involves creating a sense of engagement with whatever they are doing in the classroom. Students are more likely to be interested in an experience, activity or text if they perceive it to be personally significant or relevant. A ninth grade student, Kristin, developed an interest in how females are portrayed in teenage magazine ads. She used her journal to describe her descriptions of these ads. Based on her reading of a number of different kinds of magazines, she discovered that females were frequently portrayed in stereotyped ways, often in terms of appealing to the perspective of the "male gaze." By describing her own intuitions about stereotyping in her journal, she developed a stronger interest in the value and significance of her topic—the fact that the stereotypical portrayals were shaping her friends' and her own self-images. Her personal investment in the topic motivated her to keep writing about her critical reactions to the ads.

Chapter Five

Journal Writing Activities in the English Class

In Chapters Two and Three, we discussed some general approaches to using the journal in the classroom, with special emphasis on the variety of uses to which journals may be put. As some critics have argued recently, We may be limiting students' education if we adhere to a pure version of the "doctrine of educational formalism," providing them with only "strategies" empty of the kinds of knowledge and content that they ought to be learning (Hirsch, 1987). In conservative curriculums, students are enjoined to memorize facts and dates, or to become familiar with capsulated bits of knowledge that are thought to constitute our nation's "cultural literacy" (Hirsch, 1988). Journal writing provides an ideal bridge between these two quite different visions of learning: they are *strategic* in the way they encourage critical reflection and provide students with many ways to examine and learn about a topic; and they are *content-driven* in their potential to focus students' attention on many subjects both personal and academic. Unlike the static, information-driven methods outlined by advocates of cultural literacy, journals encourage students to learn new knowledge at deeper and more sophisticated levels than lists of facts or three-sentence definitions of widely known information.

But what sort of "content" might give life to students' journals? The answer to this question must be in the specific goals of a curriculum, discipline, course of study and teacher. The purpose of this chapter is to turn from the "why's" and "how's" of journal writing to the "what's," the content that can fill a journal's pages and lead to principled intellectual change and positive learning. Our goal is to suggest some topics and ideas for students to write about—to open possibilities for new and imaginative uses of the journal.

Writing Autobiographically

Today was stressful for Terry. She learned that her boyfriend, Mike, had developed an interest in one of her friends, creating a sense of betrayal or what David Elkind (1981) describes as "peer shock." On the same day, she scored two goals for her soccer team. After she scored the second goal that won the game, she was elated when she was mobbed by her teammates.

These emotional ups and downs are a part of adolescents' daily lives. Even during one day, their emotional states may swing dramatically from boredom and depression to exhilaration and euphoria (Csikszentmihalyi & Larson, 1984). They react emotionally to what strikes adults as even the most trivial of events—why a friend sat with someone else at lunch. Faced with set-backs and challenges, adolescents often overreact emotionally, losing all sense of perspective and rationality.

Adolescents are also exposed to a range of larger current events in their school, community or nation—the death of a popular teacher, a natural disaster in a nearby neighborhood, the shut-down of a local plant or the explosive reaction to a trial verdict. In spite of the regional or national interest of these events, adolescents may have as much difficulty sorting them out and reflecting on them as they do with matters much closer to their own personal lives.

In reacting to such personal and current events, adolescents are not only expressing their own emotional responses; they are attempting to make sense of those events by putting them into some sort of explanatory perspective or framework. While they often use their nightly telephone conversations with friends to recount and reflect on the issues in their lives, they may also use their journals to write about their emotional reactions, particularly for those events that disturb or upset them and which they may not want to discuss with others.

In writing about personal events, students can begin by framing the event as a narrative, thereby recapturing or elaborating details. Recounting the details may evoke certain feelings or attitudes which the writer may come to terms with. When a peer has a superior performance on an exam, they may respond with envy, jealously, hatred, admiration or guilt (for not studying), feelings that shape their perception of the event.

Mike, an eighth grader, recalls a time when he wrote a letter but never delivered it.

I had written an elaborate letter to a female mentioned in the last journal entry. It was three pages long, front and back, and it told about how I was attracted to her the first time I saw her which was some eight years ago. The letter told her about the first time I dreamed about her, flying wouldn't ya' know, and about how I do day-dream about her all the time. That letter was almost a month in the making. I had spilled my guts, picked them up, and spilled them again. That letter contained most of my emotions.

But I didn't give it to her. After having spilled my guts over and over, I didn't have enough to finish the job. Instead I threw it away. My greatest works are now covered in feet of garbage and are decaying at a slow rate. I couldn't even look at her for a week afterwards.

For Mike, this event represented an instance in which he was disappointed in himself: "There have been many time when I have disappointed someone," but in this case "It's me that I'm disappointing."

In recounting the event, students may also shift the point of view from "I" to "he" or "she." In *The New Diary*, Tristine Rainer (1978) suggests that altering the point of view invites a more objective, distanced perspective on one's experience similar to "tracking back, back, back with a camera to give you a wide-angle view of an entire situation" (p. 95). She cites the example of an unidentified diarist who describes the event of turning thirty from the point of view of "she":

She had turned thirty that summer. She could both feel it and see it—something was gone, some glow which she recognized from old photographs, the glow that the college students swarming all over town still had—pure youth, nothing more, but a natural juice, the energy of children which would dissipate sooner than hers had. She felt it happening as she stared at them waiting for an answer to a meaningless question, chalk covering her hand with white dust, the other one forgotten, holding her long cigarette which had gone out (p. 95-6).

Students can also reflect on the nature of the selves or aspects of their identity reflected by their behavior in the event. To do so, they can first list different attributes comprising their self: "stubborn," "outspoken," "eager," "anxious," "outgoing," etc. They then reflect on which of these attributes are reflected in a particular event.

Students can also report on events they witness. Jenny observed a confrontation between the assistant principal and her friend, Jill. The assistant principal had asked Jill to explain why she was late getting to school. Jill responded that her alarm clock hadn't gone off, a comment that the principal disliked enough to assign her a detention. Jenny then tried to explain the event, as would a reporter, by interviewing the participants. In her interview with Jill, she discovered that Jill and the principal had been at loggerheads several times before. From her interview with the principal, she found that he had interpreted Jill's remark as an insult, a violation of standards of the respect for adults that he was trying to uphold in the school. And in conversations with a number of other students, Jenny discovered a widely held perception that the principal often overreacts to what he thinks is offensive behavior.

Students may also write about events that had negative or even traumatic effects on them—a death in the family, a break-up of a close relationship, a crippling accident or a divorce. These events may evoke anger, guilt, jealously, grief, fear or envy—feelings they may reflect on and justify, rationalize, or understand in some way. Students can clarify these feelings by finding metaphors for them. In their book, *Journal Keeping with Young People*, Barbara Steiner and Kathleen Phillips (1991) cite two examples:

> "When I'm mad I'm like a thunderstorm. I bang and crash and knock things around."

> "When I'm angry I turn into an icicle, freezing cold but sharp enough to to hurt somebody. But then when somebody does something nice for me, I begin to melt." (p. 105).

Students may also use their journal to work through and understand their negative feelings. 18-year-old Alan reflects on his feelings of being hurt by a young woman—a reflection that leads to some sense of what he gained from the experience:

> An experience that I had never known. She and I were there. I thought the feeling was mutual. As it turned out, it was only a one-way street. I heard it from her friends, I thought that I knew it all. I really knew so little, it got me into a predicament. She was foreign, dark, and many of the things I wanted. She told me I reminded her of someone she had known. She said she liked my eyes and they melted her like butter. With all these hints what did I have to lose. I went ahead and asked, she said it couldn't be. She had someone and at the moment she could not get free. I shown very happily, although not inside. I think she has lied, I didn't know why. It hurts me now to feel this way, I know I can overcome it. I'm not sure how to act with her, ignore her or be nice, I guess I'll do whats natural. I am sure

this experience will help me, like others I have had. I'm
not sure how this will help me, but I shall pay attention.
(Litowitz & Gundlach, 1987, p. 103).

As Steiner and Phillips (1991) argue, by expressing these feelings students may learn to act them out vicariously rather
than through what may be destructive behavior.

Writing about other persons. As part of writing about events,
students are also writing about other people in their lives.
Journals allow them to describe these people in sufficient detail
to tease out their unique traits and attitudes. They can use a
list of the person's behaviors to generalize traits, some of which
might need further investigation, and some of which might
provide material for a draft of a descriptive or narrative paper. Paul, an eighth grader, developed the following list about
his grandmother:

- she is 92 (?)
- her husband is John
- her name is Gladys Maxson
- she cooks wonderfully
- she is busy
- she and John run a business "Jewels of Shell"
- they collect shells and make them into things
- they go to Florida to collect them
- they are retired
- they have a garden
- she cooks fish, cookies (Spanish peanut, chocolate chip, toffee)
- she's very good natured
- she's always giving us coupons
- she gets skin cancer so she always wears a hat outside
- she dresses mellowly in light colors
- she gave birth to my mom and my uncle

Students could also observe or shadow persons, taking
notes of certain unique behaviors. During interviews they can
take note of certain bits of dialogue that reflect the person's
feelings, attitudes and beliefs. Judy followed a local police
officer, Marcia, around on her local neighborhood beat. She
observed Marcia's confrontations with some vagrants and her
discussions with store owners. Using some questions she prepared in advance, Judy also interviewed Marcia about her work,
recording her comments in her journal. She then used this material, along with some photos, to write a portrait of Marcia.

Journals also offer a place for students to write about

their relationships to people in their own lives. Using freewriting and/or mapping, they can describe their links with other people (Steiner & Phillips, 1991), or discuss what they and the other person gain from and contribute to that link, what needs are satisfied by the relationships, what conflicts have occurred with that person and the ways in which they and the person are important to each other.

Writing about past events. Significant events and memories provide excellent material for students to reflect on, especially from a more mature or "distanced" perspective. Listing works well to conjure up such memories. Alternatively, they can draw a time line on which they note "high" versus "low" points. Prompts related to stories or novels can also trigger recollections of past events.

Typically, such memories will come to students in generalized form. To recall more specific details, they might use freewriting and/or mapping strategies, perhaps returning to the place in which the event occurred to observe particulars of the setting or to recall feelings. Interviews with persons who knew them at the time, photos of themselves, letters written or sent, yearbooks, songs, scrapbooks and magazines from the period all can evoke more specific memories; journal entries can be written on any or all such memorabilia. To appreciate the value of details in their writing, students can read examples of autobiographical essays or short stories, including students' writing as found in James Moffett's (1987) *Active Voices II* (middle school/junior high students) and *Active Voices III* (high school students).

To avoid summarizing what happened, students can recapture the details of setting, behaviors and dialogue that portray the event, particularly in terms of their past point of view. An eleventh grader writing about an experience as a seventh grader could try to adopt the perspective of an early adolescent. These shifts in persona help students to gain sensitivity to audience that can be useful in other, more formal writing.

Writing about life changes. As they reflect on events in the recent and distant past, students are often displaying to themselves some of the social, physical, cognitive and emotional changes that take place in all adolescents' lives. Coping with these changes is often difficult. Writing allows students to focus on many social and cultural forces influencing their experience of change. The following guided writing activity has the goal of helping students to compare their own experiences with those of a character who is undergoing change.

Writing about Change in Oneself and a Character

1. List a number of changes that have occurred in your life; these may be minor or major changes. For example, your may have experienced changes in schools, neighborhoods, friendships, group memberships, appearance, leisure time hobbies/interests, attitudes or beliefs, sports teams, interest in the opposite sex, family relationships, etc.

2. Re-read your list and pick one change that was particularly significant for you.

3. Write a narrative describing what happened during the event or events associated with the change. Elaborate on the event in some detail.

4. In thinking about that change, visualize yourself—your beliefs and traits, before, during and after the change.

5. Reread what you wrote in #3 and #4. Write about some of the particular circumstances, social forces or persons that may have been shaping your experience:
   - the time
   - the place or "world"
   - the "rules of the game" or "codes of conduct"
   - the prevailing attitudes or beliefs
   - the group or other persons.

6. If you were to relive this experience, how would you go about making this change in a different way? How might this difference have influenced you?

7. Pick a character from a text you are reading who is or has undergone a change. They may have changed in their behaviors, feelings, identity, beliefs, attitudes or status. Adopting that character's voice, create your own version of his or her thoughts or "secret confessions" while undergoing this change. Envision the character talking to you or a friend or writing in their diary about what happened. You can make up new dialogue or characters for your narrative.

8. Review your narrative. What were some particular circumstances, social forces or persons that may have been shaping the character's experience:
   - the time
   - the place or "world"
   - the "rules of the game" or "codes of conduct"
   - the prevailing attitudes or beliefs
   - the group or other characters.

9. Compare the character's narrative with your own narrative about change. In what ways were your own experiences similar to or different from that of the character's?

Personal disclosure and the issue of confidentiality. In writing about personal experiences, some students may disclose information about drug use or violations of the law; some may even reveal information that may be life-threatening—about a suicidal tendencies, an eating disorder, or a dangerously abusive situation with a friend or family member. In some cases, they may protect themselves by creating an alternative persona, such as a "a friend of mine," or a fictional character, who is experiencing their own problems. In most cases, they are seeking some adult reaction or guidance, particularly when they have no one else to turn to.

While you may not want to discourage students from writing about matters uppermost in their minds, in some states or localities you are obligated by law to report instances of illegal behavior to school authorities. If you recognize that a student needs to be referred to counseling, the school may have so few psychologists available that the student may not be able to begin counseling for a considerable period of time. While we recommend that you do not assume a strongly therapeutic role, it is often difficult to easily distinguish between talking to students or giving advice to them about their personal problems and providing psychological counseling.

There are no easy answers on how to respond to these situations. You should inform students about your own and/or the school's policy regarding the disclosure of personal problems and concerns in their journal so that students know the consequences of doing so. You may tell students that if they do not want you to read an entry, they should put it in a "confidential" section of their journal and staple those pages together—or just do not turn it in.

Writing About Current Events

Many secondary students develop a strong interest in current events at the local, state or national level. In conjunction with an English or Social Studies class, they could use their journal to describe their emotional reactions to current events. They may then write about their reasons for being angered, pleased, shocked, upset, intrigued, annoyed, etc., by various events. They could also compare these various events with other historical events. By writing about these events, students gain some personal perspective on the meaning of the events based on their own beliefs and attitudes.

In some cases, students have difficulty responding to current community or national events because they generally learn about these events second hand through the media. They may therefore not know how to connect with these events in the same direct, emotional manner as with responding to personal events. They may also experience a sense of distancing alienation from the singular, sometimes sensationalized interpretation of an event by the media. Rather than writing about the "event" per se, they are also writing about their response to the media's portrayal of an event. In doing so, they are most likely recognizing media bias by comparing different newspapers' and/or television news coverage of the same event.

Given the influence of the media on constructing the meaning of events, students could use their journals to analyze alternative perspectives on the same event. They could read different accounts of this event in different newspapers or magazines or they could watch or listen to different television or radio news coversage of that event. In their journals, students could describe their reactions to the different versions or accounts, noting which they believe to be the most valid versus least valid or convincing. They could then compare their perceptions with other students by discussing the different versions or accounts as a group. In all of this, students may be using their writing to reflect on the ways in which reality is constructed in relatively arbitrary ways. From this experience, students begin to recognize the limitations of one singular, absolutist perspective. As Barry Kroll (1992) found in giving his students disparate accounts of the same Vietnam War battle, students then grappled in their journals with the dissonance associated with competing perspectives.

Using Journals to Respond to Texts

Journal writing about texts can assume a central role in the English class. Informal journal writing about literature represents a different way of knowing and experiencing literature than is the case with formal essay writing or summary book reports (Marshall, 1990; Parsons, 1990). Informal writing about texts allows spontaneous, exploratory reactions about one's engagement with a text. It is often assumed that more "personal" reactions result in little or no interpretation of texts. However, in one study (Newell, Suszynski &Weingart, 1989), responding to more reader-based prompts such as "What character was your favorite?" "Why?" or "If you could be any character in the story, who would you be?", students were more likely to analyze or criticize their reading than in responding to the summary prompts such as "Tell me about your book."

In writing in their journals, students may use a number of different response strategies: engaging, retelling/recounting, inferring/explaining, connecting, constructing cultural worlds, interpreting, and judging (Beach & Marshall, 1991). Knowing these different response strategies may be useful in formulating prompts for writing in their journals.

Engaging. In responding to literature, including media texts, students are doing more than summarizing or describing what happened in a text. They are also describing their emotional reactions and experience with a text. They are engaged in what Louise Rosenblatt (1994) describes as an "aesthetic experience" of living through their transaction with a text as an event. Engaging with a text involves a range of different subjective experiences—emotional reactions and associations, involvement, empathy and identification. Readers gain a heightened sense of these emotions by attending to their own "felt-sense" experience with texts. They may be aware of a welling up of a lump in the throat or a sense of apprehension over a character's impeding doom.

Students often begin their entries with what David Bleich (1978) describes as "response statements" about their experience with a text, i.e., "I really was upset by the ending;" "I felt drained after I finished the story;" "I felt close to her description of her first date;" "I was confused by why he did what he did." They may also describe their vicarious experience of a character's anger, sadness, pity, envy, intimacy, grief, fear, bewilderment, sympathy, love, vulnerability, shame, greed, etc. In the process, they are experiencing what Robert Solomon described as the "language of the emotions," which he defined as a particular way of perceiving or judging reality. Having experienced the depths of despair and self-anguish of an Othello, grieving over the loss of his wife, readers may then acquire a new way of perceiving the vanity and jealously the Iago played on. Having experienced the seething anger of Maya Angelou in coping with the adversities of poverty, segregation and prejudice in *I Know Why the Caged Bird Sings*, highlighted by a scene in which a dentist refuses to treat her, saying, "I would rather put my hand in a dog's mouth," readers gain a sense of the emotional trauma associated with racial prejudice.

To learn how to recognize and express the "language of emotions," students could adopt a character's perspective and compose stories or poems as told through the eyes of that character. In this way, students are perceiving experience in terms of what it would be like to be anxious, envious, jealous, angry, guilty, etc. In response to Roethke's "My Papa's Waltz," a student describes the experience of the boy's and the father's love:

There is much love in this poem. Love from the little boy, showing it by holding on and not letting go, even when his ear is scraped. And also love from this father. He is taking time-out to spend with his son. He could have just come home and sat in front of the television. But instead, he dances with the boy and takes care to put him to bed (Newton, 1991, p. 477).

When they reflect on their engagement responses, readers often shuttle back and forth between "reader-based" engagement responses to a text and "text-based" perceptions of those aspects of the text associated with those reactions (Hynds, 1994). To move back and forth between "reader-based" and "text-based" responses, they need to know *how* to extend their responses beyond their initial responses. In order to extend their responses, students need to be open to exploring what Mariolina Salvatori (1989) describes as the "unfolding, rather than the concealing, of the drama of knowing—with all it uncertainties, obstacles, anxieties, resolutions, complications" (30). Teachers may also demonstrate a tentative stance by modeling their own on-going, specific emotional reactions to a text. Wendy Bishop (1990) hands out her written description of her responses; in responding to the lines from William Stafford's poem, "Traveling Through the Dark," ("her side was warm; her fawn lay there waiting, alive, still, never to be born"), she writes:

> These lines overwhelm me with sensory and emotional detail. I, who have been dragging a stiff, dead deer, find, with a shock, that she is warm. As I register this information, I continue reading and learn that which I already half-guessed: "her fawn lay there." Then, a second shock occurs, equal to the first, in the alliterative emphasis given to the words "warm" and "waiting." The fawn is personified and vivified . . . " (12).

After her responses, Bishop noted that: "I learned a great deal about timing. To read, I moved backwards and forwards through the lines in a manner I've never charted before. I also detected the in and out movement of reader identification with the narrator and reader distance from the narrator . . . " (13-14).

Students also use visual images or icons to explore their engagement responses. Given the directions, "Think of your mind as some sort of box that contains the sights and sounds you have collected as you have read. Empty that box and write down its content in the next few minutes," students report the specific images they recall after reading a text (Anderson & Rubano, 1992). Or students list images that capture the ways in which a character is thinking about the world. Students then reflect on their pool of images, discussing the relationships between images, why certain images may be particularly important, and similarities between the types of images recalled by the entire class.

Adopting a character's perspective. Another form of engagement response involves students adopting the main character's perspective and creating their own version of the story from that character's perspective. The student adopts the main character's voice by mimicing that character's thoughts, feelings and reflections. In doing so, a student thinks about that character's perspective—what it would be like to be experiencing story events through the eyes of that character. In a study of eight eighth graders' adoption of characters' perspectives, Marjorie Hancock (1993) found that the students enjoyed responding in this mode. She cites the example of Lori, who adopts the perspective of Brian, the main character in Gary Paulsen's *The River*, a novel about surviving a raft journey down a river. Lori assumes Brian's perspective when he is thrown from a reft just before a waterfall:

> I can't breath I can't get air . . . need air I can't hold it any longer. There is so much pressure on me. The pressure keeps pushing me and pulling me in every direction but to the surface to get air . . . I wish it would stop for a littlebit just for a . . . breath . . . breath as much as you can. Oh, no! the raft it . . . it's gone. gone. no where to be seen and I can't breath again. The water is all over closing me in and I . . . can't . . . get . . . up . . . [The ellipses are Lori's, modeled after the writing technique of Gary Paulsen]

In preparing students for this activity, Hancock recommends that you read aloud some first person narratives. She also has students select only one episode in a chapter, as opposed to all of the events in a chapter. She provides students with the option of choosing characters other than the main character. And she encourages students to provide their reactions in their own word as readers, using parentheses, to their engagement with the character's voice. Students may also react to each other in a peer-dialogue journal using their characters' voices. In reacting to students' journals, she initially encourages them to maintain their level of involvement with a character. As students' become more comfortable adopting the character's voice, she respond to the students as if that students wee the character.

Within an entry, students can also alternate between a range of different roles or "voices" for writing their journals—

themselves as "student," "teacher," "employee," "partner," "narrator," "character," etc. In responding to the story, "A & P," by John Updike, Donna adopts a range of different roles in responding to her partner, Terry.

> Let's see, the teacher wants us to share our responses— "try to make explicit your thoughts" [TEACHER]—Terry, I don't know if I can make explicit ALL of my thoughts. You said that you felt uneasy about doing that, especially when someone else's reading [PARTNER]. Hey, as my mother said, you can always talk to me [MOTHER]. Not that I always did. About the checkout boy in "A & P," he thinks that he's hot stuff. He imagines somehow that if he quits in front of them—he says, "hoping they'll stop and watch me" [NARRATOR] that they will be impressed. Typical male attitude— "I'm the hero and you're the damsel in distress" [MALE]— what a bunch of garbage.

In this entry, Donna is adopting the roles of a teacher, partner, mother, story narrator and a critic. She is drawing on knowledge of the "outer dialogue" as described in Chapter Two—the larger conversations occurring in society regarding gender roles to extend her own "inner dialogue."

Students may extend these experience to create their own fictional dialogue, creating "mini-exchanges" between two characters—someone asking someone to dance, two strangers at a bus stop, an employer interviewing a candidate, etc., material that could be developed in a short story or play.

Prompts for Engagement Responses

Some student benefit from prompts that trigger off different types of engagement responses. The following are some prompts devised by Mary Kooy (1992) of the University of British Columbia:

I was impressed or struck by . . . .
I noticed that . . . .
I wonder about . . . .
I predict . . . .
Some questions I have . . . .
I don't understand . . . .
I now understand why/how/what . . . .
Something I noticed/ appreciate/ don't
     appreciate/wonder about is . . . .
An interesting word/ sentence/ thought is . . . .
This part of the story makes me feel _____.

Recalling/recounting. Another important strategy is recalling or recounting what happened in a text. Students may also use their journal as a reading log to record their descriptions of and inferences about characters' names, actions, traits, beliefs and goals, as well as key events in the text. The very act of writing down these perceptions helps students keep things straight, particularly with longer novels. In keeping their logs, students are also learning to attend to certain aspects of the text—titles, beginning or closing lines, names of characters, events central to the storyline or, in essays, key points. When they encounter episodes they do not understand or character refer back to events or characters they've forgotten, they can refer back to their logs.

Students can also use their logs to predict story outcomes as they are reading. In making predictions, they are constructing emerging "text models" that define the story development (Collins, Brown, & Larkin, 1980). When readers discover that their predictions are not valid—that their expectations conflict with what actually happens, they revise their predictions, creating an alternate model of the text. In order to make predictions, students review what they have already inferred about a text and match that up with their knowledge of prototypical story development. Knowing that a story is a comedy, they can predict that it will probably be resolved with a "happy ending." It is important that students should feel free to create any predictions.

Inferring/explaining. In inferring/explaining, students use character's actions to infer their attributes, knowledge, beliefs, plans and goals, inferences that serve to explain a character's actions. In keeping their logs, students could list their perceptions of characters' actions or of key events on the left side of the page and then their inferences about the meaning or significance of these actions or events on the right side. As illustrated below, giving students categories as prompts helps them visually define connections between perceptions and meanings:

characters' actions/key events   **meaning/significance**

Students can also use charts or maps to visually portray their perceptions of characters' acts, traits, beliefs and goals, as well as the relationships between characters. As illustrated below, an eighth grade student used herself to portray the relationships between two stories about revenge, Richard Peck's "Priscilla and the Wimps" and F. Scott Fitzgerald's "Bernice Bobs Her Hair." Based on freewrites about both stories, for each story, the student created a spider map with

Figure 5.1
Mapping to Compare Stories

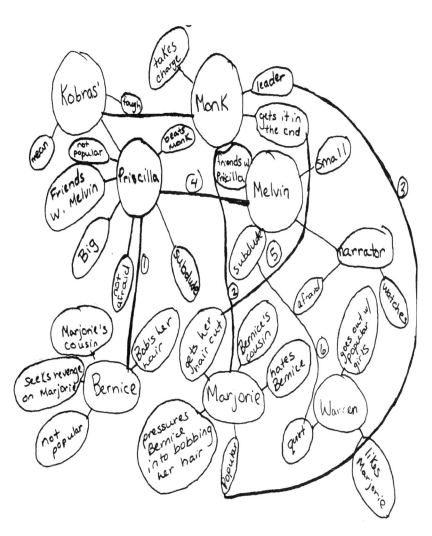

the characters in the central circles. She then drew spokes out from the central circles to smaller circles for inferences about traits, beliefs, and goals. Then, she connected these perceptions by lines to indicate similarities between the two stories.

Students can also use their logs to list questions about or aspects of characters' actions they do not understand. Richard VanDeWeghe (1987) cites the example of how a student initially perplexed by a poem is able to use her entry to generate some hypotheses and reach some understanding of the poem:

> I don't really like this poem. I can't figure out what it is saying. The last two lies, about the girl's red hair lighting the wall really throws me. I just can't figure out what it means. This poem seems to reveal human experience by comparing one's life to the life of a town. Phillipsburg was once a lively and happy town. Now it has died. It is depressing. I think maybe Hugo is trying to say that people go through the same cycle. They live happy lies but in the end they must get old, break down, and die. The speaker of this poem is, I would guess, a man who is realizing that he's getting older. He looks back on the way life used to be and becomes depressed because his life is no longer like this. The setting of this poem is a dying town, Phillipsburg. It is written in the second person point of view. I believe that the purpose of this poem is that the speaker is feeling that he is dying with the town. Maybe the last part of the poem is saying that one doesn't have to die with his surroundings. The girl is young and vibrant, indicating perhaps that life goes on (p. 45).

Defining what it is that she does not understand; "the girl's red hair lighting the wall really throws me," sets up a schema for reviewing the text in order to entertain possible answers. Having worked through the relationship between the dying town and the speaker, she then achieves an understanding of the girl as "young and vibrant," indicating perhaps that life goes on.

To help students engaged in problem-finding/solving, you could give them categories such as these:

things I don't understand	information that may help me understand	possible "answers"

Connecting. Another process of engagement is that of connecting past autobiographical experiences or previous reading to a current text. In related autobiographical experiences, the more students elaborate on those experiences, the more they can use those experience to interpret stories (Beach, 1990a). In elaborating on the details of actions or events in their experiences, they began to explore their own attitudes about those experiences, often in terms of the character's perspective. They then used their recalled attitudes to reflect on the text. For example, in responding to the grocery store manager who fires Sammy in Updike's "A & P," a high school student recalled in her journal:

> I have worked under a manager who would play favorites with his female employees. I was miserable when he played favorites between us. I thought of quitting but instead I talked to

him about the way we felt about his favoritism game. Although from that day I was never his "favorite" again, he never expected me to brown nose because he knew how I felt and why I felt that way (Beach, 1990a, p. 224).

She then reflects on this experience: "I'm glad I was honest. I maintained both a job and the respect I deserved by thinking before acting" (224). This leads her to distinguish between her own and Sammy's perspective: "To quit was irrational and immature. I realize what he stands for as a character. Sammy is something that I am not—the heroic, romantic worker. He puts himself into his job and stands for what he believes" (224). Thus, by elaborating and reflecting on her own experience, she then gains further insight into the story.

> Similarly, Terry recalls an experience of working in a grocery store:

> "Just like Sammy, I was working at the check out counter at one of these all-night 7-11 type stores. One night I was working pretty late, when in comes this guy who looked like he'd had one too many drinks. I was the only one in the store, so I was really nervous. Well, this guy starts weaving down some of the isles. Then, all of a sudden, he knocks over this pile of peaches. And the peaches start rolling all over the place. And then he steps on one, which made a mess, so he gets really angry and starts yelling. But then I started to feel angry, so I yell at him that he'd better leave the store, so he starts towards me, and I pick up the phone and start to dial 911. I guess that he saw me pick up the phone so he heads for the door. It's like I had some control over the situation, some kind of power that Sammy didn't have.

As illustrated below, having reflected on the meaning of that event, they then compare and contrast their own experience with their perceptions of current text.

Collecting related texts. As previously noted, students may also use their journals as working folders or scrapbooks to collect other texts related to the current text: newspaper clippings, magazine articles/ads, letters to the editor, photos, previous writings, quotes, etc. In this way, they are defining their own intertextual connections between and among a number of different texts. In responding to the novel, *The Chocolate War* by Robert Cormier, Caryn became intrigued with the topic of school administration, particularly the differences between effective versus less effective school principals. In reading newspapers and magazines, she clipped out and/or xeroxed various articles about this topic and stapled them into her

Figure 5-2
Phases of Connecting Responses

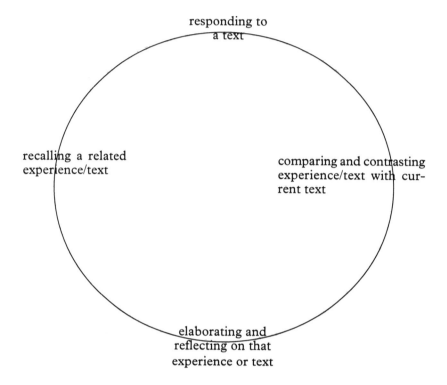

responding to
a text

recalling a related
experience/text

comparing and contrasting
experience/text with cur-
rent text

elaborating and
reflecting on that
experience or text

journal. She then circled and highlights key points, drew lines between related points, and added her own reactions to the articles. By including these other related texts in her journal, she used the journal to connect her responses to the novel to other texts, intertextual links that served to further illuminate the novel. Similarly, Bryan, an eleventh grader, was writing an autobiographical narrative about his experiences during his eighth-grade year. As part of his research for writing his narrative, he collected materials associated with his eighth-grade year: essays, letters, selections from his yearbook, photos of himself as eighth grader and clippings from magazines and newspapers published during that year. Adjacent to each clipping, he wrote what each item suggests about his attitudes and point of view as an eighth grader. He then used his reflections to describe differences between his past and present point of view and how his past point of view reflects his past beliefs and attitudes.

The fact that students are using their journal as a scrapbook/working file may encourage them to read for and collect materials relevant to their own needs. Thus, when they spot a newspaper or magazine article that relates to their interests, they not only read that article in terms of their topic, but they also store that article for future use.

Constructing cultural worlds. In responding to a text, students need to do more than simply identify the physical location of the setting. They may also describe the texts as consisting of distinct cultural worlds. They need to define the different norms or conventions operating within a certain cultural world. In responding to a text, students draw on their knowledge of differences between cultural beliefs and attitudes. However, students unfamiliar with these cultural differences need to rely on characters' actions or events in the text that represent certain cultural conventions. By noting the consequences of actions—how character actions are perceived to be appropriate or inappropriate—they construct a set of norms constituting cultural attitudes. Thus, students construct cultural worlds by attending to those character behaviors that mark or signal cultural beliefs and attitudes.

Constructing cultural worlds is difficult for most students. As fish in water, they have difficulty stepping outside their own culture to recognize cultural differences. In some cases, they impose their own cultural attitudes or stereotypes onto texts (Jordan & Purves, 1993), judging characters of color according to white, middle-class norms. Given this difficulty, it is helpful to relate writing about cultural worlds in text to writing about cultural worlds in their own experience (see activities below for writing about cultural worlds).

Interpreting. In interpreting a text, students are inferring the larger symbolic meaning of events or character's actions. This often involves relating the text to larger issues associated with need for power, freedom, identity, love, etc. Students often draw on the other response types to interpret texts. For students who have difficulty interpreting, you may ask them to review their other writings, reflecting on possible interpretive meanings.

Judging. Students may judge characters' actions or the quality of the text. In making judgments, students need to cite reasons for their judgments. In judging a character as "a failure," a student may review a novel and list instances that verify that judgment.

Prompts for Different Response Strategies

Engagement
- what are your feelings about or reactions to the text or experience?
- what were your experiences in entering into the world of the text or experience?
- which characters or people did you identify or empathize with and why?

Recalling/recounting
- what happens in the story or experience?
- what are the characters' or persons' traits, beliefs, goals, plans and knowledge of each other?
- what is the setting or world of the text or experience in terms of social, psychological or cultural forces?
- what are your predictions of story outcomes or consequences of the experience?

Inferring/explaining
- what are some reasons for the characters' or persons' actions in terms of their traits, beliefs, goals, plans and knowledge?

Connecting
- what are some autobiographical experiences or other texts the current text or experience reminds you of?
- how are these experiences or other texts related to the current text or experience?

Constructing cultural worlds
- what are the different cultural worlds operating in the text, worlds defined by peer group, school, community, family, class, region, race, nationality?
- what are the norms constituting these different worlds?
- what is the main character's relationship to these different norms?

Interpretation
- what meanings do the characters' or persons' actions represent?
- what ideas or beliefs are being addressed in the text or experience?
- what have you learned from responding to the text or experience?

Judgment
- how would you judge or assess the characters or persons?
- how would you judge the quality of the text?

Encouraging a range of response strategies. In her year-long analysis of eight of her eighth grade students' dialogue journal writing, M. Cyrene Wells (1992) found that certain students adopted certain preferred ways of responding to texts:

> Anne . . . uses journal letters for evaluation of text/author, metacognitive analysis, as a vehicle for explaining how she connects with characters. She never retells stories, and she abstracts plots only when necessary. Ricky, on the other hand, connects to situations rather than characters. He likes to ask questions in his letters and often retells or abstracts plot. Mark focuses on plausibility. Evaluation of text and author are also important to him. . . Ruth uses letters to teachers for self-assessments and often abstracts plots for her friends (299-300).

These students have adopted certain preferred, habitual ways of responding that may inhibit exploration of different ways of responding. Given these preferred responses, you could ask students to review their entries and describe their consistent use of certain response strategies, noting those strategies in the margins of their journals. Students could then explore alternative ways of responding. A student who notes that he consistently responds with description/retelling responses may explore the use of connection responses.

Combining strategies: Formulating guided assignments for journals. In giving journal assignments, you may also consider ways of combining strategies. In writing about a text, students may first recount the storyline, followed by a connecting that story to another related story, followed by an interpretation of the original text. Or a student may first explain a character's action, followed by defining the cultural norms shaping that character's action, followed by judging the character's actions.

In formulating a guided assignment, you consider the sequence of strategies you want students to employ, each strategy leading to the next (Beach & Marshall, 1991). You then develop prompts, questions or activities (listing, mapping, freewriting, role-play, etc) designed to elicit the use of that strategy. In doing so, you are constantly thinking about the need for "first things first"—that certain strategies serve as prerequisites for other strategies.

A sample guided assignment: Writing about conflicts in *Yellow Raft in Blue Water*. As part of a Themes in Literature course at South High School in Minneapolis, Minnesota, Ms. Lilja gave her students a guided assignment for writing responses to the novel, *Yellow Raft in Blue Water*, by

Michael Dorris, a Native American writer (Beach, in press). This novel depicts the experiences of a family of three Native American woman, Rayona, a 15-year-old; Christine, her mother, and Ida, Christine's mother. Each of the three sections of the novel is told through the eyes of these three main characters. The novel revolves around conflicts between these women, particularly Christine and Ida, who hate each other.

In order to help students examine these conflicts, Ms. Lilja asked students to write an essay about the conflicts in the novel. In setting up the assignment, she asked students to complete a series of journal assignments designed to help students focus on family, gender and cultural conflicts.

Illustrated below is how one twelfth-grade student, Chris Ayers, used the journal assignments to develop her own ideas for an essay about cultural conflict in the novel. We will cite the assignments and excerpts from her journal writing.

In Chapter One, what do we find out about Rayona and Christine? What are your inferences about these characters?

> Rayona is part Native American, part African American. She's Christine's daughter. Chirstine is Native American. Rayona and Christine do not have the best of relationships. Elgin, Ray's dad, is not connected with the family much anymore although his reasons for leaving aren't told yet. I can infer that Christine is an alcoholic by the fact that she likes to party a lot; too much. She's spent a lot of time in the hospital. They are poor, another inference by their junky, run-down car and their few belongings when they decide to move.
>
> Christine is a very troubled woman with many problems as shown by her crazy actions: driving to Tacoma, kicking Ray out of the car, talking about suicide, etc.

Relate your own experiences to those of the character.

Chris related her own experiences of zoning-out to Rayona:

> I liked the part where Rayona rides the bucking bronco at the rodeo, although I'm not sure why. I guess maybe because it showed us a little bit of Rayona that hadn't been revealed before; a stubborness, a determination. She wanted to keep getting back up on that horse, why exactly I don't know.
>
> Sometimes you become so determined that you lose some of your consciousness and go into a zone, sometimes a stubborn zone. You let your subconcious take over and control your actions. Rayona was prob-

ably not aware of the crowd or the noise. All she saw, heard, smelled, tasted, and felt was that horse.

Trace one of the themes we've discussed through Chapters One–Four

> I think there is a lot of cultural conflict in this book (as well as family and gender conflict). Much of it stems from the fact that Christine and Elgin have (or had) an interracial marriage. Rayona is part Black and part Native American. Rayona also encounters a lot of antagonism towards her because of her "dual heritage" as Father Tom called it. I found this interesting because most often the "racial events" that we hear about are between Caucasians and another race. Little do you hear about blacks vs. Native American. At least I haven't. So it's interesting to see this type of conflict. Anyone can be racist.

Trace your conflict though the final chapters.

> My theme is cultural conflict. There is the Catholic influence still, Father Hurlburt is one of the main characters. We get a report of the Catholic influence in the last section—the letter, the nuns, the end of the world.
>
> At the very end of the book, there is a prime example of cultural differences. When Father Hurlburt and Ida are sitting on the roof on New Year's Eve, Ida begins to braid her hair, something foreign to Hurlburt. Or course, being a man with short hair he might not be familiar, but I think Dorris intended it to be more foreign than just gender! Dorris describes Ida's braiding as having rhythm, whispters of history, tradition, something that is age-old. I got the impression that it was more implicitly supporting cultural differences.

Chris used this entry to focus in on a metaphor for the cultural differences between the Father and Ida—the braid. She then developed the metaphor in her essay, "The Strands of Culture." As she noted in the introduction of the essay:

> The braid theme serves two purpose. First, it acts as a vivid metaphor for the entire book. The story focuses on the lives and relationships of three women: Ida, Christine (Ida's "daughter"), and Rayona (Christine's daughter). Each of these women represent a strand of hair being twisted and woven in the braid of life. Their paths are interwoven in history and heritage.

> This leads me to a second purpose of the braid theme. Their paths have been tied and swirled around one another, but each strand, each woman, is deeply rooted in their Native American heritage. Dorris used this braid metaphor to help express cultural conflict. [She then cites her example of Father Hurlburt not understanding the meaning of Ida's braiding her hair.]

Chris used her final entry to focus on a key theme of the novel inherent in the braid metaphor, and drew on her nine other entries to write her paper.

Using Journals for Fiction Writing

Students can also use their journals for fiction writing in which they create alternative, imaginary roles or worlds through their writing. In the process, they are experimenting with alternative versions of reality. Imaginary journals are appealing to adolescents, particularly those who enjoy reading fantasy/adventure/romance literature or playing fantasy games such as *Dungeons and Dragons*. Through creating roles or worlds that alter, reverse, ridicule, parody, attack or transform conventional versions of reality, they are testing the limits of their imagination.

The following are a few of many activities for imaginary writing.

Recording dreams or daydreams. Ninth grader Susie, whom the teacher described as a "nonwriter," wrote in a dialogue-journal to a peer:

> I had this really weird dream on Sunday night. It was really strange because in my dream, I was running and I really hate running. Anyway, while I was running around the track, I kept asking people, "how many time do I have to go around?" Nobody answered me and about the 6th time around, I finally got a response. Somebody said, "You can stop anytime you wish." It was the softest, smoothest voice that I've heard. I'm not sure what it means or if it meaning anything. I keep thinking of it though.

An eighth grade student, David, recorded his daydream:

> You are in the middle of a boring lecture in English. All of a sudden you picture yourself in a Ferrari or on a dirtbike doing 120 MPH with your hair flying around & your leather jacket puffed up like it inflates. Your beautiful girlfried

wants you to stop, but instead you punch it as fast as
it goes. Then you wake up. Everyone in the classroom is
looking straight at you. You're as beat as a red apple
and you don't even know what the question was."

Story Ideas. Students can also devise ideas or abstracts for
narratives—romance, adventure, science fiction, comedy,
detective and horror stories. For students who have difficulty generating their own ideas, you can give them story
starters—descriptions of typical situations or movie abstracts from a television schedule. Students can also generate ideas for a movie or television program and then
generate abstracts for that movie or one episode of a television program.

Alternative endings, storylines, or character letters/diaries. In response to literary texts, students can construct alternative
endings, storylines or character letters/diaries, imagining what
the characters might do in a sequel to a story or novel. Or
they can alter an event in a story or novel, describe the possible "what if" consequences, orcompose letters or diary entries characters might write.

Utopias. Students can construct their own utopian communities or worlds based on certain ecological, political, economic or educational theories, or they can create an ideal
government or formulate plans for a total overhaul of waste
management and energy production processes in their own
community.

Song lyrics. Students could write song lyrics that draw on their
story ideas or utopian visions, illustrating their lyrics with
images that could be used in a music video.

New products. Students could imagine new products along
with descriptions of how they would work and possible ad-
vertisements for the products. They could then construct
scripts or storyboards for an television commercial for their
product.

Fantasy sports. Students who are familiar with "fantasy baseball, football or basketball" may create their own "dream
team" of actual or fictional players (it's important that female
students and/or female sports stars be included). Students
could also describe games in which their "dream team" com-
pete. They could also illustrate their stories with pictures of
themselves hovering high over a basketball rim about to make
a "slam dunk."

Tabloid newspaper articles. Students could write tabloid newspaper articles in which they mimic or parody reports of bi-

zarre, unconventional, freakish events. They can then combine their articles and using desktop publishing, produce a class newspaper for distribution to the school.

Excuses or alibis for not doing something. Students could make up possible excuses for not doing something, such as not turning a paper in on time ("my word processing keys were frozen") or being late to class ("I forgot my locker combination.")

Writing about Cultural Worlds or Institutions

Drawing on recent interest in ethnographical writing, English teachers have increasingly incorporated writing about cultural worlds or institutions into the writing curriculum. In such writing, students observe life in and interview people involved with a cultural world or institution—a school, club, workplace, neighborhood, sports team or religious organization. Rather than the traditional "research report" which often consists of a rehash of encyclopedia articles, students construct their own knowledge about the cultural norms and conventions operating in this world or institution.

In the context of conducting observational and/or ethnographical research, students may keep field-note journals to record their observations of and reflections on whatever phenomenon they are studying. In taking field notes, students record what they are seeing or hearing. In observing student behaviors at a football game, Janet records not only specific aspects of students' behavior. She notes that while the opposing team had a group of cheerleaders, her own school did not. She records the fact that students from her own school frequently ridiculed or mimicked the opposing school's cheerleaders, particularly in terms of the fact that they were females. She also interviews various students from both schools about their attitudes towards cheerleaders. Based on her observations and interviews, she infers that students in the two schools have different attitudes towards cheerleaders, reflecting possible differences in attitudes towards the role and status of females. In the process, rather than simply regurgitating information from texts, she is constructing her own knowledge.

The success of using field notes depends on students understanding and ability to conduct ethnographical research. According to Louis Casagrande (1991), of the Boston Children's Museum, effective ethnographical researchers employ:

- "rich," sensory descriptions of a cultural scene or institution.
- a clearly defined, believable point of entry into the scene or institution

- distinctions between the often stereotyped expectations of the "outsider" as contrasted with those perspectives of "insiders"
- "cultural brokers" who provide an entree into a culture
- evidence to document the rituals and routines evidence in persons' behaviors
- a recognition of how their own identity and attitudes shapes their perceptions of meanings
- a sense of how beliefs of the whole culture shape behaviors in that culture
- interrogation of how members are recruited and what forces of change are operating in the culture
- an analysis of how the particular culture compares to other cultures

Working in groups, students could conduct studies of a range of different social or cultural events or sites: sports events, religious ceremonies, fairs, club meetings, amusement parks, shopping malls, schools, festivities, family gatherings, etc. In selecting topics for their research, students need to choose groups, institutions or events that are accessible, somewhat familiar, of interest to students, and which do not pose risks or dangers. It is also important that they find what Casarande defines as a "cultural broker," a person who helps them gain access to a particular culture.

In her work with eleventh graders, Linda Callendar of Blaine Senior High School, Blaine, Minnesota, found that students had more success with certain topics than other topics. Topics that worked well include studies of a day care center, skydiving club, Chinese school, group who played fantasy computer games, comedy club, family history by an adopted student from Indonesia, group of "theater tech" students and dinner time rituals for families from different cultures. For many of these topics, students knew their "cultural broker." In studying the comedy club, they worked with a teacher who performed in the club. The teacher arranged to have the students observe not only the performers but also to gain access to behind-the-scenes aspects of the club. Some topics that worked less well included a study of Indian tribal dances (students remained as total cultural outsiders that they could never gain an insider's perspective), elementary schools (students had little strong investment in the topic), and drag racers (students had difficulty working together due to tensions between the students/"cultural broker" and the other members of the group). In working with students, Callendar continually poses "reality check" questions to help the students to focus their topic and organize their strategies according to a schedule in order to avoid being overwhelmed by the project.

To understand the nature of ethnography, students can read selections from ethnographical writing: Penelope Eckert, *Jocks and Burnouts* (1989); Shirley Brice Heath, *Ways With Words* (1983); John Fiske, *Reading the Popular* (1989); Oscar Lewis, *Children of Sanchez* (1989); Margaret Mead, *Growing up in New Guinea* (1930); Alan Peshkin, *The Color of Strangers, the Color of Friends, The Play of Ethnicity in School and Community* (1991); Paul Willis, *Learning to Labor* (1977). Students could also view "cinema verite" documentaries that are studies of particular events, institutions or places. The documentaries of Frederick Wiseman portray various institutions— Aspen, Colorado; a Neiman-Marcus Department Store in Dallas, Panama City, a welfare agency, a city hospital, a high school—without any voice-over and long stretches of unedited footage. Or, Robert Flaherty's classic documentary, *Nanook of the North*, portrays the life of an Eskimo family on the eastern shores of Hudson Bay. And *Running Fence* by the Maysele Brothers portrays the reaction of members of a small town to an artist, Christo's, project to construct a twenty-four mile fence of white fabric. Students could discuss how these filmmakers selected certain material to portray the particular cultural world of an institution or place. Students could also watch the video from the PBS Writers Writing Series, *Before the First Word*, which portrays two high school students and *New York Times* writer Anna Quindlen taking notes and interviewing people in preparation from writing about Sullivan street in New York City's Little Italy. The video demonstrate ways of observing and interviewing people who live in a relatively distinct cultural world.

Keeping field notes. In keeping field notes, students are responding in both a descriptive and judgmental mode to the phenomenon they are observing. In describing a phenomenon, instead of vague, evaluative comments such as "friendly," "outgoing," "nice," "wonderful," "pleasant," or abstract summaries, students need to use concrete descriptions of behaviors. Corrine Glesne and Alan Peshkin (1992) cite the example of observing a classroom:

> After observing a class, you might be tempted to write, "The class was disorderly and noisy." This statement does not present a clear picture of the classroom, and it is judgmental because it relies on the researcher's conceptions of "disorder" and "noise." The following statements are more concrete in their descriptiveness:
>
> > The fifth grade class contained fifteen girls and twelve boys. When I entered, they were clustered loosely into six groups. One group of

> four girls was trying to see who could blow
> the biggest bubble with their gum. A group of
> five boys was imitating a Kung Fu movie they
> had seen on tv the evening before . . . .(47).

> Your eyes, ears and hands join forces to capture the de-
> tails of a setting in your field notes, particularly early in
> your fieldwork, when you are trying to capture an over-
> all picture of the setting and its people (48).

As they record notes, students record in the margins the
time of day and and the beginning and end of certain activities—the fact that people move from one activity to the next.
At a club meeting, members may move from their business
meeting to a social gathering. They may also note certain specific events within the larger activities; within the business
meeting, the group may, in a series of events, deal with a
number of different issues.

Students could also interview participants, recording
verbatim or with a tape recorder their perceptions of their
own and others' behavior as well as the conventions constituting a certain institution or culture.

In observing and interviewing, students could focus on
a number of aspects:

- *Setting.* Students can describe sensory aspects of the setting or context—the smell or the drawings on hallways
  in a school. It is useful to compare or contrast different
  parts of a setting. In observing a school, a student may
  compare their observations of different classrooms—the
  fact that students are actively engaged in activities in one
  classroom, while sitting passively listening in another.

- *People.* Students could describe the particulars of persons' behaviors, dress, hair style, gestures and manner-
  isms as well as identifying them according to their gender,
  class and race. In describing a group of people at a small
  neighborhood church, a student may note that most of
  them are women over the age of fifty and they vary con-
  siderably in their dress (suggesting a range of class backgrounds) and are continually gesturing to each other
  (suggesting that they all know each other).

- *Talk/conversation.* Students can record verbatim the conversations they overhear, noting certain words or phrases
  that are repeated. In observing young boys in Little
  League baseball, Gary Fine (1987) noted that the boys
  kept repeating certain obscene words. Fine noted that
  they often used these words to put down each other in a
  competitive, derogatory manner. Observing sales clerks

in their department store job, students may note that the clerks keep repeating the same flattering terms to describe their customers: "You look just wonderful in that coat."

- *Documents, photos, writings.* In addition to observing behaviors, students can collect documents, photos or writings from the people they are observing. In writing a family history, students could collect old letters, diaries, photos, legal documents, etc. representing the lives of previous generations of family members. And they can draw sketches of settings or take photos of the settings and people they are observing.

Reviewing and reflecting on notes. Students then review their notes, preferably on the same day while their perceptions are still fresh and add their own comments and reflections. In reflecting on their notes, they look for recurring patterns or frequencies of behavior, treating their perceptions as a jigsaw puzzle. They may also pose questions about their notes, questions that encourage them to think about different aspects of their notes. Based on her notes from her observation of males and females at a high school dance, Marlene noted that males were more likely to congregate in all male-groups than the females. She also noted that, contrary to her expectations, females were more likely to initiate dance requests than males, and that most students danced with a range of different partners.

Students may also organize their perceptions around certain categories. In *Jocks and Burnouts* (1989), Penelope Eckert observed the behaviors of students in a suburban Detroit high school. She observed the students' behaviors, dress and where they congregated in high school. Based on her notes and interviews, she defined two predominate categories shaping students' perceptions of school—"jocks"—students who were middle-class, pro-school, involved in athletics and extra-curricular activities, and "burnouts"—students who were representative of blue-collar backgrounds and less involved in school and more involved in work and neighborhood activities. The "jocks" learned to use the social networks in the school to gain the information necessary for success in the school. The "jocks" associated school with certain forms of "preppy" dress, "pro-social" behaviors and athletics. In contrast, the "burnouts," who were more accustomed to functioning in small, coherent neighborhood or workplace groups, had more difficulty coping with the large, bureaucratic structure of the school. The "burnouts" associated dress, behaviors and allegiance to neighborhood groups and workplace as cultural rejection of the "jocks'" world. Because of their symbolic display of what was perceived to be "deviant" attitudes, "burnouts" were often excluded from academic courses and social networks in the school's organizations. Thus, each group defined themselves in opposition to the other. As Eckert notes, "clothing, territory, substance use, language, demeanor, academic behavior and activities all ultimately serve as conscious markers of category affiliation . . . hat strengthens the hegemony of the category system in adolescent life and increasingly restricts individual perceptions and choice" (69).

At the same time, it is important not to let students' preconceived categories or stereotypes shape their perceptions; they also need to learn from that phenomenon. Rather than impose their own predispositions and assumptions, they need to be open to changing their attitudes and beliefs about a phenomenon. Ethnographies often describe their work as making the strange familiar and the familiar strange (Erickson, 1973). In order that they can make the familiar strange, they need to be able to question their own assumptions and expectations. By recording all they perceive, they may discover phenomena that challenge their expectations. By sharing their perceptions with a peer, they can compare and test out the validity of their inferences, a process ethnographers define as "triangulate."

Using Journals in Writing Across the Curriculum

In the school curriculum, students learn that different disciplines are constituted by different norms and practices. They go from class to class with little sense of how one subject relates to the other. Unless a teacher employs an interdisciplinary approach with a subject, they study each subject isolated from the other.

As an English teacher seeking to help students learn to write across the curriculum, you can ask students to use their journals to write about specific tasks or problems they encounter in other courses. You can help students use their journal as a learning tool for other classes by talking about the different ways of thinking or knowing unique subject matter areas. Obtaining assignments by other teachers, you can talk about knowing the ground rules in that subject for completing specific assignments. You can show students how to use their journal writing to learn specific ways of thinking or knowing the subject-matter. A useful reference source for both theoretical and classroom-based material on writing across the curriculum is Chris M. Anson, John E. Schwiebert and Michael M. Williamson's *Writing Across the Curriculum: An Annotated Bibliography* (1993). This work contains over 1,000 entries on all aspects of WAC. See additional readings cited below for each subject matter area.

You can also provide teachers in other subject areas with suggestions on how to use the journal to foster learning in their classes. But avoid telling them how to teach. Instead, share with them journal writing techniques that will improve the quality of learning in their classes.

Social Studies. In helping students in Social Studies classes, you may want to model some of the thinking processes specific to explaining or analyzing historical, economic or political events. Rosemarie is writing a paper for her American History class on the topic of the 1928 Stock Market Crash; she read some articles about the crash, but is having difficulty knowing how to organize her information. She could use her journal to list the different possible causes of the crash, followed by an evaluation of the validity of each cause. In this way, Rosemary was learning a basic thinking process associated with doing history—determining and assessing possible causes of events.

Allen, H. and Fauth, L. (1987). "Academic journals and the sociological imagination." *The Journal Book.* Ed. Toby Fulwiler. Portsmouth, NH: Boynton/Cook, . 367–74.

Brodsky, D. and Meagher, E. (1987) "Journals and political science." *The Journal Book.* Ed. Toby Fulwiler. Portsmouth, NH: Boynton/Cook. 375–86.

Hoffman, L. (1986). "Students readers and the civil war letters of an Ohio woman." *Reader 15* : 34–47.

Levitsky, R. (1991). "Journal writing in the social studies." *Social Studies Review 31.* 50–54.

Mulholland, B. M. (1987) "It's not just the writing." *The Journal Book.* Ed. Toby Fulwiler. Portsmouth, NH: Boynton/Cook. 227–38.

Segal, E. (1990). "The journal: teaching reflexive methodology on an introductory level." *Anthropology & Education Quarterly 21.* 121–27.

Steffens, H. (1987) "Journals in the teaching of history." *The Journal Book.* Ed. Toby Fulwiler. Portsmouth, NH: Boynton/Cook. 219–26.

Steffens, H. (1991). "Using informal writing in large history classes. helping students to find interest and meaning in history." *Social Studies 82.* 107–09.

Mathematics. In math classes, students could use a journal to record their thought processes involved in solving math problems. By recording the various steps, students provide teachers with a record of their problem-solving strategies. Teachers can then determine instances of faulty reasoning, commenting to students reasons for their difficulties in solving problems.

Atherton, C., Joyner, S., Pender, N., Ryerson, F., and Young, S. (1992) "Keeping math journals." *Instructor, 101.* 46–52.

Bemiller, S., (1987) "The mathematics workbook." The Journal Book, ed. Toby Fulwiler. Portsmouth, NH: Heinemann. 359–66.

Borasi, R., and Rose, B.J. (1988) "Journal writing and mathematics instruction." *Educational Studies in Mathematics.*

Connolly, P. and Vliardi, T. (1989), *Writing to Learn Mathematics and Science.* Teachers College P.

Gordon, C., and Macinnis, D. (1993) "Using journals as a window on students' thinking in mathematics." *Language Arts, 70.* 37–43.

McIntosh, M., (1991) "No Time for Writing in Your Class." *Mathematics Teacher, 84.* 423–33.

Miller, D., (1991) "Writing to learn mathematics." *Mathematics Teacher, 84.* 516–21.

Nahrgang, C., and Peterson, B., (1986). "Using writing to learn mathematics." *Mathematics Teacher, 79.* 451–65.

Sterrett, A., (1990). ed. *Using Writing to Teach Mathematics.* Washington, D.C.: MAA.

Stiy, A. (1994). "Pic-jour math: pictorial journal writing in mathematics." *Arithmetic Teacher, 41.* 264–60.

Venne, G. (1989). "High school students write about math." *English Journal, 78.* 64–67.

Vukovich, D., (1985). "Ideas in practice: integrating math and writing through the math journal." *Journal of Developmental Education, 9* : 19–20.

Science. Students in science class need to be able to accurately and concisely describe observed phenomena and engage in problem-solving strategies. Students could use their journals to record observations of natural phenomena. They could describe the various problem-solving processes they went through to write their formal lab reports. An ethnographic analysis of journal writing in a geology class found that students were able to use their journals to reflect on their geological research (Johnstone, 1993).

Jensen, V., (1987). "Writing in college physics." *The Journal Book.* Ed. Toby Fulwiler. Portsmouth, NH: Boynton/Cook, . 330–36.

Johnstone, A.(1993). *Uses for Journal-Keeping: An Ethnography of Writing in a University Science Class.* Norwood, NJ: Ablex.

Grumbacher, J. (1987). "How writing helps physics students become better problem solvers." *The Journal Book*. Ed. Toby Fulwiler. Portsmouth, NH: Boynton/Cook, . 323–39.

Meese, G. (1987). "Focused learning in chemistry research: Suzanne's journal." *The Journal Book*. Ed. Toby Fulwiler. Portsmouth, NH: Boynton/Cook, 337–47.

Zentz, G. (1992). "A personal and permanent journey through the universe." *Astronomy, 20*. 80–84. (astronomical logs)

Art/Music. In the art/music class, students could use their journals, as in the literature class, to express their responses to art or music texts to assist them in the process of composing art or music. They could use their journals to sketch out drawings or describe their ideas for songs.

Ameigh, T. (1992). "Learn the language of music through journals." *Music Educators Journal, 79*. 30–32.

Ambrose, J. (1987). "Music journals." *The Journal Book*. Ed. Toby Fulwiler. Portsmouth, NH: Boynton/Cook, . 261–68.

DeLorenzo, L C. (1990). "Early field experiences in the community." *Music-Educators-Journal, 77*. 51–53.

Duke, C. R. (1987). "Integrating reading, writing, and thinking skills into the music class." *Journal of Reading, 31*. 152–57

Larsen, C. M., and Merrion, M. (1987). "Documenting the aesthetic experience: The music journal." *The Journal Book*. Ed. Toby Fulwiler. Portsmouth, NH: Boynton/Cook. 254–60.

Prisco, K. (1990) "The aesthetic journal: A creative tool in art education." *School Arts, 90*. 24–26.

Thaiss, C. (1987). "A journal in the arts." *The Journal Book*. Ed. Toby Fulwiler. Portsmouth, NH: Boynton/Cook. 246–53.

Second Language. In the second language classroom, students need to practice using a second language. They can use dialogue journals with peers and/or the teacher to practice conversation using the second language.

Reyes, M. L. (1991). "A process approach to literacy using dialogue journals and literature logs with second language learners." *Research in the Teaching of English, 25*. 291–313.

Sandler, K. (1987). "Letting them write when they can't even talk? Writing as discovery in the foreign language classroom." *The Journal Book*. Ed. Toby Fulwiler. Portsmouth, NH: Boynton/Cook, . 312–20.

Chapter Six

Studying Published Journals and Diaries

Teachers often find that their students are immersed in their own thoughts, relationships and activities, living out their experiences with great emotional energy. Although tapping into this energy can yield exciting class sessions, teachers also find that students have difficulty engaging in the more contemplative side of academic life—standing back and reflecting on their own perceptions. In journal writing, this inexperience with self-analysis often shows up as a lack of reflection, of going beyond merely rehashing information in order to formulate new ideas about experiences and texts.

This chapter suggests ways in which students can read and respond to published journals and diaries. In doing so, students become familiar with the forms and patterns writers use to reflect on their lives. Examining the ways that writers use journals will help students explore the potential of their own journal writing for academic and personal contemplation.

Studying Published Journals and Diaries

By responding to journals and diaries, students discuss the ways writers reflect on their experiences. In response to longer journals or diaries, students chart changes in the nature of writers' reflections. Eleanor Hall asked her high school students to describe the changes in Anne Frank's levels of thinking as her famous diary unfolds. In the beginning of the *Diary*, Frank reflected primarily on her own immediate needs. As her situation became more dire, she began to reflect on larger moral and spiritual aspects of life. As part of the following unit on the drama version of *The Diary of Anne Frank*, Mary

Betland had her students relate the discrimination in the play to their own lives.

Unit Outline – *The Diary of Anne Frank*
Mary Betland

As of this year, *The Diary of Anne Frank* is the only required piece of literature for seventh graders in the White Bear Lake School District. The book *Night* is on the list of recommended books for 8th graders.

I am pleased that we have chosen *The Diary of Anne Frank*, because I really enjoy teaching it for several reasons. I am shocked at how little our students really know about that time period. I think we need to continue to talk about and teach the Holocaust so we will never forget it. It seems that in some places in the world right now, new Holocausts are beginning and many Americans think we should actually keep our noses out of it, letting it go on because it doesn't involve us. I also see many forms of prejudice at the school where I teach. The student and teacher population in our district is about 97% Caucasian. I strongly believe that every teacher in the school has an obligation to deal with the ignorance and prejudice that we see in some of our students.

I think *The Diary of Anne Frank* is very appropriate for this age level. Students can relate to the characters of Anne, Peter and Margot. We will read the book together, aloud in class. My classes are predominantly heterogeneous and while this may take more time, I believe the majority of my students will benefit by reading the play as a class.

I expect this unit to take about six weeks. Throughout this time, students will be required to read books of their choice at home for two hours each week. About three pages in a reader response journal will also be required. I will recommend books that deal with prejudice, the Holocaust and WW II, but I will not require the students to chose only from these books. I have one advanced section and I will require each of them to keep a dialogue journal with another student and continue the reader response journals they've been doing all year. They will begin this dialogue journal during the first week of the unit and will continue throughout the unit.

Resources, materials and activities

- Guest speaker from the Jewish Community Relations Council or some other organization. (Contact: Cookie Miller)
- Drama terms
- Background on the Holocaust
- Posters (I will call various organizations to see what's available)
- Extra credit opportunity: viewing the Anne Frank exhibit in St. Paul until Oct. 8
- Vocabulary, especially terms referring to WW II
- *A World of Difference—My Personal Commitment* (JCRC publication)
- At least two pieces of writing required:
  - drama
  - poem
  - letter
  - persuasive paper
  - fictional diary
  - story
  - personal narrative relating to prejudice
  - research paper
  - ethnography
  - brief biography
- Reader response journal and a dialogue journal for the advanced class
- a recommended list of books similar to the *Diary of Anne Frank*
- *Friedrich*, a book with a chronology of the removal of the rights of Jews
- The blue dot activity found in Linda Rief's *Seeking Diversity*.
- *The Wave*, a movie used as a prereading activity (I have to preview this first).
- Display various quotes throughout the room:

  "Despite everything, I believe man is good at heart."
  Anne Frank;

  "My mission is to destroy and exterminate."
  Adolf Hitler;

  "Nobody can make you feel inferior without your consent."
  Eleanor Roosevelt;

"An eye for an eye will leave the world blind."
Mahatma Gandhi;

"It is never too late to give up our prejudices."
Henry David Thoreau;

"There is more hunger for love and appreciation in this world than for bread."
Mother Teresa;

"An injustice against one human being is an injustice against humanity."
Anne Frank.

- The video based upon the play
- *Courage to Care* (video on prejudice today)
- *Weapons of the Spirit* (video on prejudice today)
- *Witnesses to the Holocaust;* A book with activities that allow students to portray actual survivors in an interview format.

WEEK 1
- Discussion and readings about the Holocaust and World War II
- The book *Friedrich* by Hans Pieter Richter (a chronology of the removal of freedoms and rights from the Jews).
- Writing responses to what they've heard and discussed about World War II and the Holocaust.

WEEK 2
- The blue dot activity found in Linda Rief's *Seeking Diversity* (101). A group of students lose particular rights and freedoms for a period of 24 hours. All students respond in writing to the activity and how it made them feel.
- We see the movie *The Wave,* the account of an experiment in a high school classroom. Students respond to the movie.

WEEKS 3–5
- We begin with the vocabulary of drama terms: set, setting, script, dialogue, cast, stage directions, props, act and scene.
- We read the play together in class. Depending upon our progress in the story, we may or may not continue reading workshop on Fridays.
- As we read the play, the students' reading teacher (reading is a separate class from communications, but all of my students have the same reading teacher) will cover difficult vo-

cabulary found in the play. I will cover terms relating to world War II.

- Students will have *Response to Reading* questions for each day of reading.
- At some point during the reading of the play, we will have a speaker from the Jewish Community Relations Council. This speaker will address the Holocaust as well as prejudice seen today in our society.

WEEK 6
- We will view the video based on the diary
- "A World of Difference": personal commitment to improving race relations, increasing cultural awareness and reducing prejudice. Students will work in small groups to define, in their own words, each part of the commitment sheet and then discuss it. Each group will write a commitment sheet that would be appropriate for their age group, and sign it if they would like. Then they will be displayed in the classroom.

WEEK 7 AND BEYOND
- We will begin a full time writing workshop. During this time, I will have students reading excerpts from *Witnesses to the Holocaust* and preparing, in rough draft form, interview questions and responses. Small groups of students can work together to bring these rough drafts to final publication and present their interviews to the class during our writing workshop sharing time. At least two finished pieces, during this 6 to 8 week workshop time, should come from ideas discussed during the Anne Frank unit. Several writing options are actually outlined in the textbook *Literature and Language*: character analysis, letter or persuasive essay, set of director's notes, diary entries for Anne or Mr. Frank, and responding to a quote taken from the play.
- Students could also use the writing workshop time to study diary writing as a form. Examples from Anne's diary, as well as a student's personal experiences with diary writing, could be the basis of this study and a final essay. I would give the students interested in this project the following guide.

DIARY WRITING   Name _____
The Diary of Anne Frank   Date _____
                                              Period _____

The "W's" of Diary Writing

WHO?   Anyone can write a diary; you do not have to consider yourself a spectacular writer in order to keep a diary. In fact, Anne Frank, who wrote one of the most famous diaries of all time, was not remembered by her teachers as a talented writer. Why do you think Anne's diary became so famous?

WHAT?   According to Thomas Mallon, author of *A Book of One's Own: People and Their Diaries*, "A diary can be your letter to the person you'll be." Anne's life was tragically cut short, but her diary became a letter to the world. What have we learned from her simple diary?

WHERE? Even though the secret annex was small and cramped, Anne found the private space she needed to write in her diary. What space do you, or would you, use to write in your diary? Why?

WHY?   Anne Frank wrote, "I want to go on living even after my death." She may have intended to go on living through her books and stories, but it was her diary that helped her accomplish this goal. She also wrote that she was "never in despair" because, she continued, "I can shake off everything if I write." Anne used her diary as a type of coping mechanism to help her through the years in hiding. What are some reasons you, or others, keep a diary?

WHEN?   Anne wrote when she was in a variety of moods and when experiences prompted her to do so. The recording of her experiences and her feelings about them is what makes her diary so valuable today. When do you find yourself writing in your diary?

HOW?   Anne didn't know that millions of people would some day read her diary. She was casual about the writing and she allowed the habit of writing to take root. Anne recorded details and she maintained a positive attitude. Everything is interesting; that's the best reason to keep a diary.

The Great Irony

While in hiding, Anne Frank also wrote a novel and a book of short stories, but it is her diary that made her famous. The Green Police had been instructed to destroy any papers left behind by the people they'd arrested. Why is it ironic that shortly before the Nazis were forced out of power in Amsterdam they failed to destroy a diary that has come to symbolize the horror of the Holocaust?

Students also read examples of journals, diaries and letters with an eye to these writers' use of certain techniques. They can practice or experiment with these techniques in their own writing. In reading Thoreau's *Walden,* a student focuses on how Thoreau uses his descriptions of nature to convey his spiritual interpretations and beliefs. In responding *as a writer* to these texts, the student can make use of similar techniques in a journal entry or more formal paper.

One writer who kept an on-going journal was the poet and novelist, May Sarton. Her book, *Journal of a Solitude* (1973) contains entries for one year in her life. In these entries, she writes about living alone in a small New Hampshire town. She is continually reflecting on the value of solitude as a writer. At the same time, she is also racked with a sense of despair. In the following entry, she gravitates between her sense of positive versus negative feelings about her life as a "solitude":

October 11th

The JOKE is on me. I filled this weekend with friends so that I would not go down into depression, not knowing that I should have turned the corner and be writing poems. It is the climatic moment of autumn, but already I feel like Sleeping Beauty as the carpet of leaves on the front lawn gets thicker and thicker. The avenue of beeches as I drive up the winding road along the brook is glorious beyond words, wall on wall of transparent gold. Laurie Armstrong came for roast beef Sunday dinner. Then I went out for two hours late in the afternoon and put in a hundred tulips. In itself that would not be a big job, but everywhere I have to clear space for them, weed, divide perennials, rescue iris that is being choked by violets. I really get to weeding only in spring and autumn, so I am working through a jungle now. Doing it I feel strenuously happy and at peace. At the end of the afternoon on a gray day, the light is sad and one feels the chill, but the bitter smell of earth is a tonic.

I can hardly believe that relief from the anguish of these past months is here to stay, but so far it does feel like a true change in mood—or rather, a change of *being* where I can stand alone. So much of my life here is precarious. I cannot always believe even in my own work. But I have come in these last days to feel again the validity of my struggle here, that it is meaningful whether I ever "succeed" as a writer or not, and that even its failures, failures of nerve, failures due to a difficult temperament, can be meaningful. It is an age where more and more human beings are caught up in lives where fewer and fewer inward decisions can be made, where fewer and fewer real choices exist. The fact that a middle-aged, single woman, without any vestige of family left, lies in this house in a silent village and is responsible only to her own soul means something. The fact that she is a writer and can tell where she is and what it is like on the pilgrimage inward can be of comfort. It is comforting to know there are light-house keepers on rocky islands along the coast. Sometimes, when I have been for a walk after dark and see my houselighted up, looking so alive, I feel that my presence here is worth all the Hell.

I have time to think. That is the great, the greatest luxury, I have time to be. Therefore my responsibility is huge. To use time well and to be all that I can in whatever years are left to me. This does not dismay. The dismay comes when I lose the sense of my life as connected (as if by an aerial) to many, many other lives whom I do not even know and cannot ever know. The signals go out and come in all the time.

Why is it that poetry always seems to me so much more a true work of the soul than prose? I never feel elated after writing a page of prose, though I have written good things on concentrated will, and at least in a novel the imagination is fully engaged. Perhapsit is that prose is earned and poetry given. Both can be revised almost indefinitely. I do not mean to say that I do not work at poetry. When I am really inspired I can put a poem through a hundred drafts and keep my excitement. But this sustained battle is possible only when I am in a state of grace, when the deep channels are open, and when they are, when I am both profoundly stirred and balanced, then poetry comes as a gift from powers beyond my will.

I have often imagined that if I were in solitary confinement for an indefinite time and

knew that no one would ever read what I wrote, I would still write poetry, but I would not write novels. Why? Perhaps because the poem is primarily a dialogue with the self and the novel a dialogue with others. They come from entirely different modes of being. I suppose I have written novels to find out what I *thought* about something and poems to find out what I *felt* about something (pp. 39-41).

In responding to this entry, students discuss a number of different aspects that are characteristic of journal writing. It is important that students begin by expressing their own engagement reactions to the entry, noting specific aspects of the entry that intrigued or bothered them and reasons for their responses. A student might be engaged by her honesty and openly discuss her feelings of despair. Students could then discuss some of the following characteristics:

*Focus/shifting positions.*Writers deliberately choose to focus on certain topics and omit others, usually for rhetorical reasons. Students could discuss a writer's deliberate choice to focus on or omit certain topics by tracing certain patterns in an entry. In formulating their focus, in contrast to the traditional formal essay, a journal writer may shift their position about their topic, entertaining different or opposing perspectives on that topic. In Sarton's entry, she consistently focuses on her shifting moods. When she is gardening, she feels "strenuously happy and at peace." When she thinks about her writing, things become more "precarious." In other entries in the book, she expresses her despair with negative reviews, leading her to question her own ability as a writer. At the same time, she finds a certain "comfort" in writing as a mission in life.

She also gravitates back and forth about her attitudes towards solitude. She relishes the "time to think" and "to be" as essential to writing. However, unless she knows that she is connecting to others, she lapses back into a sense of despair. Similarly, she examines her differences between writing poetry and writing novels or prose as emanating from different aspects of her experience. She perceives poetry to be the "work of the soul" that emerges from "a dialogue with the self." In contrast, writing novels or prose is more of "a dialogue with others" in which she is grappling with her beliefs or ideas. All of this reflects a spontaneous engagement with the polar aspects of her life: positive versus negative feelings, being alone and being with others and writing poetry versus novels/prose. In dramatizing these tensions, she reveals a mind at work honestly coping with her sense of value in life.

Having identified a certain topic in a writer's journal, students could draw connections to similar topics in their own lives. In reading about these competing feelings, students may write about competing feelings in their own lives, particularly their own mood swings between positive and negative feelings.

*Omissions.*Writers may also avoid writing or expounding on certain topics. Students may consider possible reasons for a writer's omissions of information. In her journals, Dorothy Wordsworth focused primarily on descriptions of her brother, with little discussion of herself. Knowing that her journals would be read by others, as was the custom of the period, and given her total devotion to her brother William, she may have assumed that it was her responsibility to record his life for posterity. In describing narratives in journals kept by slaves,

Toni Morrison (1992) notes that there is little mention of their own inner life. As she notes, "I'm looking to find and expose a truth about the interior life of people who didn't write it (which doesn't mean that they didn't have it) (113). Slaves may have been reluctant to reveal interior feelings for fear of potential reprisals from their owners. In her entry, other than a reference to a friend who comes to dinner, Sarton does not talk about other people in her life. The absence of others itself reflects the fact that she doesn't spend much time with other people, that her life and writing revolves around her own private thoughts. Nor does she specify the reasons for her sense of despair, possibly because those reasons are too difficult to discuss.

In reflecting on their own entries, students could note what it is they leave out. In some cases, they may be deliberately avoiding dealing with a topic or issue. In other cases, they may be so interested in or focused on a particular phenomena that they ignore other phenomena.

Purpose. As we discussed in Chapter Two, journals, diaries or letters can be used for many different purposes. Students could discuss their perceptions of the writer's purpose or function. In her entry, Sarton is exploring reasons for her sense of optimism about her "change of *being* where I can stand alone" despite her past anguish and her sense of the precariousness of life. Her purpose is suggested by the reiteration of various aspects of her life that feed this optimism—the fact that she can live on her own; that she, as a writer, serves as a "lighthouse keeper" for others; that she is able to reflect; and that she is able to write poetry.

In discussing their own purposes for writing, students may note that they do not begin writing with any set purpose in mind, but often discover their purpose through their writing.

Portrayal of time. Students may also examine a writer's treatment of time. The diary/journal writer generally reports events as unfolding in the present, creating a sense of immediacy for the reader, often conveyed through the use of recorded dates that chronicles time passing. While a reader of an autobiography can often predict what will happen next, a reader of diaries or journals may be surprised by some unpredictable revelation, which adds to the sense of immediacy (Culley, 1985).

This sense of immediacy is illusionary because the writer has had time to think about and reflect on the event. Abbott (1984) quotes Sartre, who noted, "'as to the event itself, although it is recent, it is already rethought and explained'" (28). Or, as Alex Aronson (1991) notes: "Diaries, then are metaphors of the flux of time, evocations of the writer's often capricious and fragmentary recall of the past, and his daily attempts at transforming memory into images that, once they are written down, are apprehended as if they existed outside or beyond time" (ix). In her entry, Sarton begins with a specific description of her weekend and working in the garden and then broadens out to reflect on her solitary life in her rural home. Her journal entry seems grounded in an immediate present-tense time, as evident in her use of the speculative word, "perhaps," or her openly posing a question to herself, "why is it that poetry always seems to me so much more a true work of the soul than prose." However, this sense of immediacy belies the fact that she is thinking about experiences from her entire life.

In examining their own portrayal of time, students could talk about how they record their perceptions of experience relative to the time of the event. While they may be describing the event as it unfolds, the very fact that they are recalling a past event means that they are already reflecting on the meaning of the event. In doing so, they are already changing the meaning of "what actually happened." This can lead to a discussion of the difficulty of trying to recall past events objectively. Writers of autobiography and memoir frequently note that they frequently alter or even create past experiences given the difficulty of knowing "what actually happened." Our versions of "what actually happened" keep changing as we reinterpret the past from new and different perspectives. Students recollections of themselves as fourth graders may have changed from their perspective as eighth graders to their perspectives as twelfth graders and the process of writing about it reconstitutes past meanings. In discussing her own writing, Annie Dillard (1987) notes:

> Memory is insubstantial. Things keep replacing it. Your batch of snapshots will both fix and ruin your memory of your travels, or your childhood, or your children's childhood. You can't remember anything from your trip except this wretched collection of snapshots. The painting you did of the light on the water will forever alter the way you see the light on the watch; so will looking at Flemish paintings. If you describe a dream you'll notice that at the end of the verbal description you've lost the dream but gained a verbal description (70–71).

By discussing old childhood letters, diaries or journals, students could compare their past and present perspectives. They may note how their perspectives of the world has changed and reasons for those changes, reasons having to do with changes in their own attitudes, values and self-concept.

All of this may help them recognize that through their writing, they are constructing their own versions of reality.

Self-reflexiveness. Writers also vary in the degree to which they openly reflect on their own self or writing process. In some cases, they simply report events with little or no reflection. In other cases, they introspectively reflect on their own self—their voices, attitudes, beliefs or their own processes of constructing the meaning of experience.

Students could compare differences in writer's self-reflexiveness, considering possible reasons for these differences. Students may read Joyce Carol Oates' (1991) reflection on the process of journal writing:

> Why the journal distresses me, but also fascinates: I'm required to use my own voice and to record only the truth—but not to record *all* the truth. There have been many things I've eliminated over the years or hinted at so slantwise no one could guess...for reasons too obvious to note. Still, what is recorded is always true. At least at the time it is recorded.
>
> The journal as a work-in-progress; no structure; no plot; no them, no characters really (I don't invent a character to be an intermediary here: which is why the journal distresses since I don't feel comfortable or assured with my own voice)—where, in my serious writing, I always compose a persona to observe what I myself ("myself") observe. That twist, spin to words, that sense of a queer filtering other—what I most love (342).

Oates is reflecting on her own voice as distinct from the voices of her characters. In her entry, Sarton is drawing on the voices of others. In describing her self-doubts as to "whether I can 'succeed' as a writer or not," she is referring to the voices of critics who bring their own assumptions about success to judging her writing.

Students could also reflect on their own voices inherent in their own writing—the voices of "friend," "student," "daughter," "rebel," "scientist," "politician," etc. Students could also note the degree to which they reflect on experience in their own writing. They may find that they are more likely to reflect on certain topics than others.

Social relationships with an audience. Writers may also attempt to build social relationships with their audiences. In examining these strategies, students need to recognize that *how* people communicate with each other is just as important as what they say to each other. As Deborah Tannen (1986) notes, "talk is a way of showing that we are involved with each other, and how we feel about being involved. Our talk is saying something about our relationship" (13). In an exchange of letters, the way writers respond to each other implies how they feel about each other. A writer who is constantly acknowledging their audience's feelings is communicating their concern for that audience. Through her question-asking, Sarton is adopting the voice of her audience, who might be asking her such questions.

Students may examine how writers establish social relationships in terms of power and affiliation/solidarity. In some cases, writers may use their letter or entry to assert their power or status. To maintain their status role as "teacher," a teacher may respond in a teacher/student dialogue journal, that "you didn't completely follow my directions in writing this journal." In other cases, writers build affiliation or solidarity with their audience by attempting to gain their sympathy or identification. In writing to a peer, a student may describe her struggles in a math class and, by addressing that peer as a "close friend," seek to gain their sympathy.

Students also need to recognize that the meaning of writers' texts depends on how their audience interprets those texts. A writer's use of humor to build affiliation may be read by their audience as a put-down. Or a writer who discloses their own problems or difficulties may be interpreted as attempting to control or coerce an audience into helping them. In examining a published exchange of letters or examples of dialogue-journals, students could intuit the audience's interpretation of a writer's meaning. They may then compare their own interpretation with the audience's interpretation.

Students could then apply all of this to an analysis of their own peer-dialogue journal writing. In exchanging entries, they need to be aware of "what is going on" socially in their exchange. They also need to be sensitive to the ways in which they are responding to each other's entries.

Metaphors. In depicting their own life narratives, writers also rely on metaphors that reflect their own larger beliefs and cultural models constituting their organization of experience (Lakoff & Johnson, 1980). Writers employ certain metaphors for their conceptions of the life experience as a journey—that one is continually "searching" in life as a "quest." By describing the metaphors writers use, students infer those writers' beliefs and attitudes. Sarton describes her own life as a journey, as a "pilgrimage inward," suggesting that she is searching for something within her own self. She also compares herself to being a "light-house keeper" who, as a writer read by others, serves to help others navigate "by rocky islands" in their own lives.

Thus, by studying published writers' journals or diaries from the perspective of a journal or diary writer themselves, students may begin to appreciate the richness of this genre. Further, the act of reading journals or diaries as texts serves to legitimize them as an important part of both the literature and writing curriculum.

Studying Women's Journals, Diaries, and Letters

Given the continued focus in the secondary school literature curriculum on male authors, it is important to study women's journals, diaries and letters as works of literature. Because women often had difficulty publishing novels or plays, they turned to journals and diaries as a forum for expressing their ideas. Contrary to the myth that women were more likely to keep dairies or journals given the fragmentation of their lives, during the eighteenth and nineteenth centuries, women often assumed the roles of family or social historian who chronicled the daily lives of those around them. These women would record in detail, daily events as a form of history for others members of the family and for posterity. Margo Culley (1985) cites the example of Mary Vial Holyoke's (1737-1802) diary which consists of sparse, one- or two-sentence descriptions of daily events in Salem, Massachusetts. Many of the entries dealt the births of her twelve children, only three of whom survived. The following is an excerpt from an entry written in 1767:

Sept. 5. I was brought to bed about 2'Clock A. M. of a daughter.
6. The Child Baptized Mary.
7. The Baby very well till ten o'Clock in the evening & then take with fits.
8. The Baby remained very ill all day.
9. It Died about 8 o'clock in the morning.
10. Was buried.

In these entries, Holyoke offers little or no emotional reaction to events, even the deaths of her own children. Moreover, there is little reference to herself recording these events. Based on her research on women's diaries from the eighteenth to the twentieth century, Culley notes an increasing sense of privacy during the nineteenth century, with the result that women were more likely to describe their own feelings and focus on the self as subject. She cites the example of an entry written by Mary MacLane of Butte, Montana, written in 1920:

• And at this point I meet Me face to face.

I am Mary MacLane: of no important to the wide bright
world and dealy and damnably important to Me.

Face to face I look at Me with some hatred, with despair
and with great intentness.

I put Me in a crucible of my own making and set it in the
flaming trivial Inferno of my mind. And I assay thus:

I am rare—I am in some ways exquisite.

I am pagan within and without.

I am vain and shallow and false.

I am a specialized being, deeply myself (5-6).

In contrast to the Holyoke entry, MacLane's entry reveals her own feelings and focuses on herself as subject. It is
far more self-reflexive than Holyoke's entry. Her purpose for
writing shifts from that of chronicler for the good of others to
a portrayal her own life as significant, as worthy of self-re-
gard. She is therefore using her diary to construct her own
sense of self. This shift represented a basic change in
women's willingness to openly express their own social
concerns and political power. By comparing women's writings from the seventeeth century to the present, students
could trace this shift in women's willingness to assert their
own views.

Below are some resources for studying women's journal
writing.

Women's Diaries and Journals

Ashton-Warner, Sylvia. *Myself.* Simon and Schuster, 1967.

Brewster, Mary. *"She Was a Sister Sailor": The Whaling Journals of Mary Brewster, 1845–1851.* Mystic Seaport Museum, 1992.

Blackwell, Alice. *Growing Up in Boston's Guilded Age.* Yale UP,
1990.

Chance, Sue. *Stronger Than Death.* Norton, 1992.

Fisher, M. F. K. *Stay Me, Or Comfort Me: Journals and Stories, 1933–1941.* Pantheon, 1993.

Forten, Charlotte. *The Journal of Charlotte L. Forten: Free Negro
in the Slave Era,* ed. by Ray Billington. Collier-Macmillan,
1969.

Grumbach, Doris. *Fifty Days of Solitude.* Beacon, 1994.

Hasselstrom, Linda. *Windbreak: A Woman Rancher on the Northern Plains.* Barn Owl, 1987.

Horney, Karen. *The Adolescent Diaries of Karen Horney.*
New York: Basic, 1980.

Kaufman, Sue. *Diary of a Mad Housewife.* Bantam, 1968.

Lessing, Doris. *The Golden Notebook*. Simon and Schuster, 1962 (a novel in diary form).

Morton, Andrew (ed.). *Diana's Diary: An Intimate Portrait of the Princess of Wales*. Summit, 1990.

Nin, Anais. *The Diary, Volumes I through VI*. Harcourt, Brace: 1966 - 1976.

Sarton, May. *Journal of a Solitude*. Norton, 1973.

————. *After the Stroke: A Journal*. Norton, 1988.

————. *Endgame: A Journal of the Seventy-Ninth Year*. Norton, 1992.

Shelley, Mary. *The Journals of Mary Shelley 1814–1844*, ed. Paula Feldman and diana Scott Kilvert. Oxford: Claredon Press, 1987.

Shore, Emily. *The Journal of Emily Shore, 1818–1837*. UP of Virginia, 1991.

Smart, Elizabeth. *Necessary Secrets: The Journal of Elizabeth Smart*. Grafton, 1991.

Washam, Ethel. *Lady's Choice: Ethel Waxham's Journals and Letters, 1905-1910*. U of New Mexico P, 1993.

Whiteley, Opal. *The Singing Creek Where the Willow Grows: The Rediscovered Diary of Opal Whiteley*. Ticknor & Fields, 1986.

Woolf, Virginia. *The Diary of Virginia Woolf*, ed. Anne Olivier Bell. Penguin, 1979.

Wordsworth, Dorothy. *Selections from the Journals*. New York UP, 1992.

Yates, Elizabeth. *My Diary—My World*. Philadelphia: Westminster Press, 1981.

There are a number of collections of women's diaries:

Begos, Jane, ed. *A Women's Diaries: Miscellany*. Magicircle Press, 1989.

Blodget, Harriet, ed. *Capacious Hold-all: An Anthology of Englishwomen's Diary Writing*. U P of Virginia, 1991.

Blythe, Ronald, ed. *The Pleasures of Diaries: Four Centuries of Private Writing*. Patheon, 1989.

Cline, Cheryl. *Women's Diaries, Journals, and Letters: An Annotated Bibliography*. Garland Press, 1989.

Culley, Margo, ed. *A Day at a Time: The Diary Literature of American Women from 1764 to the Present*. The Feminist Press, 1985.

Franklin, Penelope, ed. *Private Pages: Diaries of American Women, 1930's–1970's*. Ballantine, 1986.

Havlice, Patricia. *And So to Bed: A Bibliography of Diaries Published in English*. Scarecrow, 1987.

Holliday, Laurel, ed. *Heart Songs*. Bluestocking, 1978.

Lifshin, Lyn. ed. *Ariadne's Thread: A Collection of Contemporary Women's Journals*. Harper & Row, 1982.

Moffat, Mary Jane, and Charlotte Painter, ed. *Revelations: Diaries of Women*. Vintage, 1975.

For further reading about women's diaries and journals:

Bateson, Mary Catheine. *Composing a Life*. Plume, 1990.

Benstock, Shari, ed. *The Private Self: Theory and Practice of Women's Autobiographical Writings*. Routledge, 1988.

Blodgett, Harriet. *Centuries of Female Days: Englishwomen's Private Diaries*. Rutgers UP, 1988.

Bunkers, Suzanne. "Diaries: Public and Private Records of Women's Lives." *Legacy* 7 (1990): 17–26.

Davis, Gayle. "Women's Frontier Diaries: Writin for Good Reason." *Women's Studies* 14 (1987): 5–14.

Dehler, Kathleen. "Diaries: Where Women Reveal Themselvs." *English Journal* 78 (1989): 53–54.

Gristwood, Sarah. *Recordings Angels: The Secret World of Women's Diaries*. Harrap, 1988.

Heilbrun, Carolyn. *Writing a Women's Life*. The Women's Press, 1989.

Hoffman, Leonore, and Margo Culley, eds. *Women's Personal Narrratives: Essays in Criticism*. Modern Language Association, 1985.

Milloy, Jean. *The Woman Reader: Learning and Teaching Women's Writing*. Routledge, 1991.

Romines, Ann. *The Home Plot: Women, Writing, & Domestic Ritual*. U of Msasachusetts P, 1992.

Simons, Judy. *Diaries and Journals of Literary Women from Fanny Burney to Virginia Woolf*. U of Iowa P, 1990.

Smith, Sidonie. *A Poetics of Women's Autobiography: Marginality and the Fictions of Self-Representation*. Indiana UP, 1987.

Stratton, Joanna. *Pioneer Women: Voices from the Kansas Frontier*. Simon and Schuster, 1981.

Reading Journals, Letters, or Diaries about Different Topics

Consistent with the idea of organizing journal writing around students interests in certain topics, students may also read and discuss published journals, diaries, or letters pertaining to a particular topic—health issues, sports, families, school, the environment, etc. Through reading and responding to these texts, students may develop further interests in a topic, which may transfer to their own writing. Students who develop an interest in reading journals on responses to the media may begin to use their own journal to respond to the media.

For each of the topics listed below, we have suggested some titles that may be appealing to secondary students.

Fictional texts. Students could read fictional texts or epistolary novels written in the form of journals, diaries, and letters (Hassam, 1992). In responding to fictional texts, students may note the ways in which writers use various techniques to construct characters, story lines and worlds. In the epistolary novel, *The Color Purple* (Harcourt Brace, 1982), Alice Walker develops the characters of Celie and her relatives through her letters. Younger students may read Paul Zindel's *The Amazing and Death-Defying Diary of Eugene Dingman* (Bantam, 1901), noting the ways in which Eugene uses his diary to reflect on everyday problems. Or in *Diary of a Freshman* (Doubleday, 1901), Charles Flandrau describes the life of a college student in the 1800's.

They may use these techniques to construct their own fictional versions of journals, diaries or letters. They may write their journals, diaries or letters from the perspective of a number of one or more of these different fictional persona:

- a student or adult they know who is quite different from themselves
- a celebrity, famous person, or historical figure
- a familiar fictional character or narrator, perhaps taken from a text they are reading in the class.
- a martian who is visiting their classroom from outer space and who may have no understanding of the social and cultural meanings of earthlings' behaviors
- a narrator who espouses beliefs or values quite different from their own.

Defining identity and attitudes. Adolescents are concerned with defining their own identity and attitudes. At the same time, in order to be popular with their peers, they may succumb to peer pressure, compromising their own identity and attitudes. Students could compare published writers' explorations of identity and attitudes with their own attempts. In *Be True to Your School* (Theneum, 1987), a rewrite of a diary kept in 1964 about his seventeenth year, Bob Greene writes about his experiences in developing friendships, work, school, dating, music and winning a varsity letter. High school students may compare his identity and attitudes as shaped by the values of the pre-Vietnam War 1960's with their own identity and attitudes as shaped by the values of the 1990's.

Diaries/journals in fictional form
about defining identity include:

Axworthy, Ann. *Ann's Diary of France.* Whispering Coyote, 1994.

Butler, William. *The Butterfly Revolution.* Ballentine, 1967,

Cleary, Beverly. *Strider.* Morrow Junior Books, 1991.

Chambers, Aidan. *NIK Now I Know.* Harper, 1988,

Coleman, Hila. *Diary of a Frantic Kid Sister.* Archway, 1975.

Cooney, Caroline. *Among Friends.* Bantam, 1986.

Cushman, Karen. *Catherine, Called Birdy.* Clarion, 1994.

Glasser, Diane. *The Diary of Trilby Frost* Holiday, 1976.

Gottlieb, Dale. *My Stories by Hildy Calpurnia Rose.* Macmillan, 1994.

Griffith, Helen. *Journal of a Teenage Genius.* Greenwillow, 1987.

Hamm, Diane Johnston. *Bunkhouse Journal.* Scribner's, 1990.

Hirsch, Karen. *Ellen Anders On Her Own.* Macmillan, 1994.

Jones, Robin. *The Beginning of Unbelief.* Atheneum, 1993.

Lewis, C. S. *The Screwtape Letters*

MacLachlan, Patricia. *For the Very First Time.* Harper & Row, 1980.

MacNeil, Robert. *Burden of Desire.* Doubleday, 1992,

Marsden, John. *So Much to Tell You.* Jay Street, 1989.

McCenna, Colleen O'Shaughnessy. *Eenie, Meanie, Murphy, No.* Scholastic, 1990.

Robertson, Keith. *Henry Reed, Inc.* Penguin, 1989.

Sclick, Eleanor. *My Album.* Greenwillow, 1984.

Zindel, Paul. *The Amazing and Death-Defying Diary of Eugene Dingman.* Bantam, 1990.

Family relationships. Adolescents are also concerned about their relationships with other family members. Students could read *The Day the Loving Stopped,* by Julie List (Fawcett, 1983)—journal entries and letters to her parents about the breakup of a marriage and divorce—and discuss the ways List copes with her concerns through her letters. Students could also read a number of fictional novels in the form of journals, letters or diaries about family relationships. *A Solitary Secret,* by Patricia Hermes (Harcourt, Brace, Jovanovich, 1985) is a daughter's fictional journal about her father's sexual abuse. *I Only Made Up the Roses* by Barbara Porte (Greenwillow, 1987) is a journal of 17-year-old about her experiences with mixed-race parents. *Mostly Michael,* by Robert Smith (Delacorte, 1987) and *Bunkhouse Journal,* by Diane Hamm (Scribner's, 1990) are diary accounts of male adolescents coping with family difficulties. *Strider* by Beverly Cleary (Morrow, 1991), portrays 14-year-old Leigh's diary accounts of his relationships with his family. In *My Father's World* (Bethany, 1990), Michael Phillips writes about the difficulty of relationships with fathers. *Dear Bruce Springsteen,* by Keven Major (Dell, 1987), consists of a 14-year-old's letters to "The Boss" about conflicts with other family members. And *Jeb and Dash: A Diary of Gay Life, 1918–1945,* by Jeb Alexander (Faber, 1993), portrays the lifetime relationship between two gay men.

In responding to these and other texts, students could examine how the events or stories reflect certain aspects of family life: patterns of communication, family rituals or celebrations, problem-solving strategies, organizational structure, members' sense of autonomy, and shared attitudes and values.

Based on observations and interviews, students could then write journal entries about their own family members. Students could read *How It Feels When Parents Divorce* by Jill Krementz (Knopf, 1984) and *My Parents Are Divorced: Teenagers Talk about Their Experiences and How they Cope* (Everest, 1980), books based on interviews with adolescents about their experiences. For further reading on writing about family experiences, see William Hofmann, *Life Writing: A Guide to Family Journals and Personal Memoirs* (St. Martin's Press, 1982), Peter Stillman, *Families Writing* (Writer's Digest Books, 1989), and Lois Dorn, *Peace in the Family: A Workbook of Ideas and Action* (Pantheon, 1987).

Personal Problems/Health. Recent surveys of adolescents indicate an increase in physical and psychological health problems. Students may be reluctant to discuss their own personal or health problems. However, they may be more willing to vicariously cope with these problems through discussions and journal writing about other persons or characters.

Adolescents must often cope with the experience of losing a loved one. Students could discuss two adolescent novels written in journal form that depict adolescents coping with death. In *Rising Phoenix,* by Cynthia Grant (Atheneum, 1991), Jessie writes a journey about the loss of her older sister to cancer. And, in *The Year Without Michael,* by Susan Beth Pfeffer (Bantam, 1988), Jody keeps a journal about her and her family's attempts to cope with the disappearance of her 13-year-old brother. Both of these characters use their writing to deal with the grief associated with recollections of their sister and brother. In his book, *Bitter, Bitter Tears: Nineteenth-Century Diarists and Twentieth-Century Grief Theories,* Paul Rosenblatt (1991) discusses how fifty-six nineteenth century diary writers used their writing to cope with the deaths of loved ones. Contrary to stage-theories of grieving, Rosenblatt argues that the process of grieving is set off by various memories and behavior patterns as associated with the deceased. "Grief work" for Rosenblatt involves dealing with these reminders. Diary writing may contribute to or hinder this "grief work:"

> If . . . diary keeping focuses attention on a comparatively few memories, hopes, and behavior patterns, the ones recorded in the diary, it may actually facilitate grief work by reducing the number of memories, hopes, and behavior patterns one must disconnect. In addition, diary keeping may help to crystallize one's disconnecting by committing one to what one has put on paper following the loss. On the other hand, the need to write clear thoughts may force one to think about and wrestle with a relatively large number of memories, hopes, and behavioral connections (40).

Students may also read about how other adolescents cope with the problems of chemical use, pregnancy, disease, depression and crime. They can then discuss the ways in which the adolescents in these texts coped with their own adversities and compare these coping skills with those described in their own entries.

Anonymous. *Go Ask Alice*. Avon, 1975. [The diary of a fifteen year old's experiences with drugs that eventually lead to her death.]

Bell, William. *Crabbe's Journey*. Little Brown, 1986. [Fiction; portrays an adolescent's battle with alcoholism.]

Blume, Judy. *Letters to Judy What Your Kids Wish They Could Tell You*. Pocket, 1987. [Contains letters to Judy Blume concerning personal problems.]

Fraser, Craig. *Burnt A Teenage Addict's Road to Recovery*. Signet, 1990.

Gravelle, Karen, and Leslie Peterson, eds. *Teenage Fathers*. Messner, 1992.

Kaye, Geraldine. *Someone Else's Baby*. Hyperoin, 1992.

Keyes, Daniel. *Flowers for Algernon*. Bantam, 1970.

Kittredge, Mary, ed. *Teens with AIDS Speak Out*. Messner, 1991.

Miller, Robyn. *Robyn's Book A True Diary*. Scholastic, 1986. [Recounts a sixteen-year-old's girl's battle with cystic fibrosis; for a discussion of teaching this book, see Neil Glixon, "Robyn's Reach When Readers Want To Write," *English Journal* 76 (1987) 62-65].

Shanks, Ann Zane, ed. *Busted Lives Dialogues with Kids in Jail*. Delacorte, 1982. [Contains writings about the lives of thirteen young people in prison.]

Walsh, Meeka. *Ordinary Magic: Intervals in a Life.* Turnstone, 1991.

School. Students often have difficulty adjusting to a new school, particularly in moving from an elementary to junior high school. They could read *The Diary of Latoya Hunter: My First Year in Junior High* (Random, 1992) which portrays the experience of a West Indian student's coping with her seventh grade year in a junior high school in the Bronx.

Students can also read examples of ethnographic studies about classrooms or schools, noting the ways in which writers used field notes and interviews to make generalizations about the school. They could read excepts from school ethnographies such as *Jocks and Burnouts* by Penelope Eckert (1989), a study of a large, suburban Detroit high school; *Adolescent Life and Ethos: An Ethnography of an US High School* by Heewon Chang, a study of a small Oregon high school; or *God's Choice: The Total World of a Fundamental Christian School* by Allen Peshkin, the study of a rural Illinois fundamentalistic school. In her study, Eckert found two competing social groups—those occupied by the "jocks" and the "burnouts." Each of these groups was defined symbolically opposed to the other through alignments with worlds outside of the high school. The world of the "jocks" consisted of students who were "middle-class," pro-school, involved in athletics and extra-curricular activities. The "jocks" learned to use the social networks in the school to gain the information necessary for success in the school. As in the corporation, they learned how to play the corporate game to serve their own ends. The "jocks" associated school with certain forms of "preppy" dress, "pro-social" behaviors, and athletics. In contrast, the "burnouts" consisted of students who were representative of "working-class" backgrounds. They were therefore less involved in school and more involved in work and neighborhood activities. In contrast, the "burnouts," who were more accustomed to functioning in small, coherent neighborhood or workplace groups, had more difficulty coping with the large, bureaucratic structure of the school. The "burnouts" associated dress, behaviors, and allegiance to neighborhood groups and workplace as cultural rejection of the "jocks'" world. Thus, each group defined themselves in opposition to the other. As Eckert notes, "clothing, territory, substance use, language, demeanor, academic behavior and activities all ultimately serve as conscious markers of category affiliation . . . that strengthens the hegemony of the category system in adolescent life and increasingly restricts individual perceptions and choice" (69).

In her study of a much smaller high school, Chang

(1992) found a strong emphasis on the value of everybody getting along with everybody else. Students generally knew all of the students in the school. In contrast to Eckert's findings, students maintained friendly relationships with each other through heavy participation in school activities. At the same time, the students were somewhat selective in their choices of friends. They were able to assess which students were more popular than others in the school, although groups differed in their criteria for assessing popularity. This created a tension between the surface egalitarianism and an underlying elitism. Students also espoused relatively traditional gender attitudes, ostracizing those who deviated from traditional sex-role expectations. All of this suggested to Chang that adolescents face social tensions that are difficult to reconcile.

Based on these readings, students could use their journals to take field notes (see ChapterThree) on their observations of behaviors in the school. They may observe:

- the lunch room to note which students hang out with whom.
- group differences; in dress or behavior.
- classes; representing different tracks or ability levels.
- meetings of student council or school clubs.

They may also interview students on tape about their perceptions of the school. Students then reflect on their field notes and interviews tapes, noting patterns and inconsistencies. Students then summarize what they learned about the school culture.

Sports. Because many adolescents spend a considerable amount of their time participating in sports, they have a strong academic interest in the topic. In reading examples of journals and diaries written about sports, students could discuss the ways in the writers portray themselves. These writers may vary in the degree to which they portray themselves or other players in heroic or realistic terms. Students could then write their own sports journals, describing their own experiences in sports events. In doing so, they may go beyond simply recounting the events of a game to reflect on their own engagement or involvement in the game or reasons for their own or their teammates' performance.

Bamberger, Michael. *The Green Road Home A Caddie's Journal of Life on the Pro Golf Tour*. Contemporary Books, 1986.
Carroll, Jim. *The Basketball Diaries*. Bantam, 1981.

Jacobson, Steve. *The Best Team Money Could Buy The Turmoil and Triumph of the 1977 Yankees.*
Shapiro, James *Meditations from the Breakdown Lane Running across America.* [Recounts the experiences of running three thousand miles from San Francisco to New York.]
Singletary, Mike. *Calling the Shots.* Contemporary Books, 1986. [The diary of a star defensive player for the Chicago Bears championship football team during the 1980's.]

Travel/survival stories. Students could also read journals or diaries that recount travel experiences, including accounts of survival. They could discuss ways in which writers dramatize coping with adversities.

Callahan, Steven. *Adrift: Seventy Six Days Lost at Sea.* Ballantine, 1987.
Lindbergh, Charles. *The Spirit of St. Louis.* Avon, 1985.
Moon, Willian Least Heat. *Blue Highways.* Fawcett, 1984 [written in more of an essay than journal form; this describes travels in a van on secondary roads throughout America].
Steinbeck, John. *Travels with Charley.* Penguin, 1985 [recounts the 59-year old writer's travels in American with his French poodle].
Robth, Susan, ed. *Marco Polo, His Notebook.* Doubleday, 1991.

Based on their recollections of a trip or journey—even a short trip across town, students could create their own travel journal or diary. They might also reflect on what they learned about themselves or others from their trip. It is often the case that going to a different cultural context provides students with a new set of lenses for reflecting on their own culture. If they live in a small, rural community and then visit a large city, they may perceive their small-town life in a new and different light.

The Environment. Students may also study examples of journals or diaries recording experiences in nature or perceptions of one's own environment—rural, suburban or urban. In reading Henry David Thoreau's *Walden; or Life in the Woods* (Anchor), students could discuss Thoreau's spiritual orientation towards nature as well as his political beliefs about civil disobedience. For a more contemporary example, students could read *Pilgrim at Tinker Creek* by Annie Dillard. Dillard records her observations of natural phenomenon in careful, concise details. In *The Local Wilderness* (Prentice, 1987), Cathy Johnson illustrates techniques in keeping a field journal for describing natural phenomenon. Students in middle or junior high school could read Gary Paulsen's *The Island* (Dell, 1990), in which

Will, the protagonist, escapes to an uninhabited island on a lake near his Northern Minnesota town and keeps a journal of his observations of natural events on the island.

Other nature journals/diaries include:

Abbey, Edward. *Desert Solitaire*. Ballantine, 1985.
Heinrich, Beind. *An Owl in the House A Naturalist's Diary*. Little Brown, 1990.
Hubbell, Sue. *A Country Year Living the Questions*. Harper, 1983.
Leopold, Aldo. *A Sand County Almanac*. Oxford UP, 1968.
Raymo, Chet. *Honey from the Stone*. Penguin, 1987.
Woodin, Ann. *Home Is the Desert.* Tucson U of Arizona P, 1984.

After reading these and other examples of nature journals, students could write their own entries based on observations of various environmental sites (Werkenthin, 1992). Students could go to a local park and record as many different plant types or species as possible, describing the ways in which they differ from each other. Or they could observe sites that involve environmental risks—lead poisoning, water pollution, toxic waste and the like. They could also reflect on their own feelings and attitudes towards their experience with nature as distinct from their experience with non-natural aspects of their lives.

Students could also read journals or diaries written by scientists who recorded their own methods of conducting experiments. *The Plutonium Story: The Journals of Professor GlennT. Seaborg, 1939–1941* (Batello Press) contains Seaborg's thoughts as he worked on developing the atomic bomb.

Media. Students devote a considerable amount of their leisure time activity to the media: television, films, radio, tapes and CD's. They could read some examples of journal/diary responses to the media that illustrate the reflective responses to the meaning of media experiences. In a diary-like report on his viewing of television juxtaposed with his walks in the Adirondacks, Bill McKibben describes his responses to the commercialized, artificial world of cable television as distinctly different from his response to nature. He argues that despite all of the information provided on television news and talk shows, "we also live at a moment of deep ignorance, when vital knowledge that human beings have always possessed about who we are and where we live seems beyond our reach: we live in an age of missing information" ("What's On," *The New Yorker*, March 9, 1992, p. 41).

Students could also reflect on how their media experience is shaped by viewing media as part of a shared group experience. Adolescents enjoy renting a video as a group in order to share their responses to the video. Just as viewers of popular television programs have formed their own computer bulletin board fan clubs for exchanging responses to these programs (Jenkins, 1992), students could form fan clubs in the classroom based on specific favorite programs or on certain genre types (soap opera, detective, comedy, mystery, talk shows). Students could record their own reactions to their viewing over a certain period of time, reflecting on what they learned from their viewing. In some cases, students may find it difficult to reflect on what is often a mesmerizing experience. As did McKibben (1992), if they have been keeping nature journals, they could contrast their responses to experiences with nature to their responses to the media.

Students can also create their own video diaries or journals, perhaps designing a documentary about their daily life. Such a production still involves some writing, which they then record as a "voice-over" accompanying shots of their experiences.

Cultural/historical periods. Students could read journals, diaries or letters that capture the historical aspects of certain periods. Joyce Maynard's *Looking Back: A Chronicle of Growing Up Old in the Sixties* (Doubleday, 1993), and James Kunen's, *The Strawberry Statement* (Random, 1969), capture life during the decade of "the sixties," an era characterized by attitudes and values distinct from those of the 1950's or the 1980's—cultural experimentation, improvement in civil rights, the "youth movement," political upheaval and violent conflict (see Workman, 1975, for a curriculum guide to teaching the sixties.)

As part of studying a particular period, students could read journals, diaries or letters written during that period (see Milton Meltzer, *Nonfiction for the Classroom*, 1994) Students can study letters as historical documents, discussing the ways in which letters reflect the attitudes and beliefs of historical figures. In studying World War II and the Vietnam War students could read *Lines of Battle: Letters from American Servicemen, 1941-1945*, Annette Tapert, ed. (Times Books, 1992) and *Dear America: Letters Home from Vietnam*, Bernard Edelman, ed. (Pocket, 1985) or letters left at the Vietnam War Memorial collected by Laura Palmer in *Shrapnel in the Heart* (1987). The following are two letters from *Dear America*:

April 1967

Dear Ma,

How are things back in the World? I hope all is well! Things are pretty much the same. Vietnam has my feelings on a seesaw.

This country is so beautiful, when the sun is shining on the mountains, farmers in their rice paddies, with their water buffalo, palm tree, monkeys, birds and even the strange insects. For a fleeting moment I wasn't in a war zone at all, just on vacation, but still missing you and the family.

There are a few kids who hang around, some with no parents. I feel so sorry for them. I do things to make them laugh. And they call me "dinky dow" (crazy). But it makes me feel good. I hope that's one reason why we're here, to secure a future for them. It seems to be the only justification I can think of for all the things that I have done!

Love to all.

Your son,
George

29 December 1969

Hey all,

. . . Christmas morning I got off duty and opened my packages alone. I missed you all so much, I cried myself to sleep. I'm starting to cry again. It's ridiculous. I seem to be crying all the time lately. I hate this place. This is now the seventh month of death, destruction, and misery. I'm tired of going to sleep listening to outgoing and incoming rockets, mortars, and artillery. I'm sick of facing, every day, a new bunch of children ripped to pieces. They're just kids—eighteen, nineteen year old! It stinks! Whole lives of them—cut off. I'm sick to death of it. I've got to get out of here. . . .

Peace

Lynda

In studying American history, students could read Kathyrn Lasky's historical novel, *Beyond the Divide* (Morrow, 1986), an Amish fourteen-year-old's journal account of traveling west; a *Farm Boy's Year*, by David McPhail, (Atheneum, 1992) about a boy's life on a New England Farm during the 1800's; *Mercy Short: A Winter Journal, North Boston, 1692–93*, by Norma Farber (Unicorn, 1982) that portrays a 17-year-servant experiences of being possessed by "witches" during the Salem witchcraft trials of 1692 as well as her captivity by Indians; or *In Kindling Flame: The Story of Hannah Senesh,* Linda Atkinson (Lothrop, Lee and Shepard, 1985) that contains Hannah Senesh's letters and diaries about her escape from Nazi-occupied Hungary and her return to Hungary with the British army as a freedom fighter.

As part of studying a recent historical period, students could interview persons who lived during that period, using techniques illustrated in the Foxfire interviews with residents of Appalacia. These interview techniques involved in conducting oral history projects are also discussed in the following books:

And Justice for All: An Oral History of the Japanese American Detention Camps, John Tateishi (Random House, 1984)

Before Freedom: Forty-eight Oral Histories of Former North and South Carolin Slaves, Belinda Hurmence (Mentor, 1990).

Bloods: An Oral History of the Vietnam War by Black Veterans, Terry Wallace (Random House, 1984).

Everything We Had: An Oral History of the Vietnam War by Thirty-Three American Soldiers Who Fought It, Al Santoli (Ballentine, 1985).

I Didn't Say Goodbye, Vegh Claudine (Dutton, 1985), interviews of men and women who were children during the Nazi persecution of Jews.

In the Combat Zone: An Oral History of American Women in Vietnam, 1966–1975, Kathryn Marshall (Little, Brown, 1987).

Motherwit: An Alabama Midwife's Story, Onnie Lee Logan and Katherine Clark (Plume, 1991).

Working: People Talk about What They Do All Day and How They Feel about What They Do, Studs Terkel (Ballentine, 1985)

Famous authors. Students may also study the diaries or journals of famous authors they are reading in their literature classes. They could then relate the biographical background information portrayed in the journals, diaries and letters to an understanding of the writer's perspectives or autobiographical aspects of their writing. In reading Mary Shelley's *Frankenstein* (Pickering and Chutlo, 1992), students may also read her journals which describe the death of her three children and her own experience of destitution and loneliness. Students could discuss how these experiences of loss, hopelessness and isolation may have shaped her construction of a monster who has similar experiences. As Judy Simons (1990) notes:

> It is in the journal that we find the genesis of Frankenstein, in the day-to-day concerns of Mary Shelley's own life, as she wandered from place to place, establishing

homes only to have them disbanded. Motherless, isolated from her family and much of the time exiled from
her native land, she was dependent on Shelley's rather
erratic love for her succor and support. So does
Frankenstein's monster parallel Mary's daily life in his
fugitive and nomadic existence, searching for love, for a
stable home and a normal family life, unable to accept
his own difference from the human society he sees
around him (68).

Some journals, diaries, and letters by famous authors
that might appeal to secondary students include (see also list
of women writers):

Alcott, Louise May. *The Journals of Louise May Alcott.* Little,
    Brown, 1989.
Anderson, Sherwood. *The Sherwood Anderson Diaries, 1936-
    41.* U of Georgia P, 1987.
Bosell, James. *The Diary of James Boswell, 1760-1795.*
    Heinemann, 1991.
Cheever, John. *The Journal of John Cheever.* Knopf, 1991.
Dahl, Roald. *My Year.* Viking, 1994.
Emerson, Ralph Waldo. *Emerson in His Journals.* Harvard UP,
    1982.
Kafka, Franz. *Letter to His Father.* Schocken, 1953.
Lewis, C. S. *Letters to Children.* Macmillan, 1985.
Melville, Herman. *Journals.* Northwestern UP, 1989.
Mencken, H. L. *The Diary of H. L. Mencken.* Knopf, 1989.
O'Connor, Flannery. *The Habit of Being: Letters of Flannery
    O'Connor.* Sally Fitzgerald, ed. Vintage, 1979.
Plath, Sylvia. *The Journals of Sylvia Plath*, Frances McCullough
    and Ted Hughes, eds. Ballantine, 1990.
Potter, Beatrix. *Diaries.* F. Warne, 1989.
Price, Eugenia. *Diary of a Novel.* Lippincott, 1980.
Silko, Leslie Marmon and James Wright, *The Strength and
    Delicacy of Lace.*
Steinbeck, John. *Working Days: The Journals of the Grapes of
    Wrath, 1938–1941.* Viking, 1989.
Welty, Eudora. *One Writer's Beginnings.*
Wilder, Thornton. *The Journal of Thornton Wilder.* Yale UP,
    1985.
Woolf, Virginia. *A Passionate Apprentice: The Early Journals,
    1897–1909.* Harcourt, 1990.

Students could compare authors' experiences as depicted
in their journals, diaries or letters with experiences as depicted in their own fiction. The grimly depressing experiences
in John Cheever's (1991) journal is often mirrored in the depressing lives of his short story and novel characters. Stu-

dents could also apply writers' descriptions of their writing process to study a particular text. Flannery O'Connor (1979) received a letter from an English professor asking , for his students, an interpretation of her story, "A Good Man is Hard to Find." The following are excerpts from their letter and her response.

> . . . In general we believe that the appearance of the Misfit is not "real" in the same sense that the incidents of the first half of the story are real. Bailey, we believe, imagines the appearance of the Misfit, whose activities have been called to his attention on the night before the trip and again during the stopover at the roadside restaurant. Bailey, we further believe, identifies with the Misfit and so plays two roles in the imaginary first half of the story. But we cannot, after great effort, determine the point at which reality fades into illusion or reverie. Does the accident literally occur, or is it a part of Bailey's dream?

28 March 1961

> The interpretation of your ninety students and three teachers is fantastic and about as far from my intentions as it could get to be. If it were a legitimate interpretation, the story would be little more than a trick and its interest would be simply for abnormal psychology. I am not interested in abnormal psychology.
>
> There is a change of tension from the first part of the story to the second where the Misfit enters, but his is no lessening of reality. The story is, of course, not meant to be realistic in the sense that it portrays the everyday doings of people in Georgia. It is stylized and its conventions are comic even though its meaning is serious.
>
> . . . If teachers are in the habit of approaching a story as if it were a research problem for which any answer is believable so long as it is not obvious, then I think students will never learn to enjoy fiction. Too much interpretation is certainly worse than too little, and where feeling for a story is absent, theory will not supply it.
>
> My tone is not meant to be obnoxious. I am in a state of shock.

These are different topics which integrate reading and writing of journals, diaries and letters. In such integration, you may also draw on students' reading and writing in other subject areas, creating a sense of coherence about their uses of literacy.

Chapter Seven

Reading, Responding to, and Evaluating Student Journals

Unlike formal academic papers, which represent the final outcomes of careful thought and revision, journals reflect minds *at work*. For students to take journal writing seriously, they need to receive feedback and evaluation. Otherwise, grade-conscious students will continue to treat them as unimportant or marginal to their coursework.

For many teachers accustomed to evaluating students' writing for its conformity to the characteristics of familiar genres, responding to and evaluating student journals requires some new perspectives. Are sentence fragments really acceptable, even in exploratory journals? What happens if students' entries wander or become disjointed? Should long entries count more than one-paragraph snippets? Is it more important to evaluate students' thinking than simply respond "naturally" to their entries? Where should we write our comments—in the margins? At the end of an entry? How can we judge the quality of a student's "thinking," anyway?

In this chapter, we offer some suggestions for responding to and evaluating journal writing. Because we recommend more class time be devoted to journal-like writing, it will naturally take a more prominent role in the assessment of students' progress. In most classrooms that will mean having to reconcile the tentative, "messy," process-oriented nature of journal writing with the need to evaluate some sort of product.

The bulk of this chapter focuses on providing principled response to students' journal writing. The emphasis here is on the sort of social and interpersonal transactions that journal writing can inspire—that is, on the development of thinking within a context of collaboration and social interaction. Both peer and teacher response are considered. We then turn briefly to the role that journals can play in assessments of students' performance and learning, particularly how to grade or "count" journals over the span of a class or a school year.

Responding to Student Journals

The distinctions between *responding to* a piece of writing and *evaluating* it are not always entirely clear, given the context of the writing and your feedback on it. You may choose to react informally to students' journal entries every few days, but if you are also "checking" the entries in a gradebook, even on a simple scale such as "_," "_+," and "_-," your response is an evaluation. What seems like a non-evaluative remark may imply a strong evaluative judgment: "You're not exploring the concepts very deeply here, Bob; see if you can delve into the topics more fully in your entries before your journal is due in two weeks."

Yet while response and evaluation are interrelated processes, you can be clear to your students about the goals of certain kinds of commentary. Much will depend on your goals for reading and/or grading the writing. If you want to encourage students to think more deeply about ideas in your course, you can choose to provide encouraging responses, in the form of dialogic reactions to students' entries, that are explicitly non-evaluative—you do not grade, check or take notes on the quality of the entries. You may also accomplish the same goal by telling students that you will be looking for specific characteristics in their journal writing—"depth of exploration"— model these characteristics and then assess the extent to which the entries fulfilled your expectations. Either method may help students' explorations, but it is important that students know exactly what you do and why. Furthermore, it makes pedagogical sense to tie response and evaluation to the processes of writing and learning. Strong evaluations at the early stages of students' journal writing will likely squelch the freedom to explore different ideas and practice different discursive strategies. Periodic or final journal evaluations may be helpful in assessing students' performance over longer periods of time, when they have opportunities to learn and change.

Let us first consider the processes of *responding* to journals—processes in some ways more fruitful for students' development than making final assessments of their work over a period of time. There are three main ways in which students can receive principled responses to their journal writing: peer response; teacher response (sometimes in the form of teacher-student dialogue); and self-directed metacommentary. We will look at each form of response.

Responding to Students' Solo Journal Writing. In responding to students' journal writing, you become the person the students carry on their dialogue with. Here your invoked role as an evaluator becomes even more pressing for many students, potentially thwarting productive exchanges and making students feel that they must write "for the teacher." In an analysis of college instructors' comments on 3,000 papers, Connors and Lunsford (1993) found that teachers focused primarily on the effectiveness of the use of supporting evidence or examples. There was far less attention to the content of what students were saying or to the degree to which they fulfilled the assignment. Connors and Lunsford attribute this focus to the impersonal, evaluative stance adopted by the instructors:

> Many of the comments seemed to speak to the student from empyrean heights, delivering judgments in an apparently disinterested way. Very few teachers, for instance, allowed themselves the subjective stance implicit in telling students simply whether they liked or disliked a piece of writing. This kind of reader-response stance was found in 17% of the global comments; the other 83% of comments pronounced on the paper in a distanced tone, like reified personifications of Perelman's Universal Audience. (214)

While this study applied to essay writing, teachers may also apply the same evaluative stance to journal writing. They may still attend primarily to form, rather than to what students are trying to communicate.

Responding to Meaning. Rather than adopting an overtly evaluative stance for journals, you may want to respond in a more meaning-based way to what students are saying, providing them with specific on-line, "reader-based" responses. You are describing how you as "responsive reader" (Rubin, 1993) are engaged, confused, intrigued or puzzled by what students are saying (Elbow, 1981; Johnston, 1983). Students can then experience how you are constructing the meanings they are trying to convey. *How* you respond implies to them what you value in their thinking and writing. By focusing your reactions to their *opinions* about a story instead of their plot summary, you are implying that you value a critical reaction to a piece of literature over a simple rehash of the story's contents.

Providing taped oral feedback. In a study of students' perceptions of written comments on their journals, one of us asked college students in a literature methods class to indicate which comments they most preferred. Students were more likely to prefer comments written in an informal, conversational mode, those that included self-disclosure, personal experiences or specific reactions. The students responded more negatively to pro-forma, ritualistic, vague, evaluative comments such as "interesting activity" or "this would work well with students."

In our classes, we often give oral reactions to students on cassette tapes. In contrast to written comments, tapes encourage a kind of dialogic, conversational response. We react by citing our own responses to the texts under study and to the students' entries. We also *describe* our perceptions of the students' ideas, and offer them with positive comments about the ways in which they may be thinking about the material. Such comments are also useful in describing exchanges between students in a dialogue journal. We may describe the fact that the partners are acknowledging each other's ideas, asking each other questions, sharing their own personal experience or reflecting on their own and the other's responses. We hope that our descriptive comments provide students with a vocabulary to assess of what they learned from using the dialogue journals during a course.

However, students may perceive even reader-based reactions as a lot of "teacher questions" that function primarily as a reading check. All of this creates a sense of apprehension over being judged. For this reason, it is important that you react in a highly supportive, conversational mode, responding to the topics initiated by the students (Peyton & Seyoum, 1989) and discussing your own personal reactions and related experiences. If a student begins to talk about tensions in his relationship with his parents, you could share memories of your own upbringing. In the process, you are modeling ways of elaborating your own thinking. Then, as students are exposed to your modeling, over time they may begin to elaborate their own perceptions. As Fulwiler (1989) notes, "It is the teacher's responses which create the motivation and provide the models of thought and reflection of unpredictables and honesty, which students need" (56).

Using Response Icons. Occasionally you may wish to respond to journal entries by using a system of icons. Janice Knight uses several icons that represent different thinking types: recalling, comparing, contrasting, defining cause/effect relationships, moving from ideas to examples, moving from examples to ideas and evaluating. Knight placed various icons in the margins of the students' entries. She also used a letter code to describe specific response strategies: "S," summarizing; "PK," activating prior knowledge; "P," predicting;" MV," mentally visualizing; "←R," reread a passage for clarification;

"R→," read ahead for clarification of points,"PE," relating personal experiences; "GO," graphically organizing information; "SQ," self-questioning; "C," consulting a knowledgeable source; "SK," skimming; and "MP," monitoring pace of reading.

Instilling Confidence in Expressing Ideas. In writing journals, students are gaining a sense of self-confidence in their ability to express their own ideas. It is important to react to signs of this growing self-confidence by noting that you are engaged by an idea in an entry, you are serving to bolster students' self confidence.

In their analysis of exchanges between a teacher and sixth grade students with limited English proficiency, Peyton and Seyoum (1989) found that students wrote longer entries and t-units when the teacher responded to the students' topics or expressed opinions than when the teacher introduced topics or asked questions. Similarly, college students responded with shorter entries when their teacher did not respond or responded primarily with questions (Schatzberg-Smith, 1988). In an experimental study examining the effects of different types of teacher reactions to journals, Gordon (1991) randomly assigned elementary education majors to three different groups—a group that received "sharing" comments, "questioning" reactions, and no reactions. By comparing changes in entries over time, she found that the students receiving the "sharing" comments were significantly more likely to increase in the degree of elaboration, conceptualization, expression of voice, use of metacognitive stance and entry length than were students in either the questioning or no-reaction groups. Interviews indicated that the students in the sharing group developed a sense of their own professional status and responsibility through their exchanges. As one student noted, "She wrote to me like I was already a teacher. I even started seeing myself more and more like that. I got to really know her because of the journal" (Gordon, 1991, p. 145).

Sharing Your Own Responses. As in a productive conversation, when you share your own ideas with a student you convey an interest in conversing with them about a text as a co-reader or partner. Students often experience ambivalences or difficulties in expressing their ideas. They may assume that they need to impress you with their definitive knowledge as authorities on a topic. As a result, they may be reluctant to express doubts or ambivalences about an idea. In sharing your own sense of uncertainty, you are dispelling the perceived myth of yourself as an omniscient authority. You are also acknowledging that we all experience the frustration of indecision or confusion in formulating ideas.

You are more likely to motivate students to elaborate or extend their responses by sharing your response, treating students as co-learners. As Martin Nystrand (1992) notes:

> When teachers respond to students by evaluating their answers, as in the I-R-E sequence of recitation, they treat learning as remembering and students as rememberers. By contrast, when reachers respond to students by *making an observation* of their own, as in conversation and discussion, they treat learning as reflection and validate students not just as rememberers but also as thinkers. In effect, these different forms of discourse assign or impute fundamentally different roles to students, and as such, they entail an ethical choice for the teacher (18).

The extent to which true dialogic exchange occurs between you and the student depends on the quality of the social exchange. Generally in social exchanges we value and share some mutual interest in the topic and generally perceive each other to be equal social status. In talking about a political election, we are both interested in sharing our insights into candidates' strategies and successes/failures and we both consider each other relatively knowledgeable about the topic. While each of us may have an agenda—to convince the other about the validity of our positions—we don't assume that either of us is in control. Given this mutual, collaborative arrangement, both participants are invigorated by the exchange and leave feeling that they've learned something from it.

In responding to your students' entries, you may refer to your own autobiographical experiences or other texts evoked by the students' entries. A student may be describing an experience that reminds you of an experience in your own life. Or a student's description of a text may call to mind some recollections of a similar text. Becky, a seventh-grader, is writing a journal entry reflecting on her experiences growing up in a wooded area:

> . . . Trees are perfect for when you want to be alone and think. If you have something on your mind and want some privacy the forest is the best place to go. Something about coolness, and mystery that encloses around you when you enter it, makes you feel like your troubles aren't so bad after all. I love the feel of being deep in the forest where no one is watching you. The fragile bits of sunlight that fall through tiny cracks between leaves makes you feel as though your in a whole different world.

In responding in the margins to Becky's entry, her teacher writes occasional reader-based reactions such as "this gives me a good feeling" or "I feel refreshed from reading this entry." A longer comment, however, focuses on shared experienced:

> Becky, your entry reminded me of a time when I was about ten, and I used to climb a very tall but thin tree a little way from our house, and get up really high, and if there was a wind, the tree would bend a lot. It was thrilling to be able to see so far around my neighborhood from this swaying pinnacle. It was like being at the top of a ship's mast in stormy seas.

Responding to Students' Multiple Voices. In reading students' entries, you may also sense that they are employing what could be described as different, multiple "voices." Within the same entry, writing about a fishing trip with his father, a student may be shifting into the the voices of an "ecologist," "novice," "critic," "student," "experienced fisherman" and "son."

The notion of multiple voices derives from the work of Mikhail Bakhtin. Bakhtin was interested in how a writer or speaker employs a range of different, often competing voices or discourses that reflect different social and ideological perspectives. The meaning of a student's writing is social in that it is written in response to or anticipation of other voices. As Bakhtin argued (1981), every utterance reflects a previous or subsequent utterance. Every act is a reaction to another act. In a dialogue journal, students are often restating their partner's previous statements, but in their own words, or they may anticipate their partner's reactions by signals such as "I know you won't agree with me, but . . . ."

Bakhtin also wanted to call attention to the tensions between these competing discourses as a way of undermining the use of what he called "monologic" speech as opposed to "dialogic" speech. "Monologic" speech as represented in official, bureaucratic pronouncements reflects an authoritarian stance that precludes expression of alternative voices or perspectives, a "conforming literacy" in which people's behaviors are controlled or regulated (Fleisher, 1992). In a classroom discussion, teachers often resort to a "teacher talk," discourse that reflects "the voice of the teacher's manual" or "the voice of the curriculum" (Wertsch, 1991, p. 144). However, in the same discussion, students may use what Collette Daiute (1993) refers to as "youth genre" voices that reflect their own interests, needs and attitudes beyond the focus of a teacher's often monologic discourse. Within this discussion, a teacher may privilege the "teacher talk" voice by perceiving the students "youth genre" voice as less relevant to the discussion. As a result, there is a tension between the different voices in the discussion.

In their informal journal writing, students are often experimenting with a range of different voices. In some cases, these voices represents ways of thinking or knowing associated with certain disciplines. As they move through the school day, they experience the discourses of different disciplinary perspectives: scientific/ mathematic; historical; literary; vocational or artistic. In their writing, they may experiment with these voices as they learn to talk and think in the context of these disciplinary perspectives.

Their voices also reflect certain social roles or practices, the persona of a "good student," which often related to class or racial differences. James Paul Gee (1992) cites the example of two students, a five-year-old white, middle-class girl, and a seven-year-old black girl, who both told stories to their respective classes. The five year old girl told a story that was highly literary and filled with figurative language. Her teacher openly praised her for this story. In contrast, the black girl used repetition of words and phrases, a characteristic of black oral tradition. Her teacher perceived her story as an inferior deviation from the more "literary" form. From such experiences, students learn to equate certain kinds of discourse as associated with being a "good student" in the eyes of a teacher. The teacher's response to the black girl's language only served to devalue her sense of self-worth.

Students' voices also reflect various gender identities. An "adolescent" discourse is often defined in terms of prototypical male characteristics—being boisterous, loud and assertive. As a result, traits typically associated with adolescent females—being reserved, mannered or socially sensitive—may be perceived to be a deviation from this presumed male norm. Early adolescent females often suppress or disguise expression of their own thoughts or feelings (Rogers, 1993).

Finally, students' voices may reflect differences in class or racial background. A student may modulate between voices reflecting practices valued in the home or neighborhood versus those valued in the school. As Gee (1992) notes, "many minority and lower socioeconomic students have great difficulty accommodating to or adapting to certain "mainstream" Discourses, in particular, many school-based Discourses" (p. 117). By stressing surface correctness, the "mainstream," school-based discourses serve as gate-keeping criteria for excluding students whose language does not mark them as "good." Many minority or lower SES students employ what Gee describes as "borderland discourses" (p. 146) that are situated between the school and the home. In their home environment, they may use writing consistent with the culture of the home. While students come from these diverse cultural backgrounds, their social interaction is fostered in school and mediated by its discourses. At the same time, these students know that the school-based discourses are designed to exclude them.

Gee (1992) cites the example of a ninth grade Puerto Rican inner-city student, Wilma, who wrote the following text about beginning seventh grade for a study. At the time, Wilma was participating in the study, *Storytelling Rights* (9-11) (Shuman):

> When I first came to Paul Revere I was kind of scared but it was going to be my first year there but I was supposed too get used too going there. I started early in the Morning I was happy. Everybody taking about it sounded scarry, and nice. A couple of us caught the bus together. When we got there, since I was a seventh grader I was supposed to go to the autotorium—what I did. from there I appeared in the boy's gym. I didn't know until there announced where we were at. From there I appeared somewhere else. That was my home room. Which they called advisory. I copy something from the board called a Roster. After that a Bell rang. We waited from another Bell and left. I met with my friends and cought the bus hom. They explained how to used the rosters. Which I learned very quickly.
>
> The Classroom I was in like a regular elementary school which was only from one room to the other. I didn't understand that. Until our teacher explained that was called Mini School. Well we did a lot of things. Went on a lot of trips. And were treated fairly by both teachers.
>
> I didn't hardly had any friends until I started meeting a lot of them. I had a friend by the name of Luisa and Alicia. Those were the only two friends I had at the beginning of the year. Almost at the middle I met one girl by the name of Barbara. We were starting to get real closed to each other and were starting to trust each other. As you know we still are very closed and trust each other.

In illustrating "borderland discourse," Gee notes that Wilma is writing in the context of a study in which she is adopting the school-based essay form. At the same time, in contrast to school-based essay conventions, she uses an informal style deemed inappropriate from the perspective of a school writing. She is able to use her writing to portray how her friends helped her cope with a new and "scary" environment. She portrays her friends' discourse—"they explained how to used the rosters"—as helpful in coping with this seemingly hostile world. As Gee notes, she also effectively captures the experience of her dissociation and bewilderment as she wanders through the school, passively "acted upon" by events and routines. While she is able to effectively employ this borderland discourse, it would not be evaluated positively from the perspective of the school discourse because it "is defined in part in opposition to the school's Discourses. In becoming a full member of school-based Discourses, she would be defining herself in opposition to herself" (p. 151).

Instead of irradicating or disowning their community-based discourse, teachers can help students to become aware of the range of alternative discourses and how they are related to differences in institutional power. By recognizing the mixture of different voices in their own writing, students may then begin to define their own heterogeneous voices. As Thomas Recchio (1991) notes:

> As Bakhtin argues in "Discourse in the Novel," "One's own discourse and one's own voice, although born of another or dynamically stimulated by another, will sooner or later begin to liberate themselves from the authority of the other's discourse" (348). In order for the student to begin to realize her own voice, she has to liberate it from the other voices [in her writing], not in a process of rejecting those voices but in managing them, using them as a background against which she can sound her own (450).

Identifying and Responding to Different Voices. In responding to journal entries, you can help students recognize their different voices. You may identify these different voices by asking the question, "who is speaking here?" You can also describe the tensions you perceive between the different voices. You may note that a student is dependent on the voices of an adult and/or teacher authority.

By describing these different voices, you are giving students a meta-knowledge of how different kinds of discourses shape their writing and thinking. They may then become more aware of the tensions or complexities in their own thinking, awareness that may lead to some critical self-assessment. Consider the following entry by Adell, a tenth grader:

> The qualities for a typical male and female have lessened in the last decade, although I feel the general basis is still here. In my family I notice that my mother and I do most of the housework and I help her cook and set the table, just because it is proper or the acceptable way.

> My dad comes home to watch the game or play
> some sports with my brother, and we serve them dinner.
> After dinner usually mom and I clean-up.
> I guess I don't mind doing that, but I do realize I am
> brought up to do "what is proper for a lady" in an age
> that will hopefully move away from that.

In this entry, Adell invokes several voices. In the initial sentence—"the qualities for a typical male and female have lessened in the last decade," she is using a "school" or "social science" discourse extracted from not only the writing prompt but also from the essayist tradition of the thesis statement. As she talks about her and her mother doing most of the work, she shifts into a more personal, narrative discourse. Then in characterizing that activity as the "proper or acceptable way," she adopts a more ironic voice, mimicking what might be described as a "community" or "cultural" voice regarding traditional gender roles in the family. Her more cryptic description of her father and brother ("We serve them dinner. After dinner usually mom and I clean-up") implies an angry, resistant voice reflecting an emerging feminist perspective. In the final sentence, the fact that she puts "what is proper for a lady" in quotation marks reflects the tension between this community or cultural discourse and her own feminist perspective.

In responding to Adell, we would provide some "reader-based" descriptions of these different competing school voices, her personal experience, the community and her feminist perspective. By doing this, we may help her recognize the range of different discourses that are shaping her thoughts about her family and her own gender role.

Reflecting on your own voices or discourses can provide students with important models for their own development. You may note that you are shifting from an evaluative "school" discourse to a "literary" discourse to the discourse of "personal experience." Each of these types of language shapes how you respond to students' writing and influences students' perceptions of your responses and your role as a teacher. If you use only a school discourse, students may think of your role as unchanging and inflexible (teacher/judge). But if you also describe your own personal experiences evoked by their writing, they may then recognize how your own role and self consists of different voices that can be used productively for intellectual explorations and social exchange.

Fostering Change in Thinking. Another purpose for response involves fostering change in the students' thinking. For students to change their thinking, they need to recognize the limitations of their own beliefs, knowledge and prejudices. Based on hermeneutic theory, Richard Haswell (1991) proposes a theory of development or "transformation" beginning with "an initial state of internal instability [which] is shocked into . . . unlearning and revising old knowledge or skills" (131). For Haswell, there are four phases of this transformation, which we apply to the dialectical exchange between two journal writers or between a journal writer and a reader (such as a teacher).

1. *Self-contradictions.* Rather than perceiving growth as simply tensions between developmental stages, current theorists also focus on the student's inner conflicts or self-contradictions. By openly sharing their own doubts about ideas in their journal, students begin to entertain self-contradictions.

2. *Alienation.* For students to question their own beliefs and ideas, they often need to be challenged by some external force or perspectives. This leads to a sense of alienation from their own familiar beliefs and assumptions, a sense that, as ethnographers note, that the familiar is strange. As Haswell notes, "the inner developmental state of students is necessary but not sufficient to promote most learning" (141).

3. *Re-action.* Students' experience of alienation leads to a re-action in which students reexamine their beliefs. For Haswell, "change then proceeds as much backward as forward" (143). In sharing their beliefs with others, students are "risking the very prejudices that make our world and articulate our truth" (Crusius, 1991, p. 38), particularly when they realize that their evidence no longer supports their beliefs.

4. *Appropriation.* In the final phase, students adopt or appropriate a new, alternative perspective or set of beliefs. In order to affirm their new beliefs, students need further verification from experience.

Haswell's categories suggest the need to respond in ways that challenge students' firmly-held beliefs or convictions. If a student argues that certain books that offend people should be censored, then you may want to challenge that belief, reacting in a way that supports and destabilizes the student's assumptions. In doing this, you may ask the student to cite reasons for their beliefs. A student may state that he believes offensive books should be censored because readers of such books may be so offended that they stop reading altogether.

You can then ask the student to reflect on the underlying premise or assumption, perhaps citing some counter-examples—readers seeking out material deemed to be offensive. This response strategy helps students to critically examine the validity of their beliefs and convictions.

Encouraging Recognition and Exploration of Ambivalence. As we have argued, students are free to express their own ambivalent, mixed feelings about experiences or texts in their journal writing. Their responses to various texts—even to their own or others' journal writing—may suggest conflicting roles—supporter vs. judge, friendly reader vs. critic. In a dialogue exchange between two students in a graduate literature methods course, one student noted about her partner's journal:

> Your journal did not deal with class assignments in great depth, yet I am not sure if this is good, bad or neither. Instead, you use your journal as more of a daily writing assignment. You put a lot of your feelings and ideas in your journal, but don't expand very much. This gives me a sense of you as a person, but not in great detail.

These comments may have intended to be descriptive, but her partner may have readily interpreted them as highly judgmental. Despite our attempts to "be descriptive," students still read these reactions as implying an evaluation of their performance. While we are attempting to be solely descriptive, we also know that our comments may be read as implying judgments.

Students may also perceive ambivalence in terms of people's social roles and behaviors. To help students identify external versus internal voices, Greenhalgh (1992) recommends "ear training" by giving students "occasion to eavesdrop on the written conversations between teacher and students . . . pairs of student writers, and between teachers writing research and their reviewers" (409). As part of this training, students learn to identify references to external authorities versus their own personal experience with a text. Students may also input a teacher's motives—whether or not a teacher is attempting "to master and overthrow [students'] voices or, rather, to redescribe and expand the pictures of reality represented in their writings" (409).

Students may also experience ambivalence towards conforming to or violating cultural norms. On one hand, they may want to conform to cultural norms in order to please those who hold to those norms and on the other hand, students may resist norms they object to. Thus, they experience a tension between the need to "go along with the system" and the need to break out of the system.

Reacting to Students' Literary Responses. Much of students' journal writing in English classes consists of responding to literature. In reacting to students' literary responses in a "reader-based" mode, you are describing your own perceptions of their responses—the fact that they are engaged or perplexed by the text, connecting to other experiences or texts or judging a character's actions. In doing this, you are providing students with a mirror of how they are responding, a mirror they use to better understand their own response processes.

You may also engage in a conversation or written dialogue with the student based on your own responses to the text. You are responding less as the evaluator/teacher and more as a co-reader. In reacting in a dialogic mode, you are sharing your own responses as triggered by the student's responses. In reading your responses, the student may appreciate you taking his or her responses seriously enough to engage in a conversation of equals. As in a peer-dialogue journal, the students may then react to your responses in writing or in casual conversation.

In responding to literature, students experience ambivalent, alternative ways of reading gender roles, and roles defined in terms of class, race or ethnicity. In the process, they are invited to adopt different stances associated with cultural attitudes towards gender, class or race. These stances, "reading formations" or "subject positions" (Bennett & Woollacott, 1987) are acquired ideological orientation or desired ways of responding that locate readers as members of communities. Based on his analysis of viewers' responses to a British soap opera, *EastEnders*, David Buckingham (1987) found that "viewers are not merely 'positioned' by television: They are also positioned in society and history, and will therefore bring different kinds of prior knowledge to the text . . . " (115). During the 1950s and '60s, readers' responses to James Bond novels were shaped by a host of different kinds of texts: films, film reviews, interviews with and publicity about Sean Connery and Roger Moore, fan magazines, etc. In acquiring this "reading formation" within the context of the Cold War, readers learned to perceive Bond as representative of Western, anti-Communist, masculine values and therefore aligned themselves to communities that shared those values.

Students' responses to literature may therefore reflect a tension between dominant and subordinate values associated with these stances. Students may also be responding in terms of a range of different social roles that are evident in how they react to the tasks or ways in which they identify with or resist certain characters. In responding as a "macho jock" a student may strongly identify with a Hemingway character who defines his masculinity in traditional male terms.

You may react to students' responses in a number of different ways. We will illustrate these different reactions with some examples of eighth graders' journal responses to the science fiction novel, *Z for Zachariah*, by Robert O'Brien, which depicts two characters, an adolescent female, Ann, and a older man, John Loomis, coping with life after a nuclear war.

1. *Topic focus.* You may notice that the students become preoccupied or occasionally even obsessed with certain topics or phenomena that intrigue them. A student focuses on the topic of impeding death in *Z for Zachariah*. The student repeatedly writes about instances when Ann and Mr. Loomis confront death and expresses concerns about these characters' safety. Because you are able to discern a particular focus suggests to the student that you are carefully attending to their writing. And defining a topic focus serves as a springboard for responding with your own thoughts on that topic.

   In your reaction, you might show the student that you discerned a certain focus in their response. You may note that, "In reading over your entries, I see that you were very concerned with Ann and Mr. Loomis were constantly flirting with death. I had the same feeling; they always sense that whatever they do may lead to over exposure to radioactivity and their own death."

   You may also adopt a perspective on the same focus, possibly stimulating the student to reflect further or simply become aware of this focus. You may react to the student's focus on impending death by noting that you suspect that the characters will be able to survive because they have the desire to survive.

2. *Expression of beliefs and attitudes.* You may also note instances where students express their own beliefs and attitudes about characters or events in the text—a sign that they are going beyond recounting events and reflecting on the meaning of those events. You may describe your own beliefs and attitudes. For example, Annalisa has ambivalent feelings about Mr. Loomis:

   > You have to wonder if Mr. Loomis was never really nice to Ann, but he was only nice because he

was so sick. That being nice was really just a put-on
or a cover-up. Maybe Mr. Loomis became mentally
sick from being out in the radiation-filled world. It's
hard to believe that a human being can be so cruel
to another human being. After all, he even went as
far as shooting her in her ankle.

In reacting to Annalisa, you may respond positively
because she is expressing her own beliefs about the cru-
elty of Mr. Loomis' actions. Therefore you are acknowledging the value of her willingness to express her own
beliefs and attitudes. And, as previously noted, you may
respond as a "critical friend," unpacking students' reasons for beliefs, along with the underlying premises and
assumptions.

In reading students' responses, you may be able to
attribute their beliefs or attitudes to certain social/gen-
der role or group allegiances. A student's responses may
reflect a traditional macho role or a membership in a
fundamentalist religious group. In some cases, you may
hold totally different attitudes and beliefs than those associated with these roles or group allegiances. It is important that you recognize your own biases in responding
to attitudes or beliefs distinct from your own. Rather than
criticize the students for adopting attitudes or beliefs you
do not subscribe to, you may simply describe what you
perceive to be the relationship between their responses
and their social role or group allegiances. You may note
to a student who is assuming a traditional macho role,
"You seem to be adopting a traditional male perspective
in your responses." In that way, you are helping them
recognize how their own attitudes and beliefs are linked
to their social affiliations.

You may also disagree with the student's positions
by presenting your own values and beliefs. In reading or
listening to your alternative position, a student may further reflect on their own position.

3. *Expression of self-doubt and ambivalence.* In some cases,
students may express their self-doubt—they are unsure
about their hypotheses or they are entertaining two contradictory, conflicting opinions or perspectives. A student may proffer an opinion about a text, noting that
they believe a character is doomed to die. At the same
time, they also express doubt about the validity of their
opinion as representing only tentative, immature guesses.
They may therefore express some uncertainty about their
hypotheses, noting that "maybe she won't die because

she seems so determined to survive." By noting that self-doubt is a natural to exploring ideas, you are acknowledging the value of expressing rather than suppressing self-doubt.

Encouraging Self-Directed Response Through MetaCommentary

Whereas students may be encouraged to reflect on and write informally about their own production of a formal paper—as is often the case in introductions to portfolios of their work—journals are not often "critiqued" like drafts of formal papers. However, through careful analysis of their own journal writing, students may gain a higher awareness of the roles that writing can play in their lives and of the relationship between writing and various forms of thinking and reasoning.

In responding to the world, their own lives, their academic study or works of imaginative literature, students use a range of different response strategies: engaging, recalling/recounting, inferring/explaining, constructing cultural worlds, connecting/contrasting, interpreting and judging (Beach & Marshall, 1991). In reacting to their response journals, we describe the students' practices, thereby, modeling the metacognitive process of describing one's strategies.

1. *Engaging.* In describing their engagement response, students write about their experience of entering into, being engaged by a text world and reflecting on their lived-through experience (Langer, 1989). They may also describe their identification with or empathy for certain characters or authors. Another form of engaging involves adopting a character's or writer's perspective in order to create their own fictional version of events as told through the eyes of a character.

2. *Recounting/retelling.* In writing about an experience or text, a student may also recount or retell in a narrative form, a process that helps students organize their perceptions of a text according to certain narrative schema.

3. *Inferring/explaining.* In inferring/explaining, students use character's actions to infer their attributes, knowledge, beliefs, plans and goals; inferences that explain a character's actions.

4. *Constructing cultural worlds.* In responding to a text, students need to do more than identify the physical location of the setting, they also need to perceive the text as a distinct cultural world often constituted by different, competing subcultures, each with its own beliefs and attitudes.

5. *Connecting*. In responding to texts, students may be reminded of other related texts or autobiographical experiences. By elaborating on these related experiences or texts, students begin to reflect on the meaning of these related texts or experiences/related texts. They then apply these meanings back to understanding the current text. In all of this, students are moving beyond retelling the story or analysis of aspects of form to actively construct their own understanding.

6. *Interpreting*. In interpreting a text, students are inferring the larger symbolic meaning of events or character's actions. In some cases this involves relating the text to larger issues associated with need for power, freedom, identity, love, etc.

7. *Judging*. Students may judge characters' or writer's actions or the quality of the text.

In responding to students' entries, we also try to identify the potential development of their responses. As Peter Elbow (1993) notes:

> I increase the chances of my liking their writing when I get better at finding what is good—or *potentially* good—and learn to praise it. This is a skill. . . what we must learn to do is to read closely and carefully enough to show the student little bits of *proto*-organization or *sort of* clarity in what they've already written. We don't have to pretend the writing is wonderful. We could even say, "This is a terrible paper and the worst part of it is the lack of organization. But I will teach you how to organize. Look here at this little organizational move you made in this sentence. Read it out loud and try to feel how it pulls together this stuff here and distinguishes it from that stuff there. Try to remember what it felt like writing that sentence—creating that piece of organization. Do it some more." Notice how much more helpful it is if we can say, "Do *more* of what you've done here," than if we say, "Do something different from anything you've done in the whole paper." (pp. 202-203).

In thinking about the potential for a student's response, we envision a continuum from an initial, undeveloped use of a strategy to an extended or elaborate use of a strategy. In reacting to the student's response, we might try to raise the strategy to a level of consciousness that the student will recognize and then be able to extend in further entries.

To illustrate this way of encouraging students' own meta-awareness of their writing strategies, we turn to an entry by Hadley, an African-American 12th grade student. She is responding to the novel, *A Yellow Raft in Blue Water* by Michael Dorris (1988), a Native American writer. This novel depicts the experiences of three generations of Native American woman, Rayona, a 15-year-old; Christine, her mother; and Ida, Christine's mother. Each of the three sections of the novel is told through the eyes of one of these three main characters.

Hadley's response entry. As illustrated below, we note how we would respond (in italics) to Hadley's entry by identifying the strategy we perceive her using and then noting the value of using such a strategy. We are providing students with a vocabulary for reflecting on what they are doing when they respond. And, as suggested by Elbow, we note what we like about their response and ways to further develop their responses. In all of this, we had to keep reminding ourselves that we are responding to her on-line unfolding thoughts rather than an essay.

> If you look up plot in the in dictionary, it reads: The scheme or pattern of the events, incidents or situations of a story, play, or poem, etc. So when you relate that to the book, the plot becomes pretty plain and simple. A women named Christine has major problems with her mother, leaves the reservation, learns of her brother's death in war, meets a black man named Elgin who she madly falls in love with, has his baby while he's out with other women drinking, raises her daughter, Rayona, by her herself, learns she's sick, put her in the hospital, leaves hospital with Ray, and goes back to the reservation, gets upset w/mother, and leaves Rayona there to fend for herself.

Hadley, I enjoyed you summary of the key events in the novel. Your summary may help you consider the ways in which these different events are related to each other.

> I feel that this plot is very well thought out and set up nicely. The only thing is when the story repeats itself in a few places. In a way, it a waste of time to read the same thing over again. But it is also through a different point of view, because we're dealing with another character's thoughts and feelings at that exact moment of the situation. LIke, when Christine and Rayona are in the car headed back to Montana and the car breaks down. In each story, both are thinking of each other even though they really don't say it, show it or express it.

In judging the story development, you cite a reason for the story repetition—that it serves to portray characters' "thoughts and feelings" about the same events. You also describe how this repetition of event from the characters' different perspectives gives you a sense of their own unique feelings and attitudes.

When I think of theme I think to myself, what's the meaning of this story, what was the author trying to get across to the reader and what effect the story had on me. In this story there are many different themes that come to mind. The first is the relationship between Ida & Christine and how Christine was treated when she was growing up and how it had an effect on the way she raised her daughter. Like on pg. 233 when Christine is talking about how people want to live their lives over through their children, who dream their kids can avoid every mistake. She said, "I wanted to go back and do Aunt Ida's part better and mostly I did." That part really touched me. I thought how nice & thoughtful. That was because Christine never received any of that.

You focus in on the key themes of the novel—the fact that Christine wants to be the mother she never had. You make that interpretation by comparing Ida's relationship with Christine and Christine's relationship with Rayona.

When she said that she never wanted her to be anybody but who she was, I can recall a time when I was in grade school. My best friend's name was Annie. She was smart, sweet, good at everything she did. Well one day in the car my mom kept talking about how great Annie was and I said something like what do you wish Annie was, your daughter. She turned and looked at me and said, honestly, sometimes I wish you were Annie or just like her. That really hurt. To think that your own mother would say a thing like that. I got over it and forgave her but it still lingers in the back of my mind. So the relationship that Ida and Christine had reflects on Rayona and Christine's life.

Here you are connecting your own mother's treatment of you with Ida's treatment of Christine. Elaborating on how your mother treated you meant that you could define your own attitude toward your mother, an attitude you compared with Christine's attitude towards Ida. There's also a sense of ambiguity in your own and in Christine's attitudes—the fact that although they were angry with your own and her mothers, you and she still loved them.

In reacting to Hadley's responses, we are providing her with a mirror of what she is doing in her own responses—what response strategies she is using. This meta-commentary may then help her to reflect on her own response strategies so that she can consider the further development of her journal writing.

Peer Response to Journal Writing

In Chapter Three, we presented several ways in which students can write to and for each other, ideally responding to each other's entries in a kind of ongoing dialogue. There are many advantages of such exchanges. Students learn the importance of exploring multiple perspectives on various issues or experiences. They can focus on the meaning of their exchanges without the fear of an authority making judgments on their ideas. Perhaps most importantly, peer response takes an enormous burden off the teacher who, faced with the prospect of reading 150 journals, may simply abandon them rather than assume that other students can do the work of challenging a writer's ideas, relating to a writer's narrative account to a personal experience or creating the dissonance that leads to new thought.

But peer response does not rid you of all teacherly responsibility. First, the context of response must be carefully established, with certain ground rules and procedures that students must follow if the exchanges are to be meaningful.

Strategies for Fostering Peer-Dialogue Exchange. Once students are starting to share journal entries, your role as orchestrator of the exchanges will be supplemented by an important role as responder to their dialogues. As we argued in Chapter Two, peer dialogue journals serve to build social ties between students. As partners build their social relationship, their writing benefits. At some point, you may wish to evaluate the quality of peer responses. As the exchanges are proceeding, there are a number of strategies for fostering students' dialogues that can encourage growth both in the nature of students' social exchanges and in the quality of their thinking and writing.

One problem with responding as a "reader" to students' writing is that students may also perceive you as a teacher who is evaluating them. As a result, even though you attempt to provide descriptive, reader-based comments, they will still read those comments as judgmental. As Cheryl Geisler (1991) suggests, to avoid being perceived as the teacher/evaluator, teachers need to adopt the role of "coach," helping students from the sidelines to write for other audiences—peers, adults, implied readers and even the teacher herself. "As coach, you enter into a 'time-out,' 'rehearsal', 'reflective' space by speaking *about the reader* rather than speaking *as the reader*" (22).

The role of coach allows you to describe the way you interpret the students' interactions. You may note the ways partners perceive each other. If students perceive their partners as superior, they may be reluctant to disclose doubts or invite verification. They may also think that disagreements are attempts to maintain authority, not signals of engagement in genuine dialogue. In order to save face and avoid any conflicts, some students may agree with any position their partner poses, or they may not respond. After a session at a conference (Ruddell, 1992), a group of four female academics agreed to share journal entry responses to the book *Women's Ways of Knowing*. After one year, there were no exchanges. When asked to reflect on reasons for the lack of exchange, the academics cited reasons that related to their social roles and relationships. They noted that they were reluctant to share matters of a personal nature with colleagues they did not know well. Given their unfamiliarity, they lacked a sense of trust. If students lack a sense of trust, teachers may have them share their concerns or misgivings, which may create more cohesion and community.

You may also respond to how fully students are inviting responses from each other. In a study of college students' peer-dialogue exchanges that involved no teacher intervention (Beach & Anson, 1993), we categorized whether or not the students invited a response from their partner or responded to their partner. If a student issued one invitation during an entry or made one response to a partner, that entry was categorized positively with respect to interpersonal connection. The students' entries were also categorized as they were summarizing the readings, using narratives to illustrate ideas or metacognitively reflecting on their own learning. The overall results indicated little extensive social exchange. Only 20–30 percent of the students invited a response from their partner or responded to their partner. While 60–75 percent of the students went beyond simply summarizing the material, no more than 30 percent reflected on what they were learning. While the lack of social exchange may not necessarily be related to the quality of the students' thinking, further analysis of individual pairs points to a number of specific social characteristics that restricted the extent to which students engaged in dialectical thinking. In part, the absence of a teacher's "supervision" of the exchanges, or the lack of some whole-class commentary on how to go about doing the journals, may have contributed to monologic nature of the entries.

Students who did not develop a strong social relationship often did not engage each other in a dialogic exchange. Some students ignored each other, treating the teacher, rather than their partner, as the real audience. In some extreme cases in our study, a few students addressed their partners in the third-person. The "dialogue" was really two monologues in which each student talked about his or her partner to the teacher as their primary audience. Because to them, the teacher was the most important reader, these students may have been more concerned about showing they were "on task" (responding to an assigned reading) than with engaging in dialogue with their partner.

You may also wish to examine the degree to which students are willing to challenge their partner. If they do respond, they may simply agree with their partner's position in lieu of setting up an intellectual challenge. Students may be reluctant to disagree because they are just beginning to establish a social relationship with each other. In our study students were reluctant to disclose their own doubts, questions, and self-contradictions to unfamiliar partners.

Evaluating Students' Journal Writing

At some point in a course that makes heavy use of journals, you may want to formally evaluate your students' work—that is, assess the quality of the writing as part of a total course grade. In some of our own courses, the "academic journal" may count as much as 50% of the overall course performance. In defining your purpose for evaluating, you are determining outcomes—what it is that students have learned in your course. These outcomes reflect what it is that you value. If you value students' ability to correctly recall information from their reading, then you may look for evidence of correct recall and evaluate accordingly. Or if you value students' ability to write in a manner that matches your vision of an "ideal text," then you may evaluate the degree to which students' have accomplished this. In contrast, if you value students' ability to express their own ideas, you may look for the degree to which they explore different points of view or perspectives. Thus, evaluation means more than simply making judgments. It also means looking at students' journals in a manner that both fosters and assesses certain kinds of learning consistent with your purposes. You are asking yourself how the students' writing reflects what they are learning in your course.

Some teachers judge or grade students' journal writing on simple criteria such as the number of pages or entries. One advantage of this "counting" approach is that it is fast and efficient. It may not require reading and responding to entries at all. And it may also work particularly well for "fluency journals," in which the main focus is generating material.

Teachers may depend on the counting approach as a way to avoid judging the quality of journal writing; as we have seen, the informal characteristics of journal writing make it difficult to apply standard criteria to it. This may communicate to students that journal writing is less important than formal papers, which may limit the classroom potential of the journal.

We are, however, opposed to grading each and every journal entry a student may write. Rather, we suggest looking at students' journals two or three times during a course in order to focus on change or improvement in their journal writing. In reading entries from the beginning, middle and end of a course, you are able to determine some changes in their writing. Yet without a set of descriptive criteria, it may be difficult to reach any conclusions.

Norm-based versus criterion-based evaluation. In defining your criteria, you need to consider whether they apply to the entire group or to individuals. Imagine one of your classes; you have students with a range of abilities and attitudes, some write a lot in their journal while others write very little, some enjoy journal writing while others do not. In evaluating their journal writing, you may judge each journal relative to group norms—how their writing stacks up against other students' writing. You may evaluate a student's writing as "below"or "above" this group norm. One drawback to norm-based evaluations is that they often perpetuates students' negative self-images. Students who receive "average" or "below average" evaluations may assume that they will always be in the middle or at the bottom of the group. As a "below average" student, they may assume that they are never good enough to be a "good student." And, the "above average" student may assume that they "have it made" and be unmotivated to improve.

In contrast, you may evaluate each student individually, relative to his or her own abilities and attitudes. In adopting a "criterion-based" approach, you are evaluating each student in terms of how much they change over time. You are evaluating students against themselves rather than against the group norm. If students demonstrate marked growth over time, they may then receive a higher evaluation than if they demonstrate little or no change. Sensing that they are no longer competing against the "above average" students, the "below-average" students may now be motivated to change. To make sure that students know you are using a criterion-based approach, you need to tell them that you are evaluating them against themselves, and discuss the criteria with them.

Criteria for Evaluating Journals. For criterion-based evaluation to work, students need to know the criteria which they are evaluated. These criteria should be consistent with your purposes for evaluating writing. If you employ "check plus," "check" or "check minus" categories, you may want to specify criteria associated with each of those categories. You also need to recognize that you get what you ask for. Your criteria therefore need to be consistent with what you asked students to do.

Criteria for evaluating journals may include the ability to:

- *generate a certain number of pages or entries* While this may seem like the "counting approach" we have criticized, you may use it to determine changes in the amount of writing, along with more qualitative criteria.

- *reformulate responses to reading* In responding to course readings, students may simply restate or summarize information as opposed to reformulating that information in their own words—which reflects the degree that they understand the reading.

- *elaborate on responses/perceptions.* You may examine students' ability to elaborate on their responses or perceptions. In responding to a short story, students may describe their reactions to the story, then elaborate by citing reasons for their reactions, noting that they were intrigued by a character because the character reminded them of a close relative. Or they may connect the text to other related texts, describing reasons for the similarities between texts.

- *describe difficulties in understanding.* Students may demonstrate their ability to describe difficulties in understanding a text or experience. The fact that students admit to or define something that they do not understand serves to help them further their thinking.

- *relate entries to previous entries* Students may also demonstrate an ability to define connections between entries. In writing about a certain topic or issue, they may recall a previous related entry, building on a previous idea.

- *reflect on the meaning of texts or experiences* Students may be able to reflect on the meaning of their responses to texts or experience, inferring the larger significance of those responses.

- *reflect on different "voices" in their entries* Students may note that they adopt a range of voices or styles—formal and informal, personal and impersonal—in their entries.

- *reflect on the nature or types of responses employed* Students may also be able to reflect on the nature or types of responses they employ, noting, that they are using more engaging responses.

- *socially interact with partners* In responding to peer dialogue journals, you may also evaluate the quality of the social interaction with partners. You may note the extent to which students acknowledge or invite their partner to respond; their respect for each other's ideas, attitudes and beliefs; and their ability to collaboratively explore topics or ideas.

To use these criteria to evaluate classes, you may provide students with a chart listing the various criteria. For each criterion, you may also include a scale such as "little change," "some change," and "extensive change." Then, when you return students' journals, you can check or circle the descriptor that assesses the extent of change and growth.

None of this should substitute for the value of dialogic, descriptive, reader-based feedback. In the long run, it is this more subjective and free-flowing response that stimulates further thinking. While summative evaluation may provide students with an indication that they have changed, it is frequent formative feedback that actually promotes that change.

Encouraging Self-Evaluation Through Portfolios

Student portfolios have become common enough that some teachers are asking students to include kinds of discourse that are widely different in style, form and content. It is not unexpected that certain types of journal entries serve as the basis for portfolio assessment. In assessing the contributions of journal entries, you will follow many of the same suggestions for assessing journals on their own.

Much of the literature on portfolio assessment emphasizes self-assessment of change over time. By comparing writings in the beginning of a course to those written at the end of a course, students can reflect on ways they have change or improved. In order to foster self-assessment of change, students need to select certain entries, and then describe the writing processes represented in those entries. In addition to general commentary, you might want to guide your students' attention toward some of the following characteristics of their writing:

- reasons for writing
- thought process employed in writing
- value or usefulness of the writing
- contribution of the writing to developing ideas for other texts
- reasons for selecting certain pieces of writing or entries
- ways in which their writing involved taking risks

Once students document changes that did or did not occur from the beginning to the end of a course in their entries, they could then cite reasons for changes or the lack of changes. In our own research on changes in dialogue-journal writing during a ten-week undergraduate linguistics course (Anson & Beach, 1993), we found that, as a group, the students changed in some areas, but not in others. To determine those changes, we analyzed the initial journal entry and then two entries from the beginning, the middle and the end of the course.

The students' entries were categorized in terms of whether or not they were summarizing material, employing narratives or reflecting on the material. There was no consistent pattern of change in the extent to which the students summarized material, employed narratives or reflected on the material. The students were more likely to use their journals to reflect on (75%) than summarize (25%) the course material.

We also categorized whether the entries were "formal" versus "informal" and "unfolding" versus "preplanned." There were consistent shifts in the percentage of students employing these features. In the beginning of the course, 72% of the journals were categorized as "formal," as compared to 28% informal. By the end of the course, the percentages were about equal. There was a slight increase in the percentage of students whose entries were categorized as "unfolding" as opposed to "preplanned," from 76% to 81%. Over time, the students shifted to using a more informal, exploratory approach.

However, focusing on change assumes that change or improvement occurs in a continuous, linear pattern. It assumes that students will make marked changes in their writing in a relatively short period of time. In his discussion of portfolios, Jeffrey Sommers, drawing on Knoblauch and Brannon, notes that teachers hold to a "myth of improvement." While different pieces of writing may reflect "symptoms of growth" (Knoblauch & Brannon, 1992, p. 169), it may be difficult to compare earlier and later work. Writings from different times in a course may deal with topics or texts and may represent quite different modes or genres. In comparing apples and oranges, it may be difficult to discern a clear direction of improvement.

It has also become common practice for students to select writing that they find to be most versus least satisfying to include in their final "showcase portfolio" (Tierney, Carter, & Desai, 1991). In order to judge what is most versus least satisfying, students need to discern a norm across their writing according to which they assess their writing. When students are comparing apples and oranges, it may be difficult to discern a norm. While it it important for students to be able to note their strengths and weaknesses, it may also be asking students to create a norm based on quite different kinds of writing.

Thus, in addition to determining improvement or to determining a norm, we propose that students also compare their entries to determine differences between their writings. They may note differences in their beliefs and attitudes or in their degree of interest in a topic. By making these comparisons, students may recognize their own complexities, inviting them to explore their own ambivalences. Students may then consider possible reasons for their ambivalences, reasons related to membership in different communities.

Comparison with others' responses. As Haswell suggests, in order to achieve a sense of alienation from one's own beliefs, students need to experience alternative perspectives that serve to challenge their own perspective. As part of their portfolio assessment, students might compare their own responses with others' responses that represent different stances and value assumptions. If students have been exchanging journal entries with partners, they may compare their own and their partner's responses. Or, they may compare their responses with other students in the class or published responses. These comparisons may lead students to critically examine their own beliefs, assumptions or prejudices. Through these comparison, students may, in the words of Don Bialostosky (1989), "keep talking to themselves and to one another, discovering their affinities without resting in them and clarifying their differences without resolving them" (p. 224).

References

Abbott, H. P. (1984). *Diary fiction: Writing as action.* Ithaca, NY: Cornell University Press.

Anderson, P., & Rubano, G. (1992). *Enhancing aesthetic reading and response.* Urbana, IL: National Council of Teachers of English.

Anson, C. M. (1988). Book lists, cultural literacy and the stagnation of discourse. *English Journal, 77,* 14–18.

Anson, C. M., & Beach, R. (1989). *Characteristics of effective versus less effective dialogue Journals.* Paper presented at the Annual Conference of the National Council of Teachers of English, Baltimore.

Anson, C. M., & Beach, R. (in press). Argument in peer dialogue Journals. In D. Berrill (Ed.). *Perspectives in argument.* Cresskill, NJ: Hampton Press.

Anson, C. M., Maylath, B., & Loupe, M. J. (1991). Using writing to assess skills in scientific inquiry. *Notes from the National Testing Network in Writing, 10,* 13–14.

Anson, C. M., Schwiebert, J. E., & Williamson, M. M. (1993). *Writing across the curriculum: An annotated biliography.* Westport, CT: Greenwood Press.

Anson, C. M., & Wilcox, L. E. (1987). Writing in context. New York: Holt Rinehart & Wintson.

Applebee, A. (1991). *Literature in the Secondary School.* Urbana, IL: National Council of Teachers of English.

Applebee, A., et. al. (1994). *NAEP 1992 writing report card.* Washington, DC: Office of Educational Research and Improvement.

Aronson, A. (1991). *Studies in twentieth-century diaries: The concealed self.* Lewiston, NY: Edwin Mellen Press.

Bahktin, M. (1981). *The dialogic imagination: Four essays.* Austin: University of Texas Press.

Baldwin, C. (1991). *Life's companion: Journal writing as a spiritual quest.* New York: Bantam.

Beach, R. (1990a). The creative development of meaning: Using autobiographical experiences to interpret literature. In D. Bodgan & S. Straw (Eds.), *Beyond Communication* (pp. 211–236). Portsmouth, NH: Boynton/Cook.

Beach, R. (1990b). Evaluating writing to learn: Responding to Journals. In B. Lawson, S. Ryan, & W. R. Winterowd (Eds.), *Encountering student texts* (pp. 183–198). Urbana, IL: National Council of Teachers of English.

Beach, R. (1991). *Tenth graders' exploration of tensions and contradictions in story writing and literary responses.* (ERIC Document Reproduction Service No. ED 335 672)

Beach, R. (in press). Evaluating students' writing about literature. In C. Cooper & L. Odell (Eds.), *Evaluating Writing: The second edition.* Urbana, IL: National Council of Teachers of English.

Beach, R., & Anson, C. M. (1993). Using peer dialogue Journals to foster literary response. In G. Newell & R. Durst (Eds.), *Exploring texts: The role of discussions and writing in the teaching and learning of literature* (pp. 191–210). Norwood, MA: Christopher Gordon.

Beach, R., & Anson, C. M. (1988). The pragmatics of memo writing: Developmental differences in the use of rhetorical strategies. *Written Communication,* 57–83.

Beach, R., & Marshall, J. (1991). Teaching literature in the secondary school. Orlando: Harcourt Brace Jovanovich.

Belanoff, P. (1991). Freewriting: An Aid to rereading theorists. In P. Belanoff, P. Elbow, & S. Fontaine (Eds.), *Nothing begins with N: New investigations of freewriting* (pp. 16–31). Carbondale, IL: Southern Illinois University Press.

Belanoff, P., & Dickson, M. (Eds.) (1991). *Portfolios: Process and product.* Portsmouth, NH: Heinemann.

Bennett, T., & Woollacott, J. (1987). *Bond and beyond: The political career of a popular hero.* New York: Methuen.

Bereiter, C., & Scardamelia, M. (1987). *The psychology of written communication.* Hillsdale, NJ: Erlbaum.

Berlin, J. (1988). Rhetoric and ideology in the writing class. *College English,* 477–494.

Berthoff, A. (1981). *The making of meaning: Metaphors, models, and maxims for writing.* Upper Montclaire, NJ: Boynton/Cook.

Bialostosky, D. (1989). Dialogic criticism. In D. Atkins & L. Morrow (Eds.), *Contemporary literary theory* (pp. 214–228). Amherst: University of Massachusetts Press.

Bishop, W. (1990). "Traveling through the dark": Teachers and students reading and writing together. *Reader,* 1–20.

Bleich, D. (1978). *Readings and feelings.* Urbana, IL: National Council of Teachers of English.

Bleich, D. (1988). *The double perspective: Language, literacy, and social relations.* New York: Oxford University Press.

Bloome, D., Puro, P., & Theadoreu, E. (1989). Procedural display and classroom lessons. *Curriculum Inquiry,* 265–91.

Bolin, F. (1988). Helping student teachers think about teaching. *Journal of Teacher Education,* 48–53.

Bourman, A (1990). *Meeting of minds: Writing, discussion, and research activities.* Tucson, AZ: Zephyr Press.

Brandt, D. (1990). *Literacy as involvement: The acts of writers, readers, and texts.* Carbondale, IL: Southern Illinois University Press.

Brent, D. (1992). *Reading as rhetorical invention.* Urbana, IL: National Council of Teachers of English.

Britton, J. (1977). *The development of writing abilities.* London: Macmillan, 11–18.

Britzman, D. (1991). *Practice makes practice: A critical study of learning to teach.* Albany, NY: State University of New York Press.

Brooke, R. (1991). *Writing and sense of self: Identity negotiation in writing workshops.* Urbana, IL: National Council of Teachers of English.

Bruce, B., & Rubin, A. (1993). *Electronic quills.* Hillsdale, NJ: Erlbaum.

Bruner, J. (1986). *Actual minds, Possible worlds.* Cambridge, MA: Harvard University Press.

Buckingham, D. (1987). *Public secrets: "Eastenders" and its audience.* London: BFI.

Burke, K. (1969). *A rhetoric of motives.* Berkeley: University of California Press.

Calkins, L (1991). *Living between the lines.* Portsmouth, NH: Heinemann.

Cassagrande, L. (1991). Methods for conducting ethnography research. Paper presented at the University of Minnesota.

Chang, H. (1992). *Adolescent life and ethos: An ethnography of a US high school.* Bristol, PA: Falmer Press.

Clark, G. (1990). *Dialogue, dialectic, and conversation.* Carbondale: Southern Illinois University Press.

Clift, R., Houston, W. R., & Pugach, M. (Eds.) (1990). *Encouraging reflective practice in education.* New York: Teachers College Press.

Collins, A., Brown, J., & Larkin, K. (1980). Inference in text understanding. In R. Spiro, B. Bruce, & W. Brewer (Eds.), *Theoretical issues in reading comprehension* (pp. 385–407). Hillsdale, NJ: Erlbaum.

Connors, R., & Lundsford, A. (1993). Teachers' rhetorical comments on student papers. *College Composition and Communication,* 200–3.

Cooper, J. (1992). Using Journals to Teach Multicultural Students on Interactive Television. In T. Hilgers, M. Wunsch, & V. Chattergy (Eds.), *Academic Literacies in Multicultural Higher Education* (pp. 145–149). Manoa, Hawaii: Center for Studies of Multicultural Higher Education, University of Hawaii.

Cooper, L. (1990). On the teaching of written composition. *Education,* 421–430.

Crusius, T. (1991). *A teacher's introduction to philosophical hermeneutics.* Urbana, IL: National Council of Teachers of English.

Csikszentmihalyi, M., & Larson, R. (1984). *Being adolescent: conflict and growth in the teenage years.* New York: Basic.

Culley, M., (Ed.) (1985). *A Day at a time:The diary literature of American women from 1764 to the present.* NewYork: The Feminist Press.

Daiute, C. (1993).Youth genres and literacy: links between sociocultural and developmental theories. *Language Arts,* 402–416.

Davidson, D. (1984). *Inquires into truth and interpretation.* Oxford, England:Claredon.

de la Luz Reyes, M. (1991).A process approach to literacy using dialogue Journals and literature logs with second language learners. *Research in theTeaching of English,* 291–313.

Delpit, L. (1988).The silenced dialogue: Power and pedagogy in educating other people's children. *Harvard Educational Review,* 280–299.

Dillard, A. (1987).To fashion a text. In W. Zinsser (Ed.), *Inventing the truth:The art and craft of memoir* (pp. 3–76). Boston: Houghton Mifflin.

Dillon, G. (1991). *Contending rhetorics.* Bloomington, IN: Indiana University Press.

Dorris, M. (1988). *A yellow raft in blue water.* NewYork:Warner.

Duckworth, E. (1992), March). Wanted: Deep understanding. *ASCD Update,* 34, 3–6.

Dyson, A. H. (1989). *Multiple worlds of child writers.* NewYork:Teachers College Press.

Eckert, P. (1989). *Jocks and burnouts.* New York:Teachers College Press.

Education Commission of the States (1981). *Reading, thinking, and writing.* Denver: National Assessment of Eduicational Progress.

Edwards, H. (1992, January). Class notes. *Notes Plus,* 7, 8.

Edwards, P. (1992). Using dialectical Journals to teach thinking skills. *Journal of Reading, 35,* 312–16.

Elbow, P. (1973). *Writing without teachers.* NewYork: Oxford University Press.

Elbow, P. (1981). *Writing with power.* NewYork: Oxford University Press.

Elbow, P. (1989). Toward a phenomenology of freewriting. *Journal of Basic Writing, 8,* 42–71.

Elbow, P. (1993). Ranking, evaluating, and liking: Sorting out three forms of judgment. *College English, 55,* 187–206.

Elkind, D. (1981). The hurried child. Reading, MA: Addison-Wesley.

Emig, J. (1977).Writing as a mode of learning. *College Composition and Communication, 28,* 122–128.

Faigley, L (1993). *The fragments of rationality:Writing in a postmodern age.* Pittsburgh, PA: University of Pittsburgh Press.

Farley, J. (1986). An analysis of written language of educable mentally retarded students. *Education and Training of the Mentally Retarded,* 99–106.

Fine, G. A. (1987). *With the boys: Little League baseball and preadolescent culture.* University of Chicago Press.

Fine, M. (1990). *"Framing" dropouts: Notes on the politics of an urban high school.* Albany: State University of New York Press.

Fishman (1993). Interaction:The work women do. In B.Thorne, C. Kramarae, & N. Henley (Eds.), Language, gender, and society (pp. 89–102). Rowley, MA: Newbury.

Fiske, J. (1989). *Reading the popular.* Boston: Hyman.

Fleisher, C. (1992). In J. Berlin & M.Vivion (Eds.), *Cultural studies in the English classroom* (pp.182–199). Portsmouth, NH: Boyton/Cook.

Flynn, E. (1983). Gender and reading. *College English,* 45, 236–253.

Fox, T. (1990). *The social uses of writing: Politics and pedagogy.* Norwood, NJ: Ablex.

Freiberg, H. J., &Waxman, H. (1990). Reflection and the acquisition of technical teaching skills. In R. Clift, R. Houston, & M. Pugach (Eds.), *Encouraging reflective practice in education* (pp. 119–138). New York: Teachers College Press.

Fulkerson, R. P. (1979). Four philosophies of composition. *College Composition and Communication,* 343–48.

Fulwiler,T. (1989). Responding to student Journals. In C. Anson (Ed.), *Writing and response: Theory, practice, and research* (pp. 149–173). Urbana, IL: National Council of Teachers of English.

Fulwiler, T, ed. (1987). *The Journal book.* Portsmouth, HH: Boynton/Cook.

Gannett, C. (1992). *Gender and the Journal: Diaries and academic discourse.* Albany: State University of New York Press.

Gardner, H. (1985). *Frames of mind: The theory of multiple intelligences.* New York: Basic Books.

Gee, J. P. (1992). *The social mind: Language, ideology, and social practice.* New York: Bergin and Garvey.

Geisler, C. (1991). Reader, parent, coach: Defining the profession by our practice of response. *Reader, 25,* 17–33.

Glesne, C., & Peshkin, A. (1992). *Becoming qualitative researchers: An introduction.* New York: Longman.

Goodlad (1984). *A place called school.* New York: McGraw-Hill.

Gordon, C. (1991). *The effects of teachers' comments on students' Journal writing.* Doctoral dissertation, University of Minnesota.

Greenhalgh , A. (1992). Voices in response: A postmodern reading of teacher response. *College Composition and Communication, 43,* 401–410.

Halliday, M. (1979). *Language as a social semiotic.* London: Edward Arnold.

Halpern, D. (Ed.) (1988). *Our private lives: Journal, notebooks, and diaries.* New York: Vintage, 332–351.

Hancock, M. (1993). Character Journals: Initiating involvement and identification through literature. *Journal of Reading,* 42–50.

Handa, C. (Ed.) (1993). *Computer and community.* Urbana, IL: National Council of Teachers of English.

Hassam, A. (1992). *Writing and reality: A study of modern British diary fiction.* New York: Greenwood Press.

Haswell, R. (1991). *Gaining ground in college writing: Tales of development and interpretation.* Dallas: Southern Methodist University Press.

Haswell, R. (1991). Bound forms in freewriting: The issue organization. In P. Belanoff, P. Elbow, & S. Fontaine (Eds.), *Nothing begins with N: New investigations of freewriting* (pp. 32–70). Carbondale, IL: Southern Illinois University Press.

Hayes, D. (1989). Helping students GRASP the knack of writing summaries. *Journal of Reading,* 96–101.

Heath, S. B. (1983). Ways with words: Language, life, and work in communities and classroom. Cambridge: Cambridge University Press.

Hillocks, G. (1986). *Research on written composition: New directions for teaching.* Urbana, IL: National Conference on Research in English.

Hirsch, E. D., Jr. (1987). *Cultural literacy.* Boston: Houghton Mifflin.

Hirsch, E. D., Jr. (1988). Cultural literacy. *American Scholar, spring,* 159–169.

Holly, M. L. (1984). *Keeping a personal-professional Journal.* Geelong, Australia: Deakin University Press.

Hunt, R. (1989). A horse named Hans, a boy named Shawn: The Herr von Osten theory of response to writing. In C. Anson (Ed.)., *Writing and response: Theory, practice, and research* (pp. 80–102). Urbana, IL: National Council of Teachers of English.

Hunt, R. (1993). Texts, textoids and utterances: Writing and reading for meaning, in and out of the classroom. In S. Straw & D. Bogdan (Eds.), *Constructive reading: Teaching beyong communication* (pp.113–129). Portsmouth, NH: Boyton/Cook.

Hynds, S. (1994). *Making connections: Language and learning in the classroom.* Norwood, MA: Christopher Gordon.

Jackson, R. (1992). The untapped power of student note writing. *Educational Leadership,* 54–58.

Jenkins, H. (1992). *Textual poachers: Television fans and participatory culture.* New York: Routledge.

Johnson, S., & Hoover, J. (1989). Using dialogue Journals with secondary learning disabled students. *Academic Therapy,* 75–80.

Johnston, B. (1983). *Assessing English.* Urbana, IL: National Council of Teachers of English.

Johnstone, A. (1993). *Uses for Journal-keeping: An ethnography of writing in a university science class.* Norwood, NJ: Ablex.

Jordan, S., & Purves, A. (1993). *Issues in the responses of students to culturally diverse texts: A preliminary study.* Albany, NY: Center on Literature Teaching & Learning.

Kennedy, M. L. (1985). The composing processes of college students writing from sources. *Written Communication,* 434–457.

Knight, J. E. (1990). Coding Journal entries. *Journal of Reading,* 42–47.

Knoblach, C., & Brannon, L. (1992). *Critical teaching and the idea of literacy.* Portsmouth, NH: Heinemann.

Kooy, M. (1992). *Responding to literature in the Journal.* Paper presented at the meeting of the National Confernce on Reading, San Antonio, Texas.

Kroll, B. M. (1980). Developmental perspectives and the teaching of composition. *College English,* 741–752.

Kroll, B. M. (1990). Teaching English for reflective thinking. In R. Beach & S. Hydes (Eds.), *Developing disourse practices in adolescence and adulthood* (pp.287–317). Norwood, NJ: Ablex.

Kroll, B. M. (1992). Teaching hearts and minds: College students reflect on the Vietnam War in literature. Carbondale, IL: Southern Illinois University Press.

Labov, W. (1972). *Language in the inner city.* Philadelphia: University of Pennsylvania Press.

Lakoff, G. & Johnson, M. (1980). *Metaphors we live by.* Chicago: University of Chicago Press.

Langer, J. (1989). *The process of understanding literature.* Albany, New York: Center for the Study of Teaching and Learning of Literature.

Langer, J. & Applebee, A. (1987). *How writing shapes meaning.* Urbana, IL: National Council of Teachers of English.

Lewis, O. (1979). *Children of Sanchez.* New York: Random House.

Lindberg, G. (1987). The Journal conference: From dialectic to dialogue. In T. Fulwiler (Ed.), *The Journal book* (pp. 119–128). Portsmouth, NH: Boynton Cook.

Litowitz, B., & Gundlach, R. (1987). When adolescents write: Semiotic and social dimensions of adolescents' personal writing. *Adolescent Psychology,* 82–111.

Lowenstein, S. S. (1982). *The personal Journal—journal keeper relationship as experienced by the Journal keeper: A phenomenological and theoretical investigation.* Unpublished doctoral dissertation, Boston University.

Lunsford, A. (1988, April). Reassessing assessment: Challenges to the tradition of testing. Sixth Annual Conference on Writing Assessment, Minneapolis, MN.

Lytle, S. (1982). *Exploring comprehension style: A study of twelfth-grade readers' transactions with text.* Doctoral dissertation, Stanford University.

Marland, M. (1977). *Language across the curriculum.* London: Heinemann Educational Books.

Marshall, J. (1989). *Patterns of discourse in classroom discussions of literature.* Albany, NY: Center for the Learning and Teaching of Literature.

Marshall, J. (1990). Writing and reasoning about literature. In R. Beach & S. Hynds (Eds.), *Developing discourse practices in adolescence and adulthood* (pp. 161–182.). Norwood, NJ: Ablex.

Martin, N. (1983). *Mostly about writing.* Upper Montclair, NJ: Boynton/Cook.

Mass, J. O. Writing and reflection in teacher education. In B. R. Tabachnick & K. Zeichner (Eds.), *Issues and practices in inquiry-oriented teacher education* (pp. 211–225). Philadelphia: Falmer Press.

McCormick, K (1990). The cultural imperatives underlying cognitive acts. In L. Flower, V. Stein, J. Ackerman, M. Kantz, K. McCormick, and W. Peck (Eds.), *Reading-to-write* (pp. 210–235). New York: Oxford University Press.

McKibben, B. (1992). *The age of missing information.* New York: Random House.

Mead, M. (1930). *Growing up in New Guinea.* New York: Morrow.

Meltzer, M. (1994). *Nonfiction in the classroom.* New York: Teachers College Press.

Miller, J. T. L. (1990). *Creating spaces and finding voices: Teachers collaborating for empowerment.* Albany, NY: State University of New York Press.

Moffett, J. (1987). *Active voices II.* Portsmouth, NH: Boynton/Cook.

Moffett, J. (1987). *Active voices III.* Portsmouth, NH: Boynton/Cook.

Morrison, T. (1973). *Sula*. New York: New American Library.

Mosenthal, P. (1983). On defining writing and classroom writing competence. In P. Mosenthal, L. Tamor, & S. A. Walmsley (Eds.), Research on writing: *Principles and methods* (pp. 26–71). New York: Longman.

Moss, G. (1989). *Un/popular fictions*. London: Virago.

Murray, D. (1985). *A writer teaches writing* (2nd ed.). Houghton Mifflin.

Myers, G. (1986). Reality, consensus, and reform in the rhetoric of composition teaching. *College English,* 154–174.

Newell, G., Suszynski K., & Weingart, R. (1989). The effects of writing in a reader-based and text-based mode on students' understanding of two short stories. *Journal of Reading Behavior,* 37–57.

Newman, J. (1988). Sharing Journals: Conversational mirrors for seeing ourselves as learners, writers, and teachers. *English Education,* 134–156.

Newton, E. (1991). Developing metacognitive awareness: The response Journal in college composition. *Journal of Reading,* 476–478.

Noddings, N. (1991). Stories in dialogue. In C. Witherell & N. Noddings (Eds.), *Stories lives tell* (pp. 157–170). New York: Teachers College Press.

Nynstrand, M. (1992, April). *Dialogic instruction and conceptual change*. Paper presented at the annual meeting of the American Educational Research Association, San Fransisco.

Nystrand, M., & Gamaron, A. (1991). Instructional discourse, student achievment, and literature achievement. *Research in the Teaching of English,* 261–290.

Oates, J. C. (1991). Excerpts from a Journal. In R. Pack & J. Parini (Eds.), *Writers on writing* (pp. 162–174). Hanover, NH: University Press of New England.

Parsons, L. (1990). *Response Journals*. Portsmouth, NH: Heinemann.

Perl, S. (1980). Understanding composing. *College Composition and Communication, 31,* 363–369.

Perry, W. (1970). *Forms of intellectual and ethical development in the college years.* New York: Holt, Rinehart and Winston.

Peyton, J. K., & Staton J. (1993). *Dialogue Journals in the multilingual classroom: Building language fluency and writing skills through writing interaction.* Norwood, NJ: Ablex.

Peyton, J. K., & Seyoum M. (1989). The effect of teacher strategies on students' interactive writing: The case of dialogue Journals. *Research in the Teaching of English,* 310–34.

Peshkin, A. (1991). *The color of strangers, the color of friends: The play of ethnicity in school and community.* Chicago: University of Chicago Press.

Phelps, L. (1988). *Composition as a human science.* Oxford: Oxford University Press.

Pinkston, J. W. (1989). Thoreau and current trends in the teaching of writing. *English Journal,* 50–52.

Powell, A., Farrar, E. & Cohen, D. (1986). *The shopping mall high school.* Boston: Houghton Mifflin.

Rainer, T. (1978). *The new diary.* Los Angeles: Jeremy Tarcher.

Recchio, T. (1991). A Bakhtinian reading of student writing. *College Composition and Communication,* 446–454.

Robertson, I. (1980). *Language across the curriculum: Four case studies.* London: Methuen Educational.

Rogers, A. G. (1993). Voices, play, and a practice of ordinary courage in girls and womens lives. *Harvard Educational Review,* 265–95.

Rose, M., ed. (1985). *When a wrter can't write.* New York: Guilford.

Rosenblatt, L. (1994). *The reader, the text, the poem* (2nd ed). Carbondale, IL: Southern Illinois University Press.

Rosenblatt, P. (1991). *Bitter, bitter tears: Nineteenth-century diarists and twentieth-century grief theories.* Minneapolis: University of Minnesota Press.

Rubin, D. (1993). *Gender influences: Reading student texts.* Carbondale, IL: Southern Illinois University Press.

Ruddell, M. (1993, December). *Researching literacy from the inside out.* Paper presented at the meeting of the Naitonal Reading Conference, San Antonio.

Salvatori, M. (1989). Pedagogy: From the periphery to the center. In P. Donahue & E. Quandahl (Eds.), *Reclaiming pedagogy* (pp. 17–24). Carbondale: Southern Illlinois University Press.

Sarton, M. (1973). *Journal of a solitude*. New York: Norton.

Saussure, F. (1959). *Course in general linguistics*. Eds. C. Bully, A. Sechehage., & A. Reidlinger. Trans. W. Baskin. New York: McGraw-Hill.

Schatzberg-Smith, K. (1988). *Dialogue Journal writing and the study habits and attitudes of underprepared college students*. Doctoral dissertation, Hofstra University.

Schon, D. (1987). *Educating the reflective practitioner*. San Fransico: Jossey-Bass.

Scott, F. N. (1926). *The standard of American speech and other papers*. Boston: Allyn and Bacon.

Scott, J. C., Davis, W., & Walker, A. (1989, November/December). A picture is worth a thousand words: The visual-print connection. Dialogue: *Arts in the Midwest*, 20–22.

Segal, E. S. (1990). The Journal: Teaching reflexive methlogy on an introductory level. *Anthropology and Education Quarterly*, 121–127.

Selfe, C. (1992). Computer-based conversations and the changing nature of collaboration. In In J. Gorman (Ed.), *New visions of collaborative writing* (pp. 147–169). Portsmouth, NH: Boynton/Cook.

Selfe, C., & Meyers, P. (1991). Testing claims for on-line conferences. *Written Communication*, 163–92.

Shaughnessy, M. (1977). *Errors and expectations: A guide for the teacher of basic writing*. New York: Oxford University Press.

Shuman, A. (1986). *Storytelling rights: The uses of oral and written texts by urban adolescents*. Cambridge: Cambridge University Press.

Shuy, R. (1988). The oral basis of written language acquisition. In J. Stanton, R. Shuy, J. Peyton, & L. Reed (Eds.), *Dialogue Journal Communication* (pp. 73–87). Norwood, NJ: Ablex.

Simons, J. (1990). *Diaries and Journals of literary women from Fanny Burney to Virginia Woolf*. Iowa City: University of Iowa Press.

Sizer, T. (1984). *Horace's compromise: The dilemma of the American high school*. Boston: Houghton Miffin.

Smith, J. (1991). Setting the cat among the pigeons: A not so sentimental Journal to the heart of teaching. *English Education*, 68–126.

Sommers, J. (1993). Grading student writing: An Experiment and a commentary. *Teaching English in the Two-Year College*, 263–274.

Spires, H., & Stone, P. D. (1989). The directed notetaking activity: A self-questioning approach. *Journal of Reading*, 36–39.

Staton, J., Shuy, R., Peyton. J., & Reed, L. (Eds.) (1988). *Dialogue Journal Communication*. Norwood, NJ: Ablex.

Steig, W. (1989). *Stories of reading*. Baltimore: Johns Hopkins University Press.

Steiner, B., & Phillips, K. (1991). *Journal keeping with young people*. Englewood, CO: Teacher Idea Press.

Sullivan, A. M. (1989). Liberating the urge to write: From classroom Journals to lifelong writing. *English Journal*, 55–61.

Tannen, D. (1986). *That's not what I meant*. New York: William Morrow.

Tannen, D. (1990). *You just don't understand: Women and men in conversation*. New York: William Morrow.

Thompson, J. (1987). *Understanding teenage readers*. Melbourne: Methuen.

Tierney, R., Carter, M., & Desai, L. (1991). *Portfolio assessment in the reading-writing classroom*. Norwood, MA: Christopher-Gordon.

Ueland, B (1987). *If you want to write*. St. Paul, MN: Graywolf Press.

VanDeWeghe, R. (1987). Making and remaking meaning: developing literary responses through purposeful, informal writing.. *English Quarterly*, 38–51.

Vipond, D., & Hunt, R. (1984). Point-driven understanding: Pragmatic and cognitive dimensions of literary reading. *Poetics, 13*, 261–272.

Wells, M. C (1992). At the junction of reading and writing: How dialogue Journals contribute to students' reading development. *Journal of Reading*, 294–302.

Werkenthin, K. (1992). Following the paths of Thoreau and Dillard. *English Journal*, 26–29.

Wertsch, J. (1991). *Voices of the mind: A sociocultural approach to mediated actions.* Cambridge: Harvard University Press.

White, B. (1990). *Writing before reading: Its effects upon discussion and understanding of text.* Doctoral Dissertation, University of Wisconsin, Madison.

White, E. (1992). The damage of innovations set adrift. *AAHE Bulletin,* 3–5.

Willis, P. (1977). *Learning to labor.* New York: Columbia University Press.

Witte, S. (1992). Context, text, intertext: Toward a constructivist semiotic of writing. *Written Communication,* 237–308.

Workman, B. (1975). *Teaching the decades.* Urbana, IL: National Council of Teachers of English.

Yinger, R., & Clark, C. (1981). *Reflective Journal writing: Theory and practice.* East Lansing, MI: Institute for Research on Teaching.

Young, R., Becker, A., & Pike, K. (1970). *Rhetoric: Discovery and change.* New York: Harcourt, Brace.

Additional Readings

Abercrombie, B. (1991). Keeping a journal. *The Writer*, 104, 12–14.

Arksey, L., Pries, N., & Reed, M. (Eds.) (1987). *American diaries: An annotated bibliography of published American diaries and journals, ll: Diaries written from 1845 to 1980.* Detroit: Gale.

Atherton, C., Joyner, S., Pender, N., Ryerson, F., & Young, S. (1992). Keeping math journals. In *Instructor* (pp. 46–47).

Autrey, K. (1991). The convergence of dichotomies in the personal journal. In K. Ronald & H. Roskelly (Eds.), *Farther along: Transforming dichotomies in rhetoric and composition* (pp. 40–51). Portsmouth, NH: Boynton/ Cook.

Autrey, K. (1991). Toward a rhetoric of journal writing. *Rhetoric Review*, *10*(1), 74–90.

Begos, J. D. (1977). *Annotated bibliography of published women's diaries.* Pound Ridge, NY: Begos.

Blanton, W. E., & Moorman, G. B. (1993). A diary as a tool for mediating reading teacher activity. *Reading Research and Instruction, 32*(4), 76–89.

Bode, B. A. (1989). Dialogue journal writing. *The Reading Teacher*, 568–571.

Bodmer, P. (1991). The reader's notebook: A tool for thinking. *Teaching English in the Two-Year College, 18*(1), 10–17.

Bowman, R. F., Jr. (1983). The personal student journal: Mirror of the mind. *Contemporary Education, 55*(1), 25–27.

Bradshaw, S. P. (1990). The effects of personal journal writing on irrational beliefs, internal locus-of-control, self-deception, and private self-consciousness. *Dissertation Abstracts International, 51*(6).

Browning, N. F. (1986). Journal writing: One assignment does more than improve reading, writing, and thinking. *Journal of Reading, 60*(1), 39–44.

Bunce-Crim, M. (1992). Use your writing to teach. *Instructor, 101*, 12.

Cameron, S. (1989). *Writing nature: Henry Thoreau's journal.* Chicago: University of Chicago Press.

Cline, C. (1989). *Women's diaries, journals, and letters: an annotated bibliography.* New York: Garland.

Cooper, J. E. (1991). Telling our own stories. In C. Witherell & N. Noddings (Eds.), *Stories lives tell* (pp. 96–112). New York: Teachers College Press.

Corbett, W. (1983). Journal poetics. In M. Palmer (Ed.), *Code of signals: Recent writing in poetics* (pp. 158–165). Berkeley: North Atlantic.

Crepps, S. (1993). Journal, what journal? *Quarterly of the National Writing Project and the Center for the Study of Writing and Literacy, 15*(2), 7–9.

Danielson, K. E. (1988). *Dialogue journals: Writing as conversation.* Bloomington, IN: Phi Delta Kappa Educational Foundation.

Davis, F. A. (1983). Why you call me emigrant? Dialogue journal writing with migrant youth. *Childhood Education, 60*(2), 110–116.

Davis, F. A. (1983). "Why you call me emigrant?" Dialogue-journal writing with migrant youth. *Childhood Education, 60*(2), 110–111, 114–116.

Dehler, K. (1989). Diaries: Where women reveal themselves. *English Journal, 78*(7), 53–54.

DeNisi, A. S., Robbins, T., & Cafferty, T. P. (1989). Organization of information used for performance appraisals: Role of diary-keeping. *Journal of Applied Psychology, 74*, 124–129.

Field, T. (1989). *Form and function in the diary novel.* Totowa, NJ: Barnes & Noble.

Fishman, A. R., & Raver, E. J. (1989). Maybe I'm just NOT teacher material: Dialogue journals in the student teaching experience. *English Education, 21*(2), 92–109.

Flitterman-King, S. (1988). The role of the response journal in active reading.

Quarterly of the National Writing Project and the Center for the Study of Writing, 10(3), 4–11.

Gambrell, L. B. (1985). Dialogue journals: Reading-writing interaction. *The Reading Teacher, 38,* 512–515.

Gillespie, J. S. (1993). Buddy book journals: Responding to literature. *English Journal, 82(6),* 64–68.

Goldman, L., Flood, J., & Lapp, D. (1992). In *Journal writing between third & sixth grade students* (pp. 1–8). Paper presented at National Reading Conference.

Hall, E. G. (1990). Strategies for using journal writing in counseling gifted students. *Gifted Child Today, 13*(4), 2–6.

Hamilton, C. (1991). *The Hitler diaries: Fakes that fooled the world.* Lexington, KY: University Press of Kentucky.

Hancock, M. R. (1992). Literature response journals: Insights beyond the printed page. *Language Arts, 69*(1), 36–42.

Hassam, A. (1987). Reading other people's diaries. *University of Toronto Quarterly: A Canadian Journal of the Humanities (UTQ), 56*(3), 435–442.

Hassam, A. (1993). *Writing and reality: A study of modern British diary fiction.* Westport, CT: Greenwood Press.

Havlice, P. P. (1987). *And so to bed: A bibliography of diaries published in English.* Metuchen, NJ: Scarecrow Press.

Havlice, P. P. (1987). *And so to bed: A bibliography of diaries published in English.* Metuchen, NJ: Scarecrow Press.

Hedlund, D. E. (1989). A dialogue with self: The journal as an educational tool. *Journal of Humanistic Education and Development, 27*(3), 105–113.

Hoagland, E. (1989). A writer's journal. *Harper's Magazine, 278,* 30–31.

Hoffman, S. (1983). Using student journals to teach study skills. *Journal of Reading, 26*(4), 344–347.

Hogan, R. (1986). Selected bibliography of books and articles on diaries and related subjects: Selected sources on women's diaries. *Auto/Biography Studies, 2*(2), 1–6.

Holland, R. M., Jr. (1989). Anonymous journals is literature survey courses. *TETYC,* 236–241.

Holliday, L. (1978). *Heart songs: The intimate diaries of young girls.* Guerneville, CA: Bluestocking Books.

Huot, B., & Williamson, M. M. (1989). The journal as an adjunct for teaching basic writers. *RTDE, 6*(1), 71–80.

Ioffe, G. (1993). From Russia with journals: Writing enhances dialogue in seminars. *College Teaching, 41*(3), 112–116.

Jeffords, S. (1991). Tattoos, scars, diaries, and writing masculinity. *The Vietnam war and American culture.* New York: Columbia University Press, 208–225.

Jenkinson, E. (1994). *Writin g assignments, Journals, and student privacy. ERIC digest.* Bloomington, IN: ERIC Clearinghouse on Reading, English, and Communication, Indiana University. (ERIC Document Reproduction Service No. ED 365 989).

Kadar, M. (Ed.) (1993). *Reading life writing: An anthology.* Toronto: Oxford University Press.

Keighron, P. (1993). Video diaries: What's up doc? *Sight and Sound, 3*(10), 24–25.

Kemper, S. (1990). Adults' diaries: Changes made to written narratives across the life span. *Discourse Processes: A Multidisciplinary Journal, 13*(2), 207–224.

Kirk, B. V. (1989). Dialogue journals: A technique to strengthen ethnic pride and achievement. *Journal of American Indian Education, 29*(1), 19–25.

Latta, B. (1991). In process and retrospective journals: Putting writers back in writing processes. *English Journal, 80.*

Latta, B. D. (1991). In-process and retrospective journals: Putting writers back in writing processes. *English Journal, 80,* 60–66.

Leacock, E. B., Rothschild, N. A., & Loring, S. (Eds.) (1994). *Labrador winter: The ethnographic journals of William Duncan Strong, 1927–1928.* Washington, DC: Smithsonian Institution Press.

Mallon, T. (1984). *A book of one's own: People and their diaries.* New York: Ticknor & Fields.

Martens, L. (1985). *The diary novel.* Cambridge (Cambridgeshire); New York: Cambridge University Press.

McDonough, J. (1994). A teacher looks at teachers' diaries. *ELT Journal, 48*(1), 57–65.

Mett, C. L. (1989). Writing in mathematics. *The Clearing House, 62,* 293–296.

Milner, M. B. (1986). *An experiment in leisure.* London: Virago.

Milner, M. B. (1987). *Eternity's sunrise: A way of keeping a diary.* London: Virago.

Morrison, M. C. (1982). *The journal and the journey.* Wallingford, PA: Pendle Hill Publications.

National Clearinghouse on Literacy Educaiton (1991). *Dialogue Journal Bibliography.* Washington, DC: Center for Applied Linguistics.

Newman, J. M. (1988). Sharing journals: Conversational mirrors for seeing ourselves as learners, writers, and teachers. *English Education, 20*(3), 134–156.

Oberg, A. (1990). Methods and meanings in action research: The action research journal. *Theory Into Practice, 29*(3), 214–221.

Pennebaker, J. W. (1991). Writing your wrongs: After 10 years of research, a noted psychologist finds that keeping a journal of your innermost feelings can improve your health. *American Health: Fitness of Body and Mind, 10,* 64–66.

Peyton, J. K. (1986). *Questions in ESL classrooms: New perspectives from written interaction.* Washington, DC: Center for Applied Linguistics.

Peyton, J. K. (1993). *Dialogue journals in the multilingual classroom: Building language fluency and writing skills through written interaction.* Norwood, NJ: Ablex.

Pinkston, J. W. (1989). Thoreau and current trends in the teaching of writing. *English Journal, 78,* 50–52.

Plath, S. (1983). *The Journals of Sylvia Plath.* New York: Ballantine.

Prisco, K. L. (1990). The aesthetic journal: A creative tool in art education. *School Arts, 90,* 24–26.

Progoff, I. (1975). *At a journal workshop.* New York: Dialogue House.

Progoff, I. (1985). *The dynamics of hope: Perspectives of process in anxiety and creativity, imagery and dreams.* New York: Dialogue House Library.

Progoff, I. (1992). *At a journal workshop: Writing to access the power of the unconscious and evoke creative ability.* Los Angeles: J. P. Tarcher.

Reed, L. (1988). Dialogue journals make my whole year flow. *Dialogue journal communication: Classroom, linguistic, social and cognitive views.* Norwood, NJ: Ablex.

Reinertsen, P. S., & Wells, M. C. (1993). Dialogue journals and critical thinking. *Teaching Sociology, 21*(2), 182–186.

Rupert, P. R., & Brueggeman, M. A. (1986). Reading journals: Making the language connection in college. *Journal of Reading, 30*(1), 26–33.

Sanders, T. G. (1970). *Members of the class will kleep daily journals: The Barnard College journals of Tobi Gillian Sanders and Joan Frances Bennett, spring 1968.* New York: Winter House.

Sarton, M. (1973). *Journal of a solitude.* New York: W. W. Norton.

Segal, E. S. (1990). The journal: Teaching reflexive methodology on an introductory level. *Anthropology & Education Quarterly, 21,* 121–127.

Seshachari, N. C. (1994). Instructor-mediated journals: Raising critical thinking and discourse levels. *College Teaching, 42*(1), 7–11.

Shuy, R. W. (1990). An argument for the use of dialogue journals to assess reading comprehension of deaf students. *Georgetown Journal of Languages and Linguistics, 1*(3), 355–369.

Simons, G. F. (1978). *Keeping your personal journal.* New York: Paulist Press.

Simpson, M. K. (1986). A teacher's gift: Oral reading and the reading response journal. *Journal of Reading, 30,* 45–50.

Singer, M. (1990). Responding to intimacies and crises in students' journals. *English Journal, 79*(5), 72–75.

Spencer, P. (1990). African passages: journaling through archetypes. *English Journal, 79,* 38–40.

Stanley, L. C. (1989). "Misreading" students' journals for their views of self and society. *Journal of Basic Writing, 8*(1), 21–31.

Staton, J. (1985). Using dialogue journals for developing thinking, reading and writing with hearing impaired students. *Volta Review, 87*(5), 127–154.

Staton, J., Shuy, R., Peyton, J., & Reed, L. (1988). *Dialogue journal communications: Classroom, linguistic, social and cognitive views.* Norwood, NJ: Ablex.

Steiner, D. R. (1993). *Historical journals: A handbook for writers and reviewers* (2nd ed.). Jefferson, NC: McFarland.

Sullivan, A. M. (1989). Liberating the urge to write: From classroom journals to lifelong writing. *English Journal, 78,* 55–61.

Surbeck, E. (1991). Assessing reflective responses in journals. *Educational Leadership, 48*(6), 25–27.

Vanderbilt, H. (1990). Journal keeping for fiction writers. *The Writer, 103,* 15–17.

Walter, W. Y. (1988). *Constructivist theory into practice in a secondary linguistic classroom: Shared teacher and student responsibility for learning.*

Wilson, N. (1989). Learning from confusion: Questions and change in reading logs. *English Journal, 78*(7), 62–69.

Wollman-Bonilla, J. E. (1989). Reading journals: Invitations to participate in literature. *The Reading Teacher,* 112–120.

Yinger, R. J. (1985). Journal writing as a learning tool. *The Volta Review, 87*(5), 21–33.

Yinger, R. J., & Clark, C. M. (1981). *Reflective journal writing: Theory and practice.* Michigan State University, East Lansing, MI.

Yinger, R. J., & Clark, C. (1985). Using personal document to study teacher thinking. *Evaluative Report. National Institute of Education No. 400-81-0014.*

Young, T. A. (1990). The dialogue journal: Empowering ESL students. *Writing Notebook: Creative Word Processing in the Classroom, 8*(1), 16–17.

The Authors

Chris M. Anson is Professor of English at the University of Minnesota, where he is the Director of the Composition Program. He recieved his Ph.D. from the Unversity of Indiana, and is an author and coauthor of numerous articles, book chapters, and books, including *A Field Guide to Writing, Writing and Response, Scenarios for Teaching Writing,* and *The Harper Collins Handbood for Writers and Readers.*

Richard Beach is a Professor of English at the University of Minnesota, and he received his Ph.D. from the Univeristy of Minnesota. In addition to writing numerous articles, he is the author of Harcourt Brace's *Teaching Literature in the Secondary School* and *A Teacher's Introduction to Reader Response Theories* published by NCTE. The former president of the National Conference on Research in English, he currently serves as a member of the National Board for Professional Teaching Standards.

Index